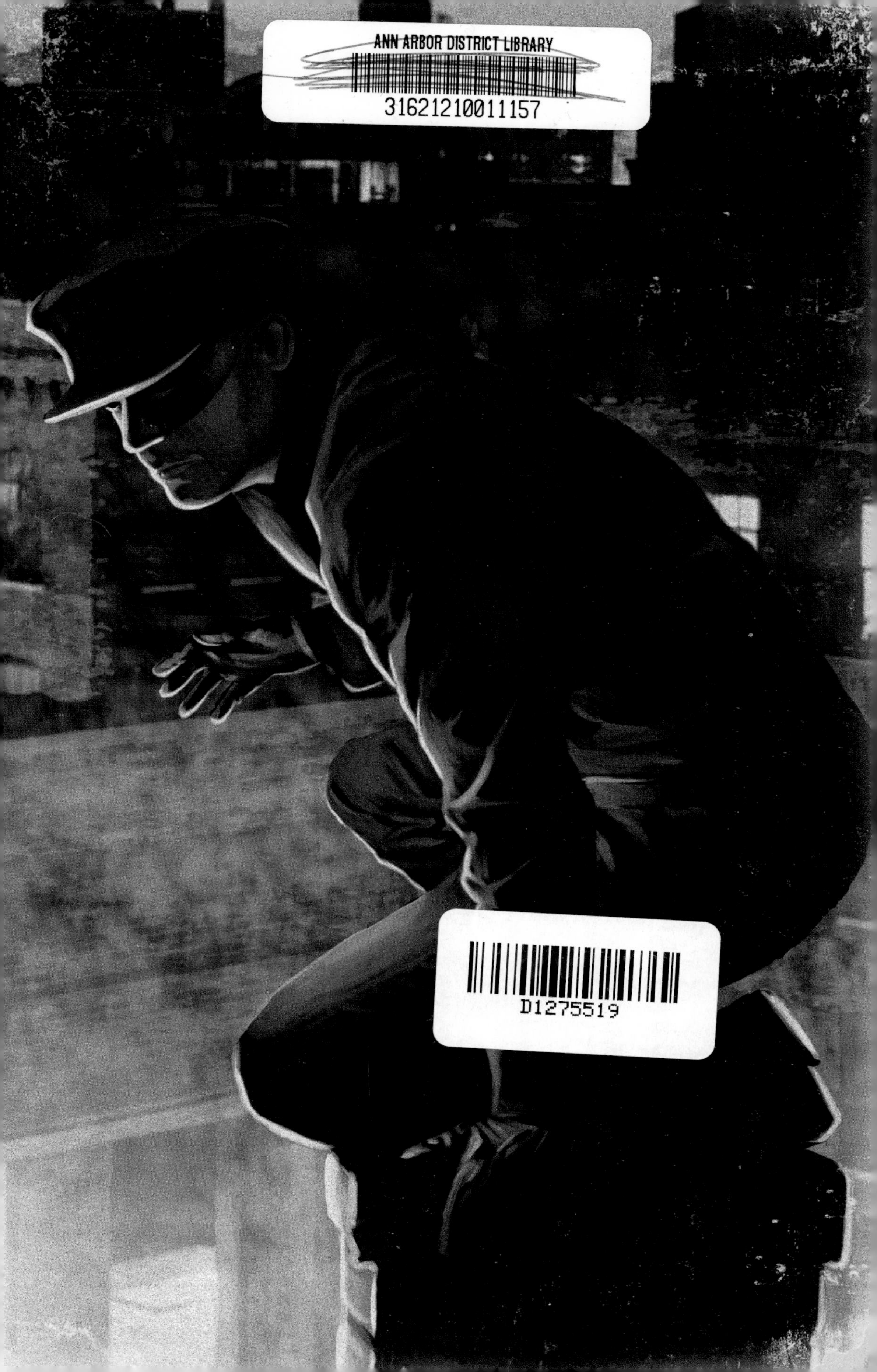

"WAY OF THE NINJA"

Written by
JAI NITZ

Pencils & inks by
COLTON WORLEY

Colors by
ROMULO FAJARDO JR.

Letters by
SIMON BOWLAND

Collection cover by
COLTON WORLEY

Special thanks to
DAVID GRACE
at Green Hornet Inc.

Collection design by
JASON ULLMEYER

ISBN-10:01-60690-155-9   ISBN-13: 978-1-60690-155-7   First Printing   10 9 8 7 6 5 4 3 2 1

For media rights, foreign rights, promotions, licensing, and advertising: marketing@dynamiteentertainment.com

DYNAMITE®
ENTERTAINMENT
WWW.DYNAMITEENTERTAINMENT.COM

NICK BARRUCCI   • PRESIDENT
JUAN COLLADO   • CHIEF OPERATING OFFICER
JOSEPH RYBANDT   • EDITOR
JOSH JOHNSON   • CREATIVE DIRECTOR
RICH YOUNG   • DIRECTOR OF BUSINESS DEVELOPMENT
JASON ULLMEYER   • GRAPHIC DESIGNER

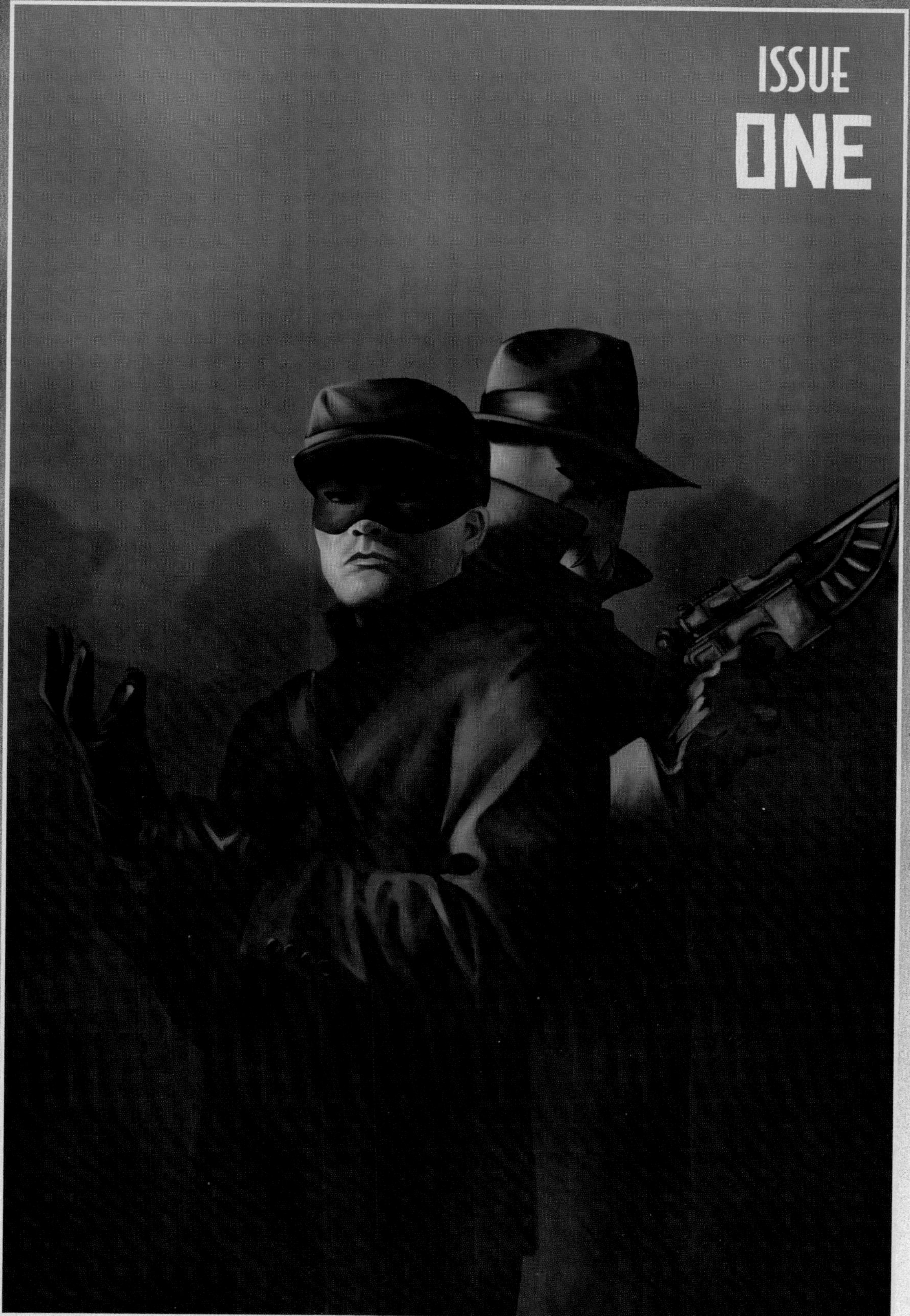
ISSUE
ONE

Issue one cover by **COLTON WORLEY**

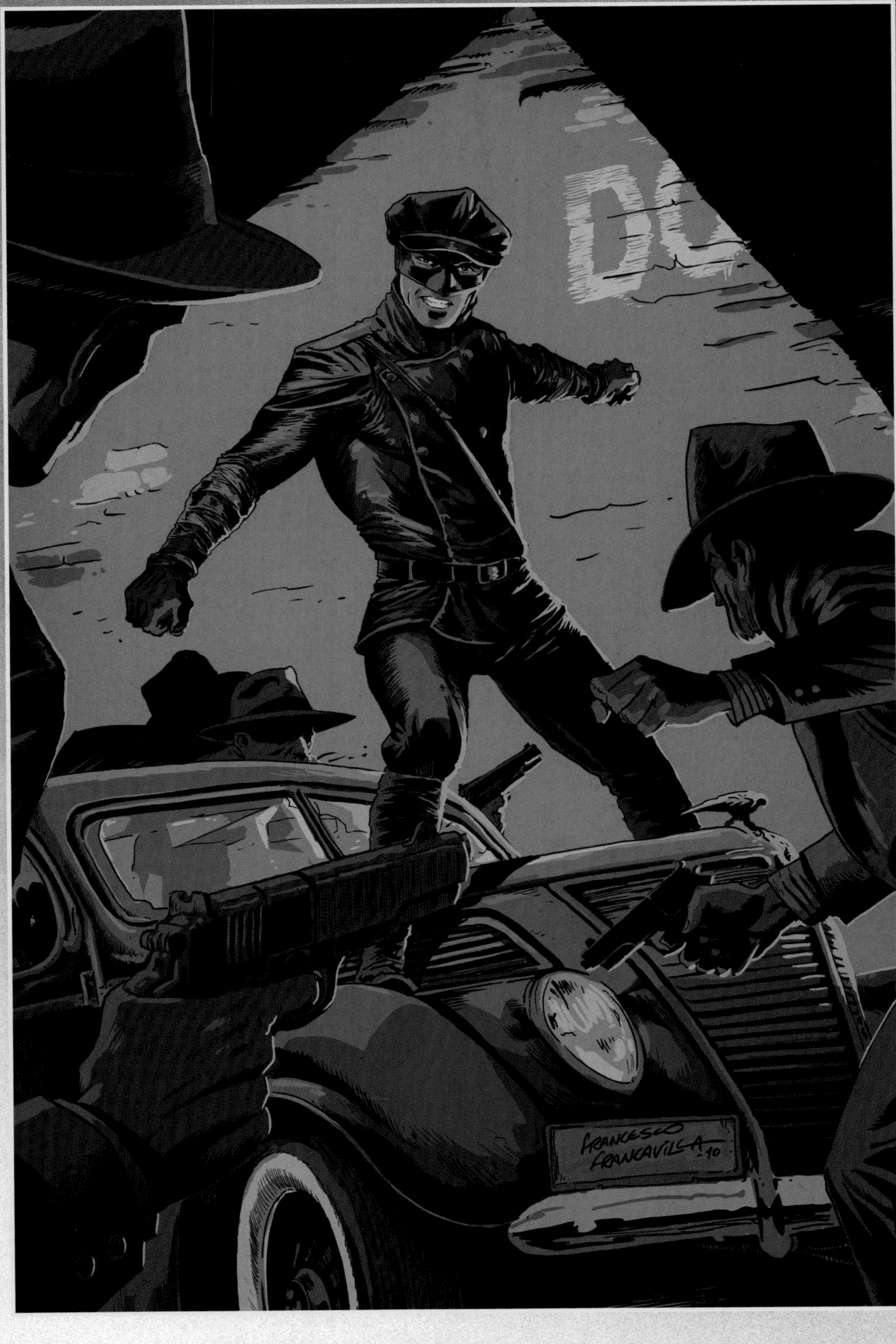
FRANCESCO
FRANCAVILLA
-10

Issue one alternate cover by **FRANCESCO FRANCAVILLA**

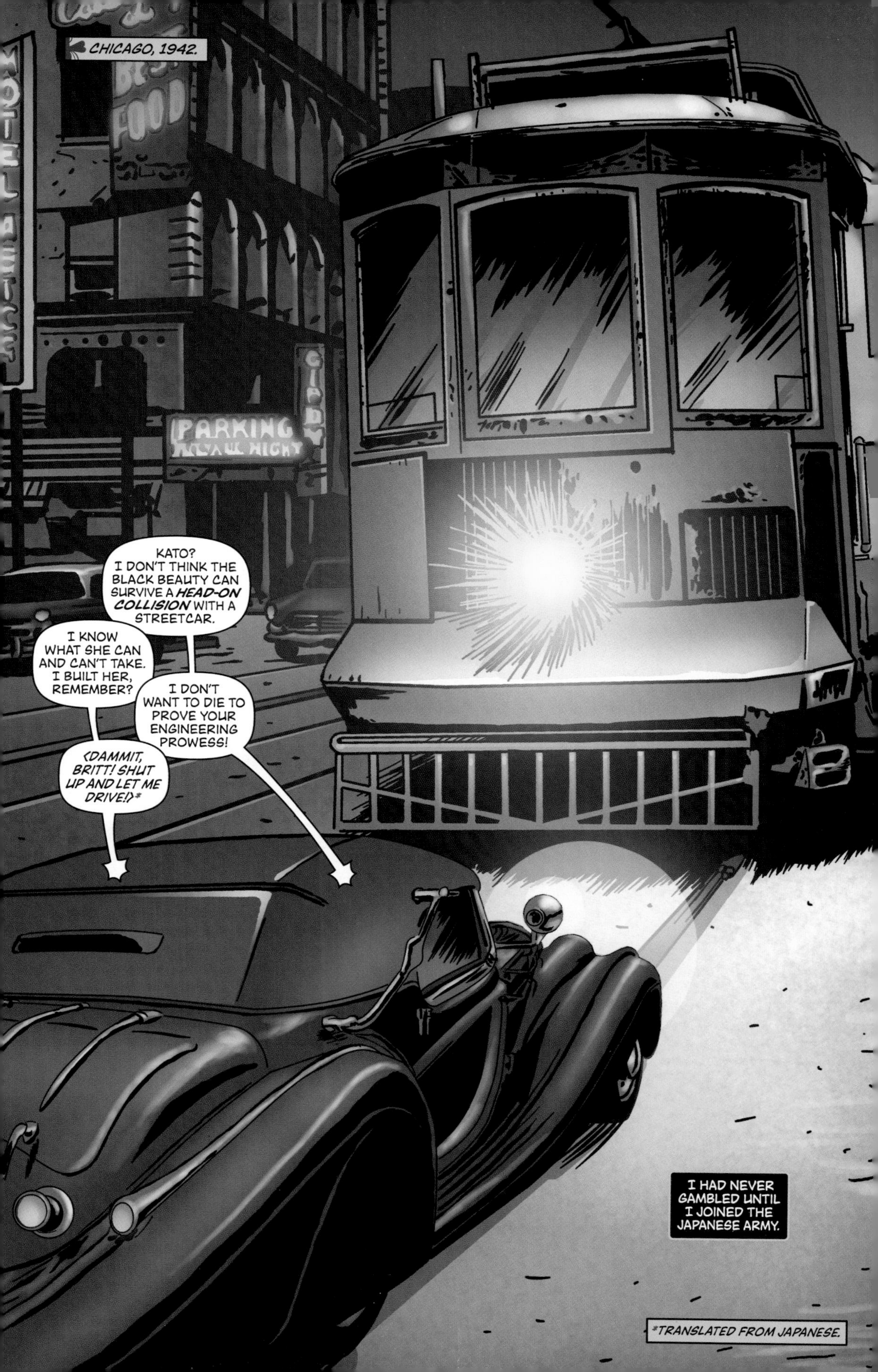
CHICAGO, 1942.
PARKING
KATO? I DON'T THINK THE BLACK BEAUTY CAN SURVIVE A HEAD-ON COLLISION WITH A STREETCAR.
I KNOW WHAT SHE CAN AND CAN'T TAKE. I BUILT HER, REMEMBER?
I DON'T WANT TO DIE TO PROVE YOUR ENGINEERING PROWESS!
<DAMMIT, BRITT! SHUT UP AND LET ME DRIVE!>*
I HAD NEVER GAMBLED UNTIL I JOINED THE JAPANESE ARMY.
*TRANSLATED FROM JAPANESE.

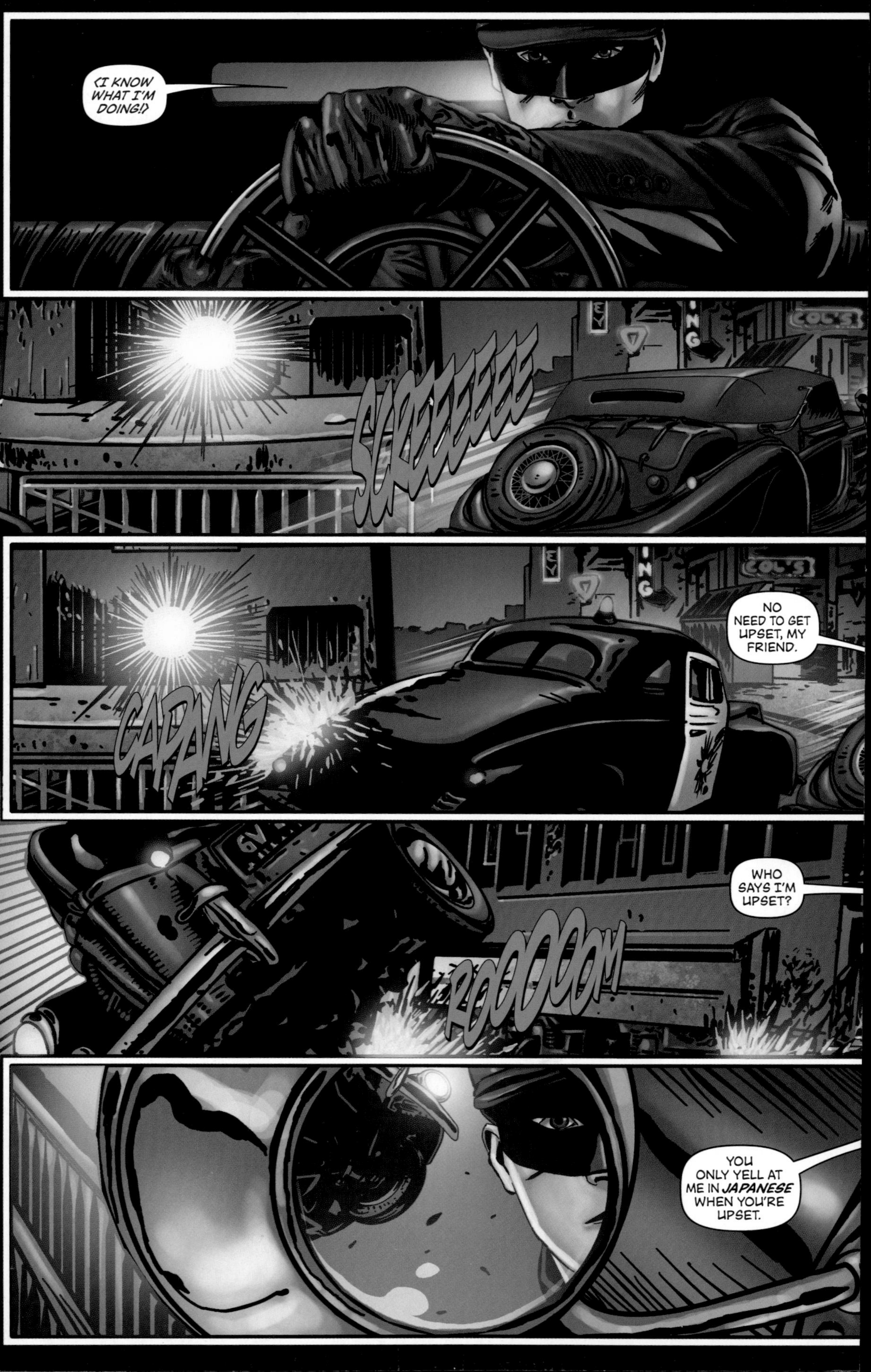
<I KNOW WHAT I'M DOING!>
SCREEEEEE
CAPANG
NO NEED TO GET UPSET, MY FRIEND.
WHO SAYS I'M UPSET?
ROOOOOM
YOU ONLY YELL AT ME IN *JAPANESE* WHEN YOU'RE UPSET.

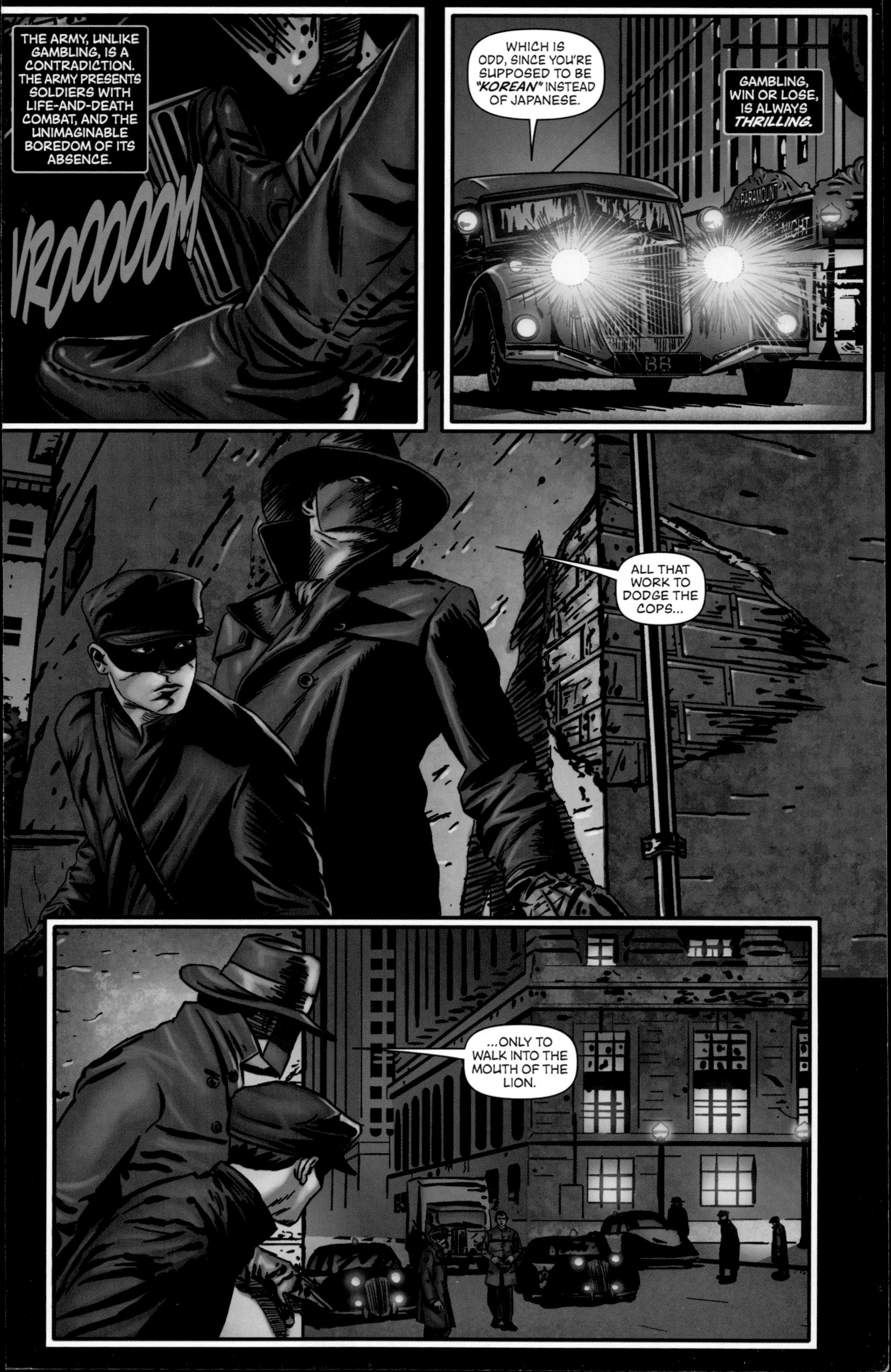
THE ARMY, UNLIKE GAMBLING, IS A CONTRADICTION. THE ARMY PRESENTS SOLDIERS WITH LIFE-AND-DEATH COMBAT, AND THE UNIMAGINABLE BOREDOM OF ITS ABSENCE.
VROOOOOM
WHICH IS ODD, SINCE YOU'RE SUPPOSED TO BE "KOREAN" INSTEAD OF JAPANESE.
GAMBLING, WIN OR LOSE, IS ALWAYS THRILLING.
PARAMOUNT
BB
ALL THAT WORK TO DODGE THE COPS...
...ONLY TO WALK INTO THE MOUTH OF THE LION.

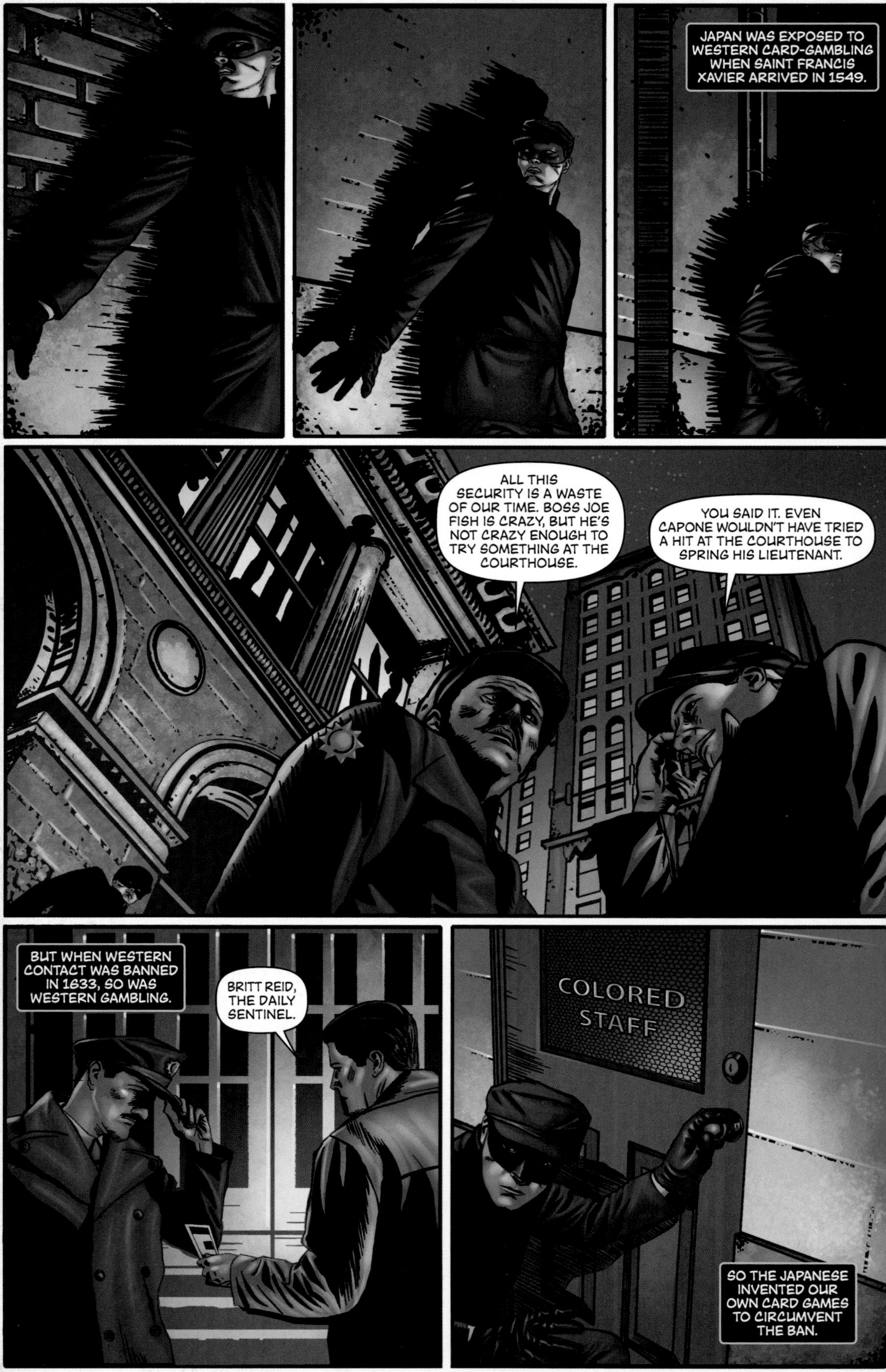
JAPAN WAS EXPOSED TO WESTERN CARD-GAMBLING WHEN SAINT FRANCIS XAVIER ARRIVED IN 1549.
ALL THIS SECURITY IS A WASTE OF OUR TIME. BOSS JOE FISH IS CRAZY, BUT HE'S NOT CRAZY ENOUGH TO TRY SOMETHING AT THE COURTHOUSE.
YOU SAID IT. EVEN CAPONE WOULDN'T HAVE TRIED A HIT AT THE COURTHOUSE TO SPRING HIS LIEUTENANT.
BUT WHEN WESTERN CONTACT WAS BANNED IN 1633, SO WAS WESTERN GAMBLING.
BRITT REID, THE DAILY SENTINEL.
COLORED STAFF
SO THE JAPANESE INVENTED OUR OWN CARD GAMES TO CIRCUMVENT THE BAN.

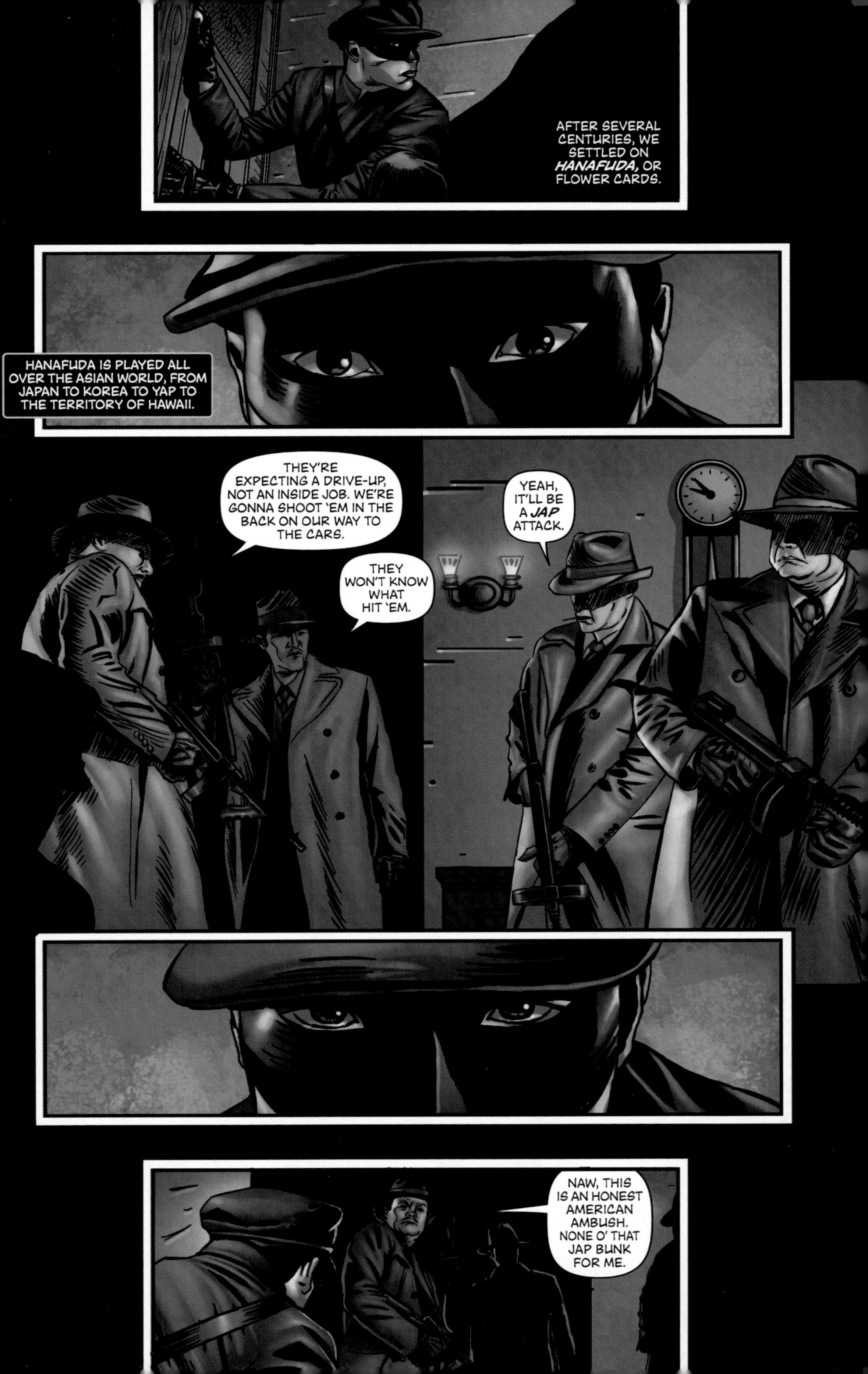
AFTER SEVERAL CENTURIES, WE SETTLED ON *HANAFUDA,* OR FLOWER CARDS.
HANAFUDA IS PLAYED ALL OVER THE ASIAN WORLD, FROM JAPAN TO KOREA TO YAP TO THE TERRITORY OF HAWAII.
THEY'RE EXPECTING A DRIVE-UP, NOT AN INSIDE JOB. WE'RE GONNA SHOOT 'EM IN THE BACK ON OUR WAY TO THE CARS.
THEY WON'T KNOW WHAT HIT 'EM.
YEAH, IT'LL BE A *JAP* ATTACK.
NAW, THIS IS AN HONEST AMERICAN AMBUSH. NONE O' THAT JAP BUNK FOR ME.

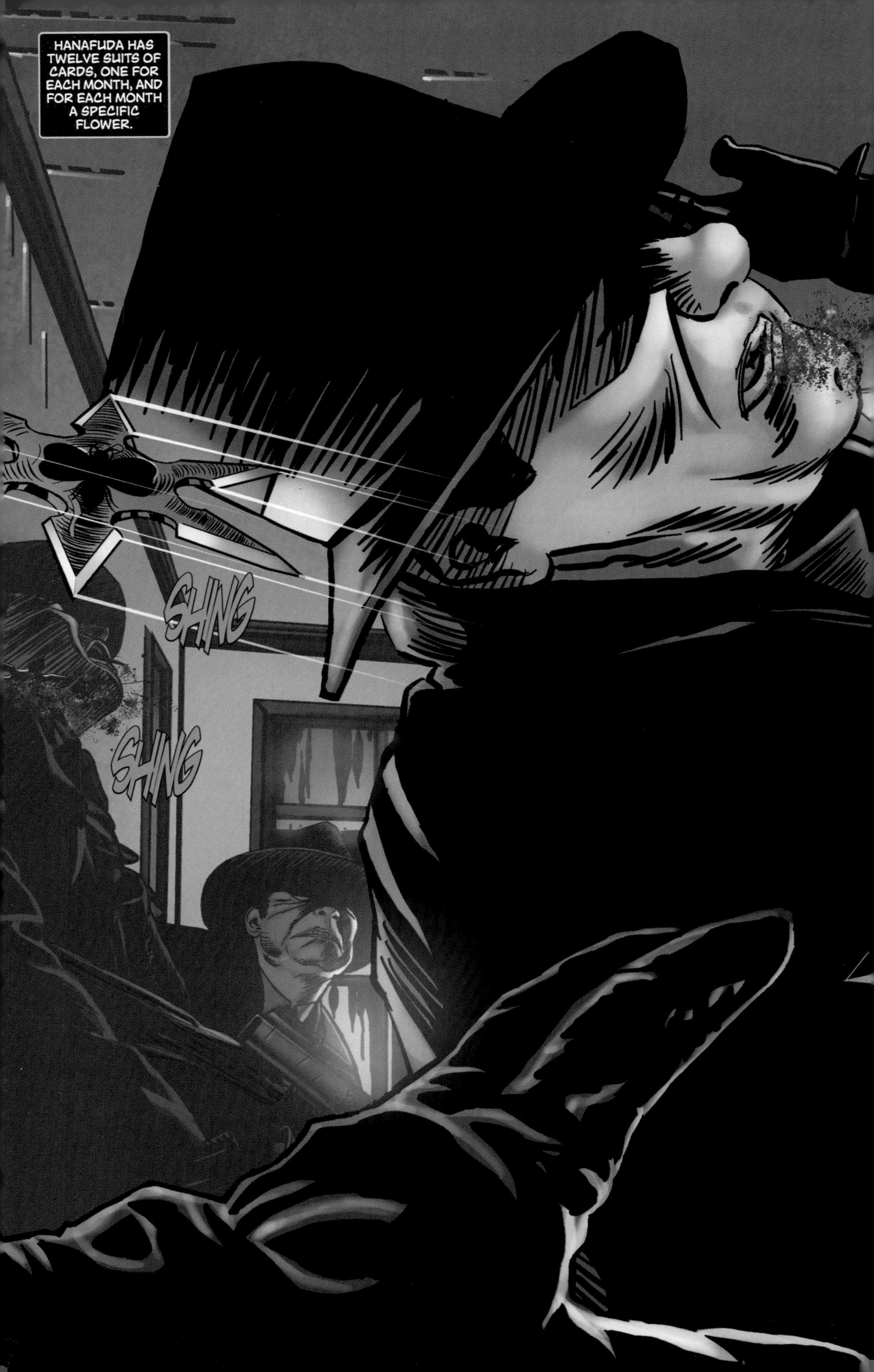
HANAFUDA HAS TWELVE SUITS OF CARDS, ONE FOR EACH MONTH, AND FOR EACH MONTH A SPECIFIC FLOWER.
SHING
SHING

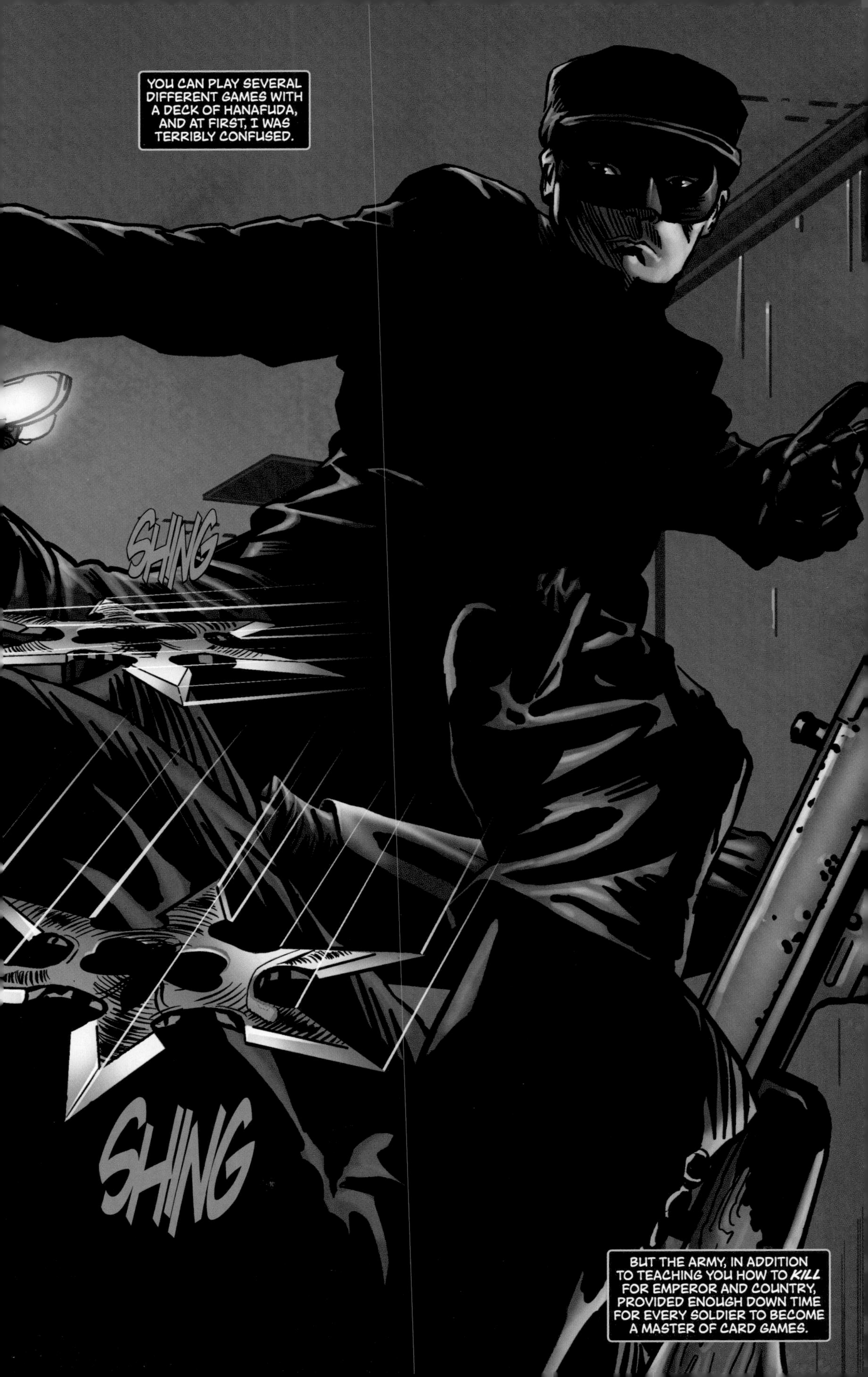
YOU CAN PLAY SEVERAL DIFFERENT GAMES WITH A DECK OF HANAFUDA, AND AT FIRST, I WAS TERRIBLY CONFUSED.
SHING
SHING
BUT THE ARMY, IN ADDITION TO TEACHING YOU HOW TO *KILL* FOR EMPEROR AND COUNTRY, PROVIDED ENOUGH DOWN TIME FOR EVERY SOLDIER TO BECOME A MASTER OF CARD GAMES.

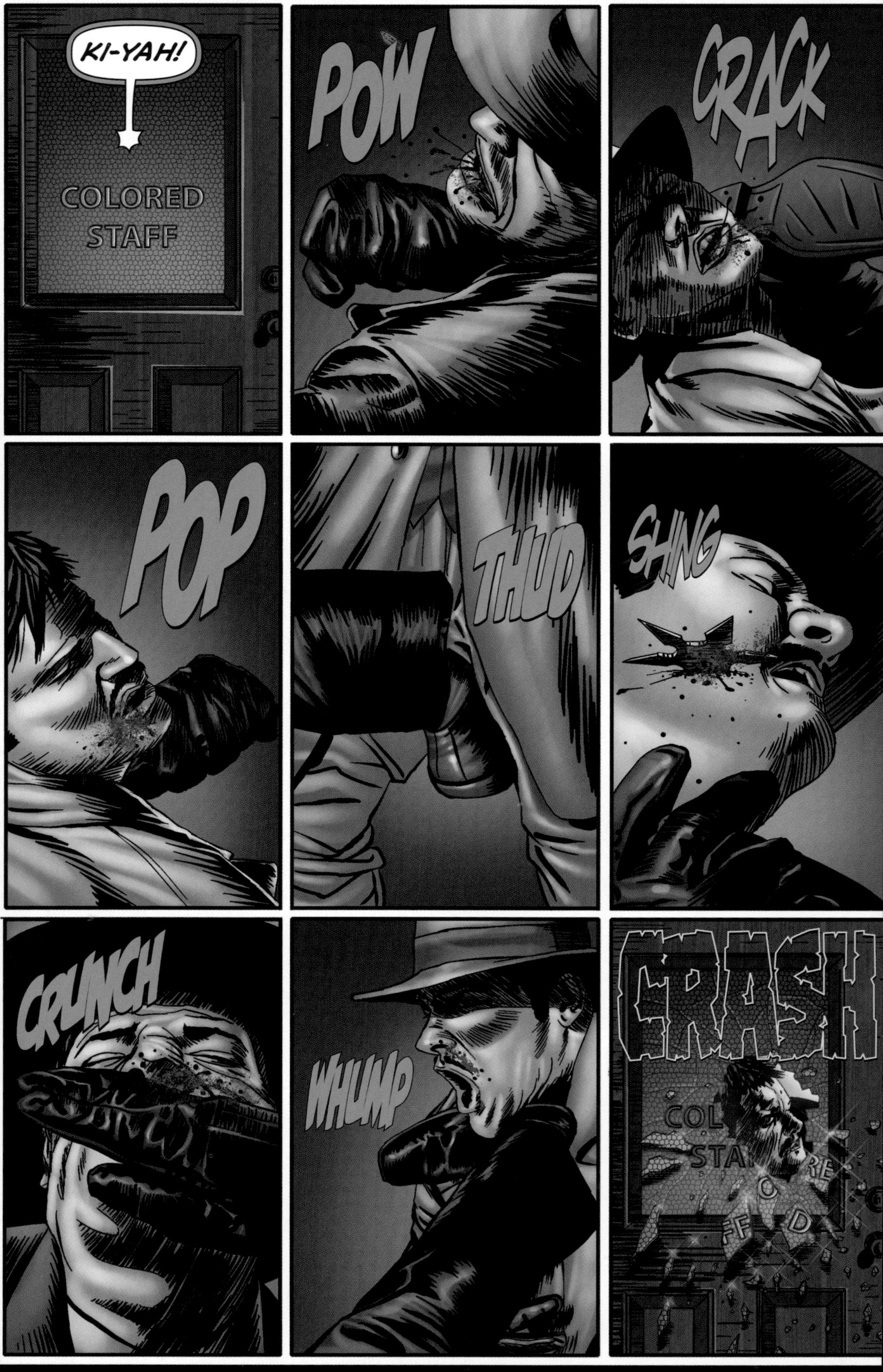
KI-YAH!
COLORED
STAFF
POW
CRACK
POP
THUD
SHING
CRUNCH
WHUMP
CRASH

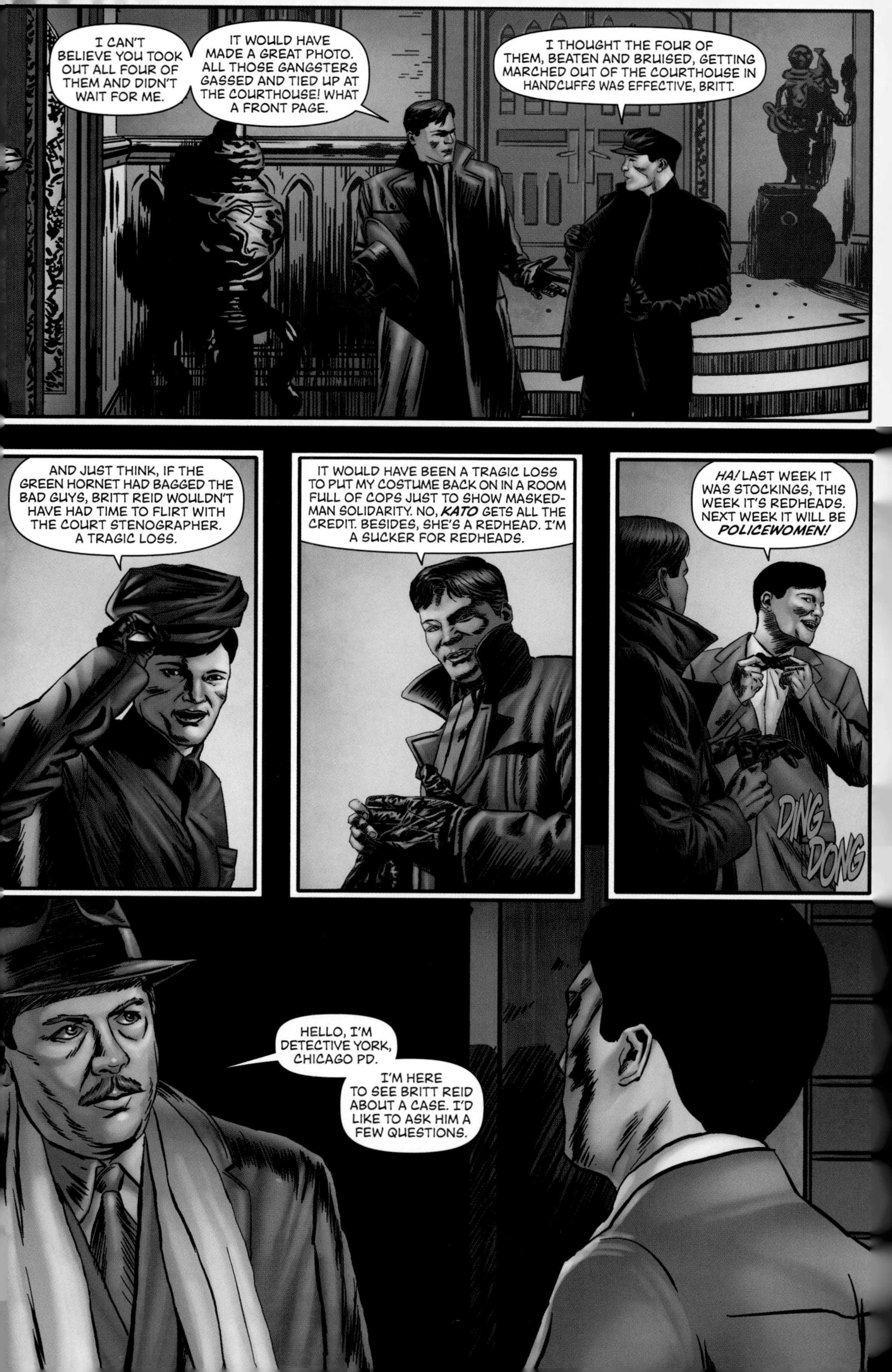
I CAN'T BELIEVE YOU TOOK OUT ALL FOUR OF THEM AND DIDN'T WAIT FOR ME.
IT WOULD HAVE MADE A GREAT PHOTO. ALL THOSE GANGSTERS GASSED AND TIED UP AT THE COURTHOUSE! WHAT A FRONT PAGE.
I THOUGHT THE FOUR OF THEM, BEATEN AND BRUISED, GETTING MARCHED OUT OF THE COURTHOUSE IN HANDCUFFS WAS EFFECTIVE, BRITT.
AND JUST THINK, IF THE GREEN HORNET HAD BAGGED THE BAD GUYS, BRITT REID WOULDN'T HAVE HAD TIME TO FLIRT WITH THE COURT STENOGRAPHER. A TRAGIC LOSS.
IT WOULD HAVE BEEN A TRAGIC LOSS TO PUT MY COSTUME BACK ON IN A ROOM FULL OF COPS JUST TO SHOW MASKED-MAN SOLIDARITY. NO, KATO GETS ALL THE CREDIT. BESIDES, SHE'S A REDHEAD. I'M A SUCKER FOR REDHEADS.
HA! LAST WEEK IT WAS STOCKINGS, THIS WEEK IT'S REDHEADS. NEXT WEEK IT WILL BE POLICEWOMEN!
DING DONG
HELLO, I'M DETECTIVE YORK, CHICAGO PD.
I'M HERE TO SEE BRITT REID ABOUT A CASE. I'D LIKE TO ASK HIM A FEW QUESTIONS.

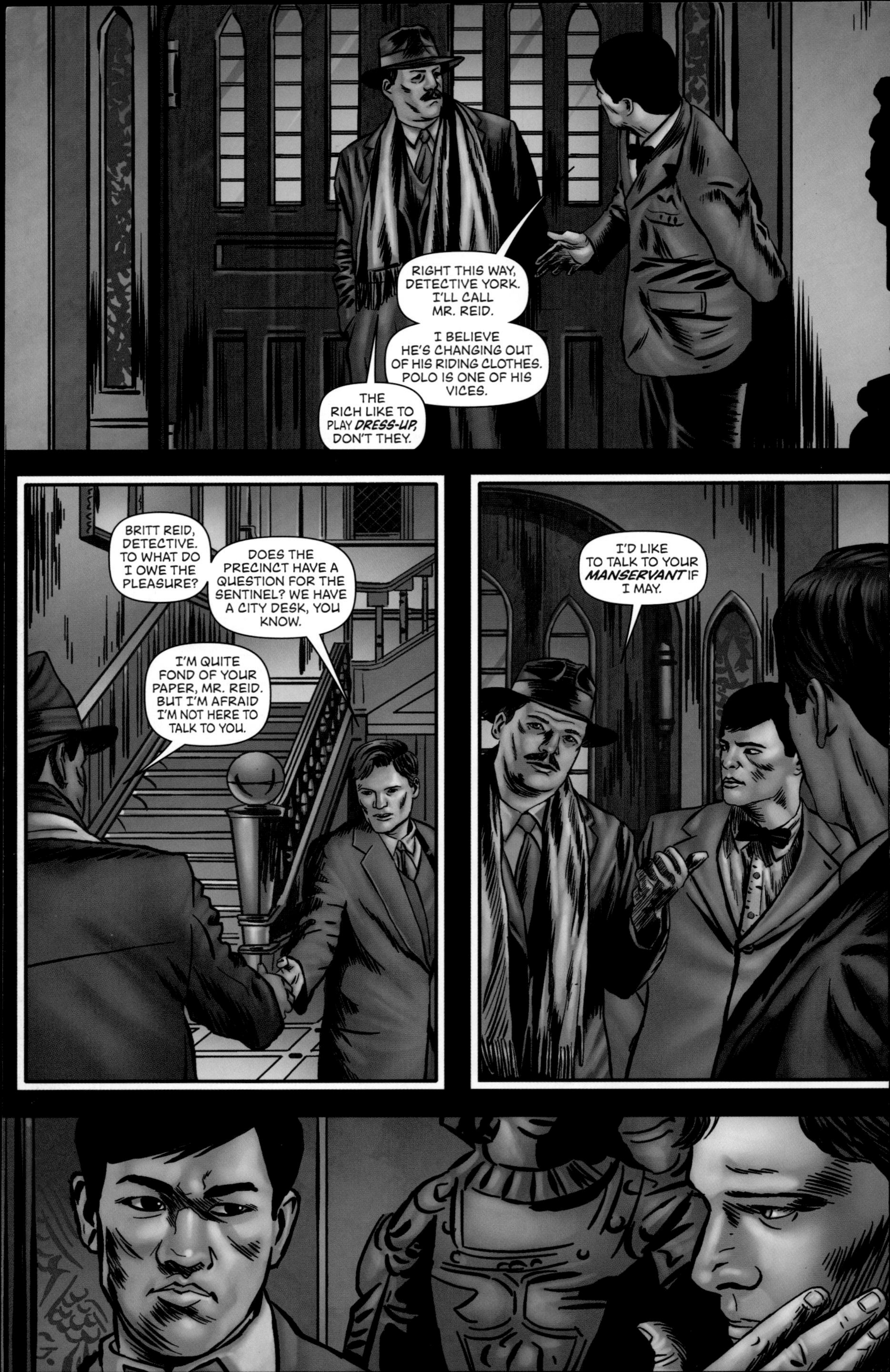
RIGHT THIS WAY, DETECTIVE YORK. I'LL CALL MR. REID.
I BELIEVE HE'S CHANGING OUT OF HIS RIDING CLOTHES. POLO IS ONE OF HIS VICES.
THE RICH LIKE TO PLAY *DRESS-UP,* DON'T THEY.
BRITT REID, DETECTIVE. TO WHAT DO I OWE THE PLEASURE?
DOES THE PRECINCT HAVE A QUESTION FOR THE SENTINEL? WE HAVE A CITY DESK, YOU KNOW.
I'M QUITE FOND OF YOUR PAPER, MR. REID. BUT I'M AFRAID I'M NOT HERE TO TALK TO YOU.
I'D LIKE TO TALK TO YOUR *MANSERVANT* IF I MAY.

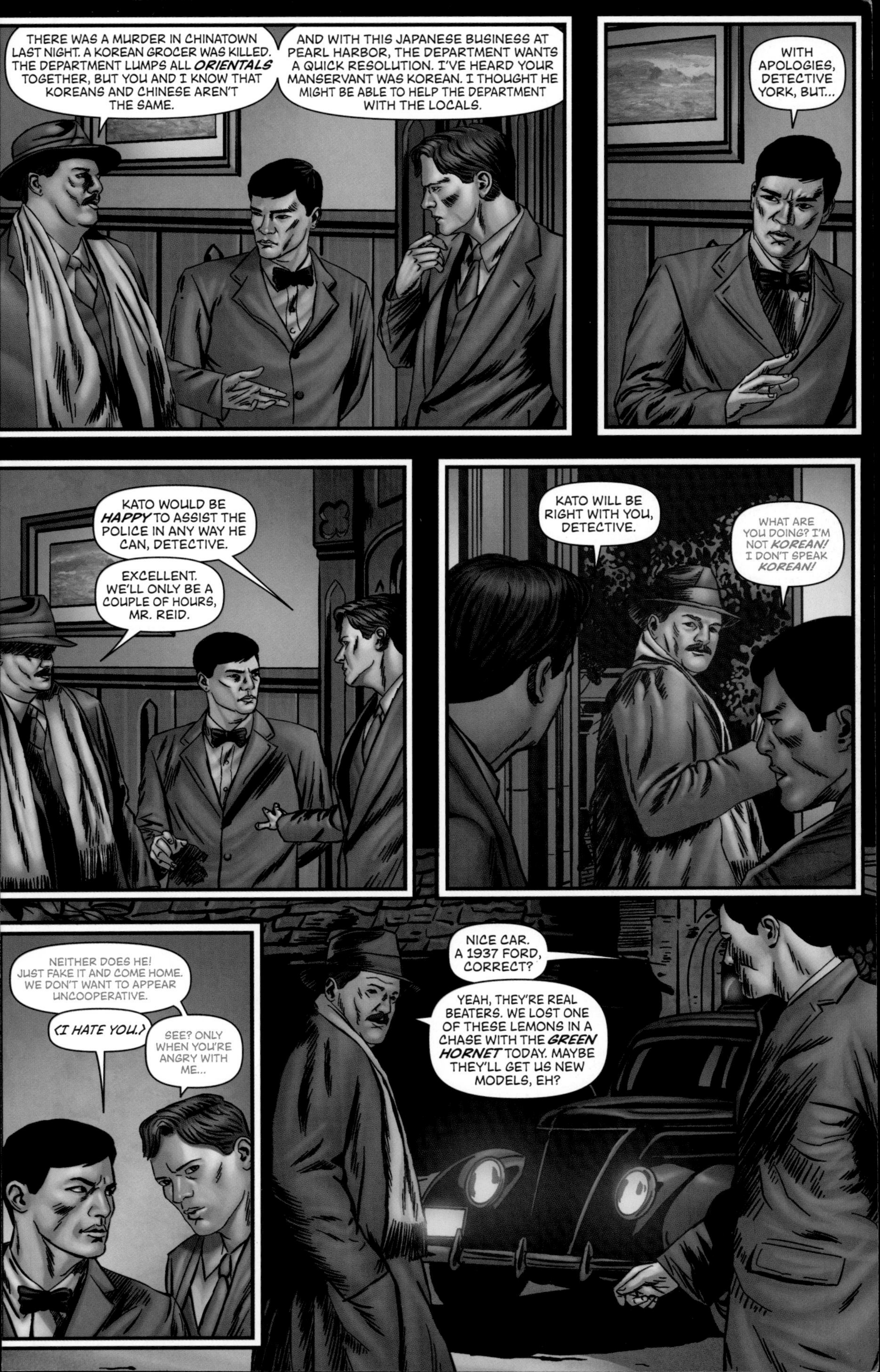
THERE WAS A MURDER IN CHINATOWN LAST NIGHT. A KOREAN GROCER WAS KILLED. THE DEPARTMENT LUMPS ALL ORIENTALS TOGETHER, BUT YOU AND I KNOW THAT KOREANS AND CHINESE AREN'T THE SAME.
AND WITH THIS JAPANESE BUSINESS AT PEARL HARBOR, THE DEPARTMENT WANTS A QUICK RESOLUTION. I'VE HEARD YOUR MANSERVANT WAS KOREAN. I THOUGHT HE MIGHT BE ABLE TO HELP THE DEPARTMENT WITH THE LOCALS.
WITH APOLOGIES, DETECTIVE YORK, BUT...
KATO WOULD BE HAPPY TO ASSIST THE POLICE IN ANY WAY HE CAN, DETECTIVE.
EXCELLENT. WE'LL ONLY BE A COUPLE OF HOURS, MR. REID.
KATO WILL BE RIGHT WITH YOU, DETECTIVE.
WHAT ARE YOU DOING? I'M NOT KOREAN! I DON'T SPEAK KOREAN!
NEITHER DOES HE! JUST FAKE IT AND COME HOME. WE DON'T WANT TO APPEAR UNCOOPERATIVE.
<I HATE YOU.>
SEE? ONLY WHEN YOU'RE ANGRY WITH ME...
NICE CAR. A 1937 FORD, CORRECT?
YEAH, THEY'RE REAL BEATERS. WE LOST ONE OF THESE LEMONS IN A CHASE WITH THE GREEN HORNET TODAY. MAYBE THEY'LL GET US NEW MODELS, EH?

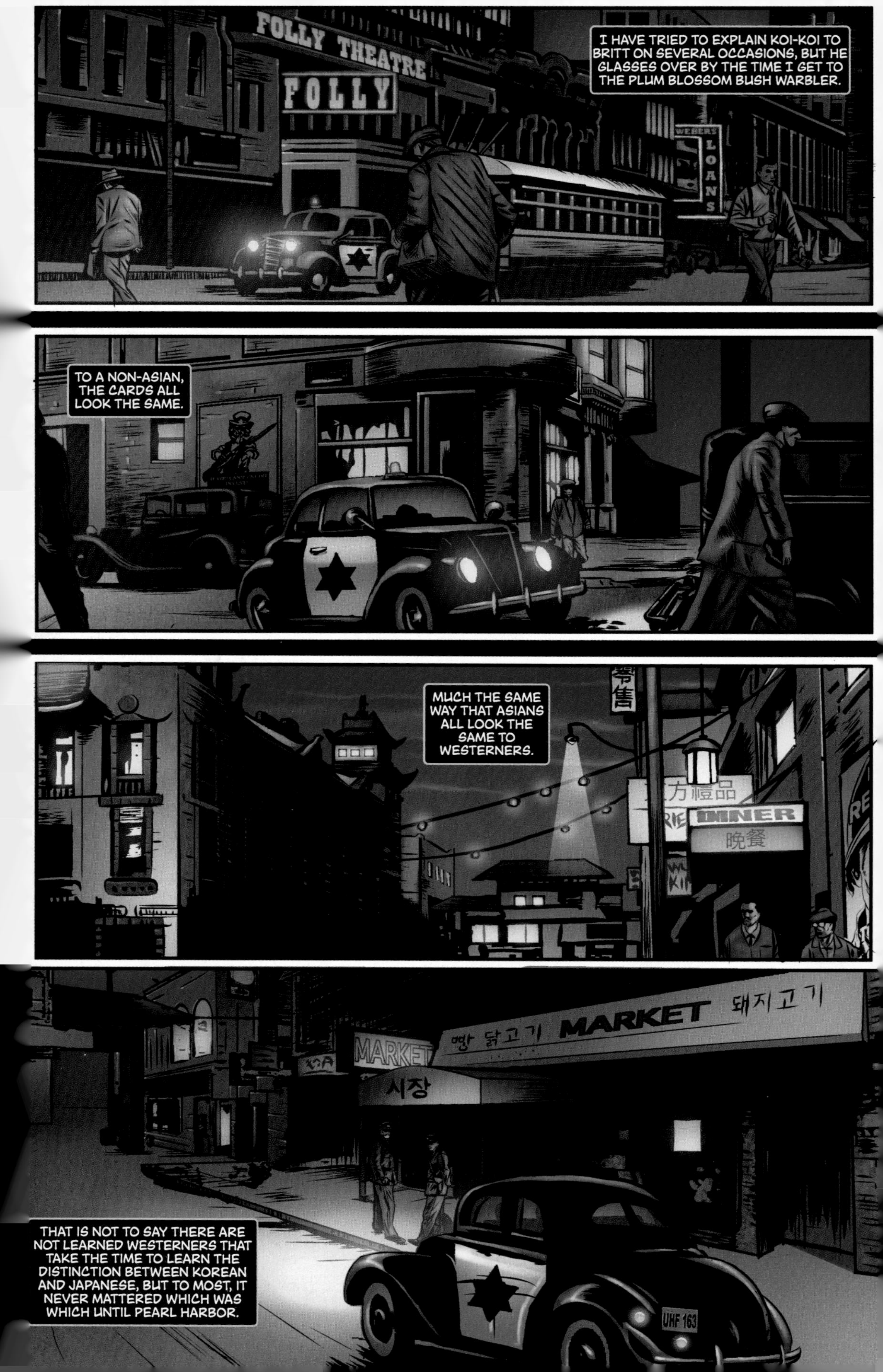
FOLLY THEATRE
FOLLY
I HAVE TRIED TO EXPLAIN KOI-KOI TO BRITT ON SEVERAL OCCASIONS, BUT HE GLASSES OVER BY THE TIME I GET TO THE PLUM BLOSSOM BUSH WARBLER.
LOANS
TO A NON-ASIAN, THE CARDS ALL LOOK THE SAME.
MUCH THE SAME WAY THAT ASIANS ALL LOOK THE SAME TO WESTERNERS.
DINER
晚餐
빵 닭고기 MARKET 돼지고기
MARKET
시장
THAT IS NOT TO SAY THERE ARE NOT LEARNED WESTERNERS THAT TAKE THE TIME TO LEARN THE DISTINCTION BETWEEN KOREAN AND JAPANESE, BUT TO MOST, IT NEVER MATTERED WHICH WAS WHICH UNTIL PEARL HARBOR.
UHF 163

NOW, THE CHINESE ARE ALLIES WHILE THE JAPANESE ARE HATED.

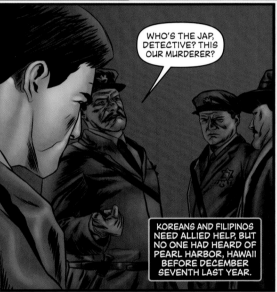

WHO'S THE JAP, DETECTIVE? THIS OUR MURDERER?

KOREANS AND FILIPINOS NEED ALLIED HELP, BUT NO ONE HAD HEARD OF PEARL HARBOR, HAWAII BEFORE DECEMBER SEVENTH LAST YEAR.

DON'T TURN YOUR BACK ON THIS YELLOW *JAPPY BASTARD*, DETECTIVE.

NOW, IT IS IMPERATIVE THAT I AM A SON OF KOREA INSTEAD OF JAPAN BECAUSE IT MATTERS TO AMERICANS THAT COULD FIND NEITHER ON A MAP.

THE NAME, THE RUSE OF THE NAME, MEANS SOMETHING TO THEM ON THE SURFACE.

LAY OFF, McLAUGHLIN.

DEEP DOWN, I DON'T THINK THEY KNOW THE DIFFERENCE.

BESIDES, HE'S *KOREAN*, NOT A DIRTY *JAP*.

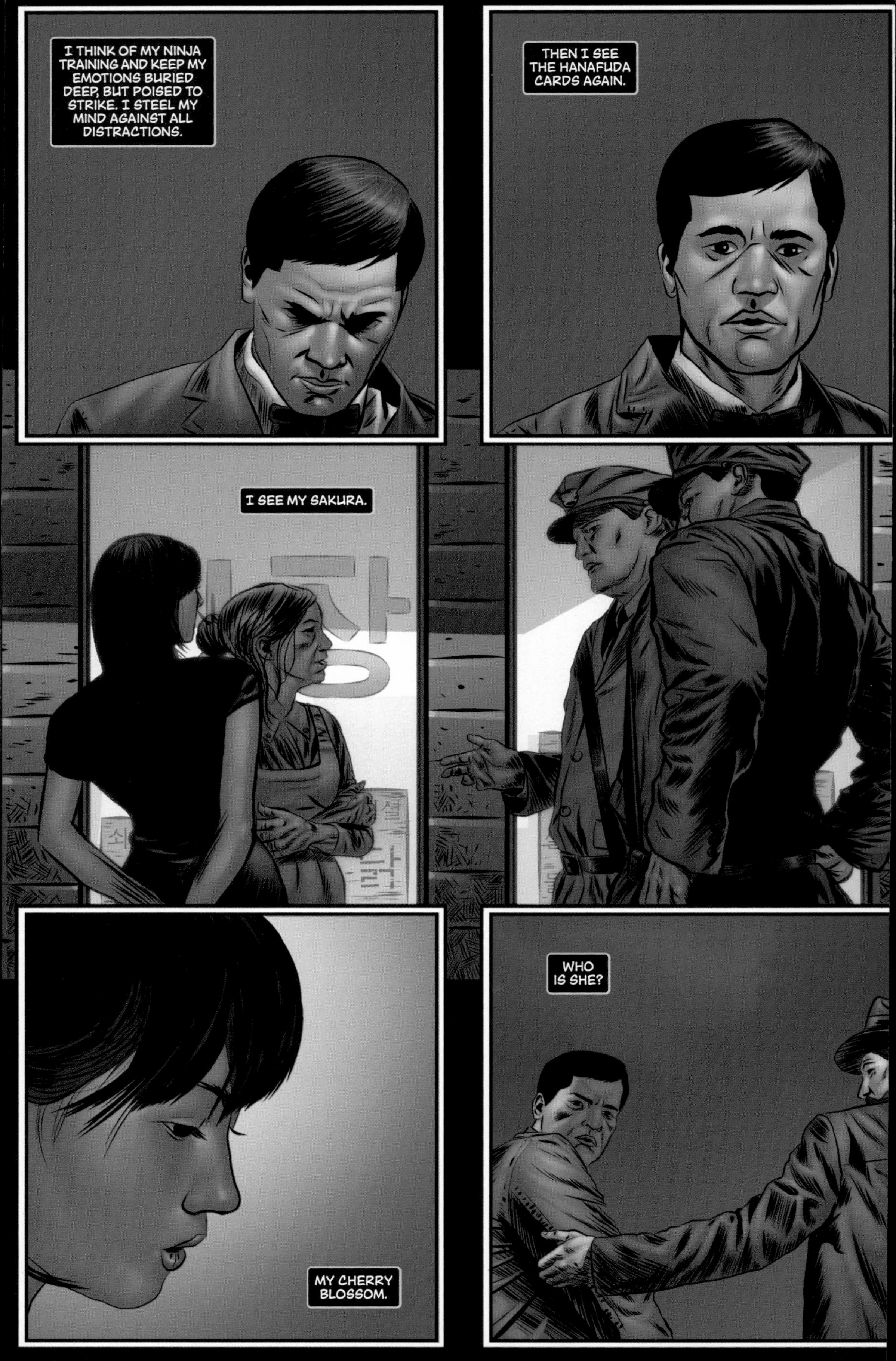
I THINK OF MY NINJA TRAINING AND KEEP MY EMOTIONS BURIED DEEP, BUT POISED TO STRIKE. I STEEL MY MIND AGAINST ALL DISTRACTIONS.
THEN I SEE THE HANAFUDA CARDS AGAIN.
I SEE MY SAKURA.
MY CHERRY BLOSSOM.
WHO IS SHE?

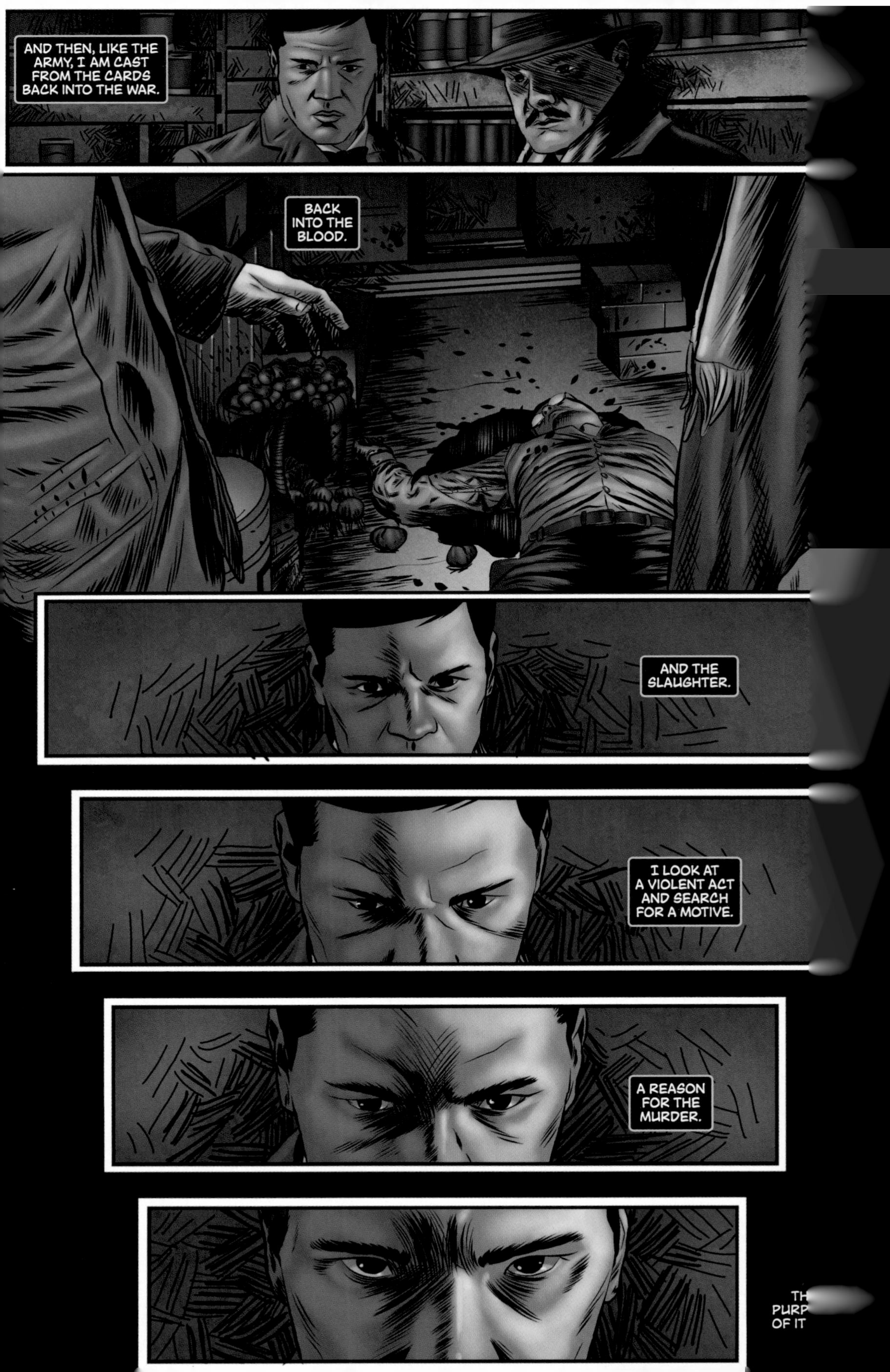
AND THEN, LIKE THE ARMY, I AM CAST FROM THE CARDS BACK INTO THE WAR.
BACK INTO THE BLOOD.
AND THE SLAUGHTER.
I LOOK AT A VIOLENT ACT AND SEARCH FOR A MOTIVE.
A REASON FOR THE MURDER.

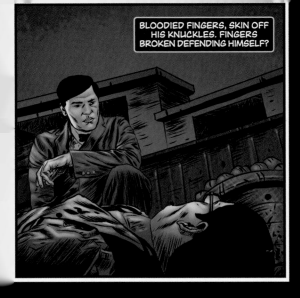

BLOODIED FINGERS, SKIN OFF HIS KNUCKLES. FINGERS BROKEN DEFENDING HIMSELF?

WHAT DO YOU SEE? SOMETHING... *KOREAN?*

DETECTIVE!

DETECTIVE YORK, A CRUISER JUST CAME BY. THE CHIEF WANTS YOU TO WRAP THIS UP AND HEAD TO THE STATION. THERE'S A MURDER *UPTOWN* HE WANTS YOU ON.

WE'RE IN THE MIDDLE OF AN INVESTIGATION HERE!

I HAVE ORDERS TO GET YOU MOVING AND PUT THE LID ON THIS ONE MYSELF, DETECTIVE.

ORDERS ARE ORDERS. CARRY ON, SERGEANT. I NEED TO GO, MR. KATO.

LET'S GO, MR. MOTO.

I SHOULD BE GLAD THAT MY FARCICAL INVOLVEMENT IS NO LONGER NEEDED, BUT THE MURDER IS UNDER MY SKIN LIKE A SPLINTER.

BEAT IT, *CHARLIE CHAN.*

EASY, SERGEANT.

I'M SORRY, MR. KATO. I'LL HAVE A DISPATCHER CALL MR. REID AND HAVE HIM SEND A CAR TO PICK YOU UP.

MY MIND SWIMS WITH INFORMATION. I THINK ABOUT THE MURDER AND THE MOTIVE.

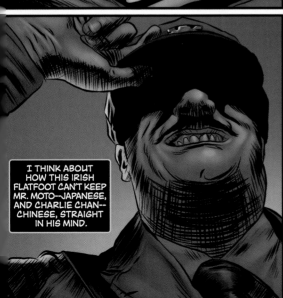

I THINK ABOUT HOW THIS IRISH FLATFOOT CAN'T KEEP MR. MOTO--JAPANESE, AND CHARLIE CHAN-- CHINESE, STRAIGHT IN HIS MIND.

BUT *MOSTLY* I THINK ABOUT MY CHERRY BLOSSOM.

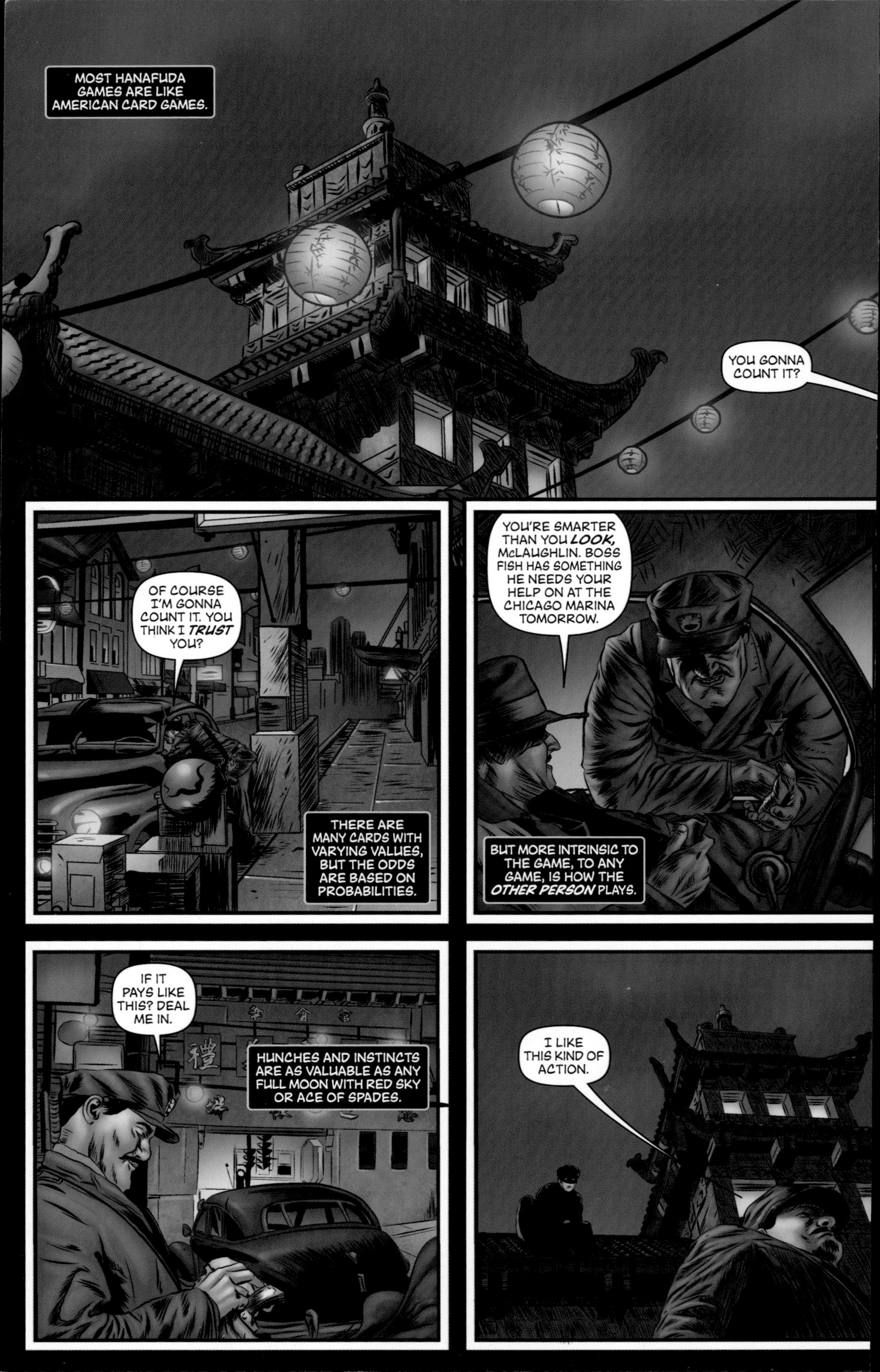

MOST HANAFUDA GAMES ARE LIKE AMERICAN CARD GAMES.
YOU GONNA COUNT IT?
OF COURSE I'M GONNA COUNT IT. YOU THINK I *TRUST* YOU?
THERE ARE MANY CARDS WITH VARYING VALUES, BUT THE ODDS ARE BASED ON PROBABILITIES.
YOU'RE SMARTER THAN YOU *LOOK*, McLAUGHLIN. BOSS FISH HAS SOMETHING HE NEEDS YOUR HELP ON AT THE CHICAGO MARINA TOMORROW.
BUT MORE INTRINSIC TO THE GAME, TO ANY GAME, IS HOW THE *OTHER PERSON* PLAYS.
IF IT PAYS LIKE THIS? DEAL ME IN.
HUNCHES AND INSTINCTS ARE AS VALUABLE AS ANY FULL MOON WITH RED SKY OR ACE OF SPADES.
I LIKE THIS KIND OF ACTION.

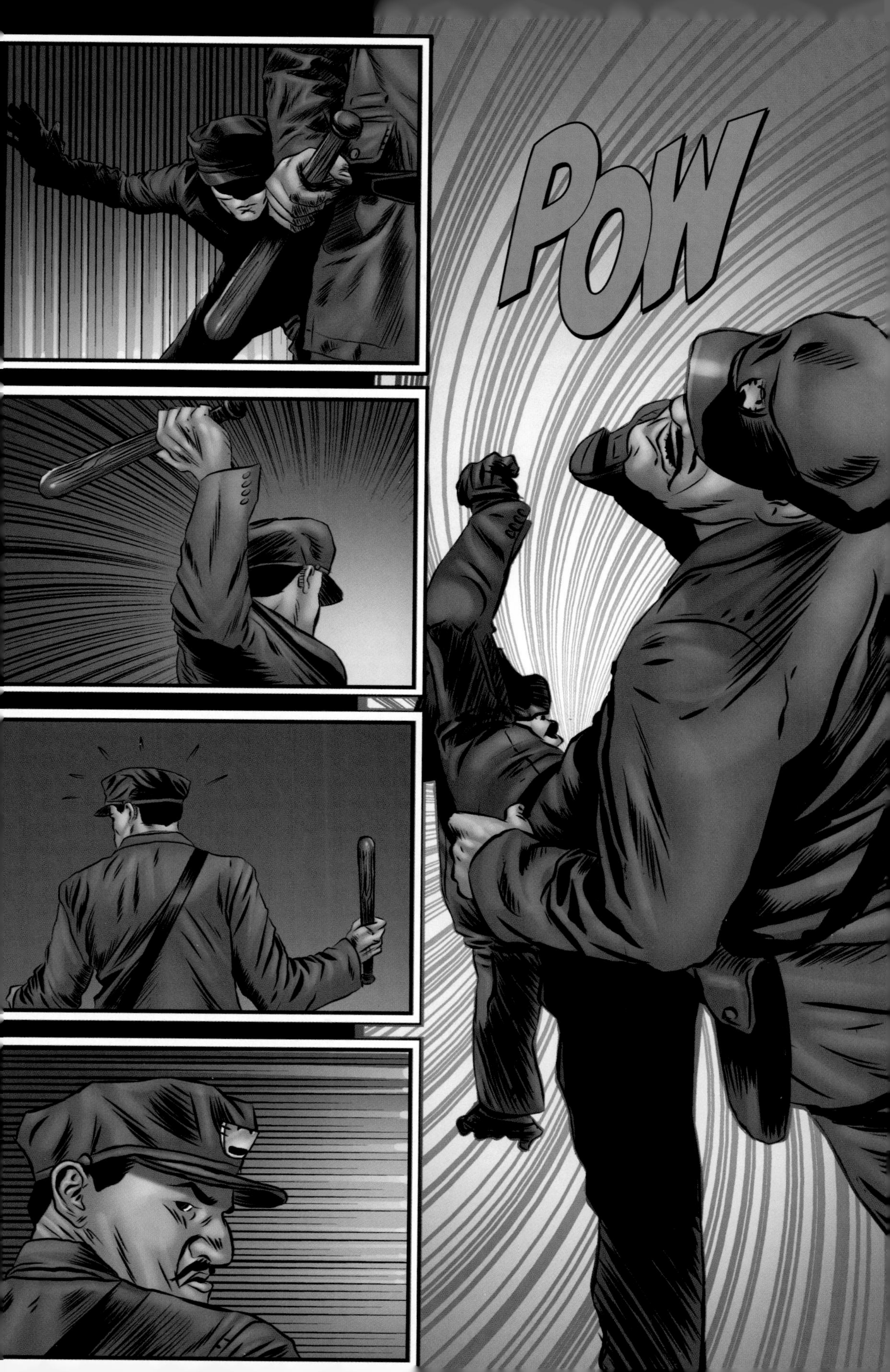
POW

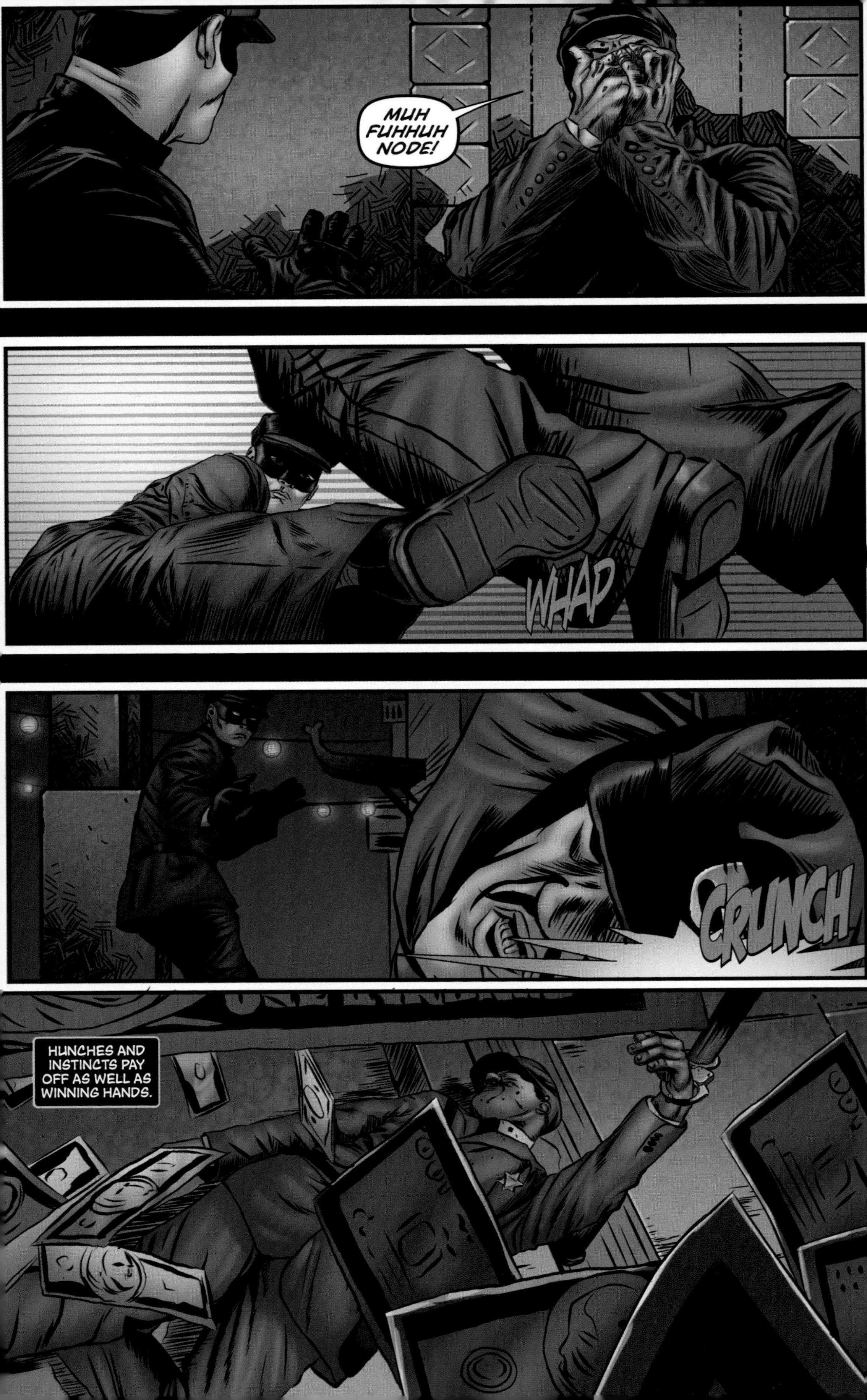
MUH FUHHUH NODE!
WHAP
CRUNCH
HUNCHES AND INSTINCTS PAY OFF AS WELL AS WINNING HANDS.

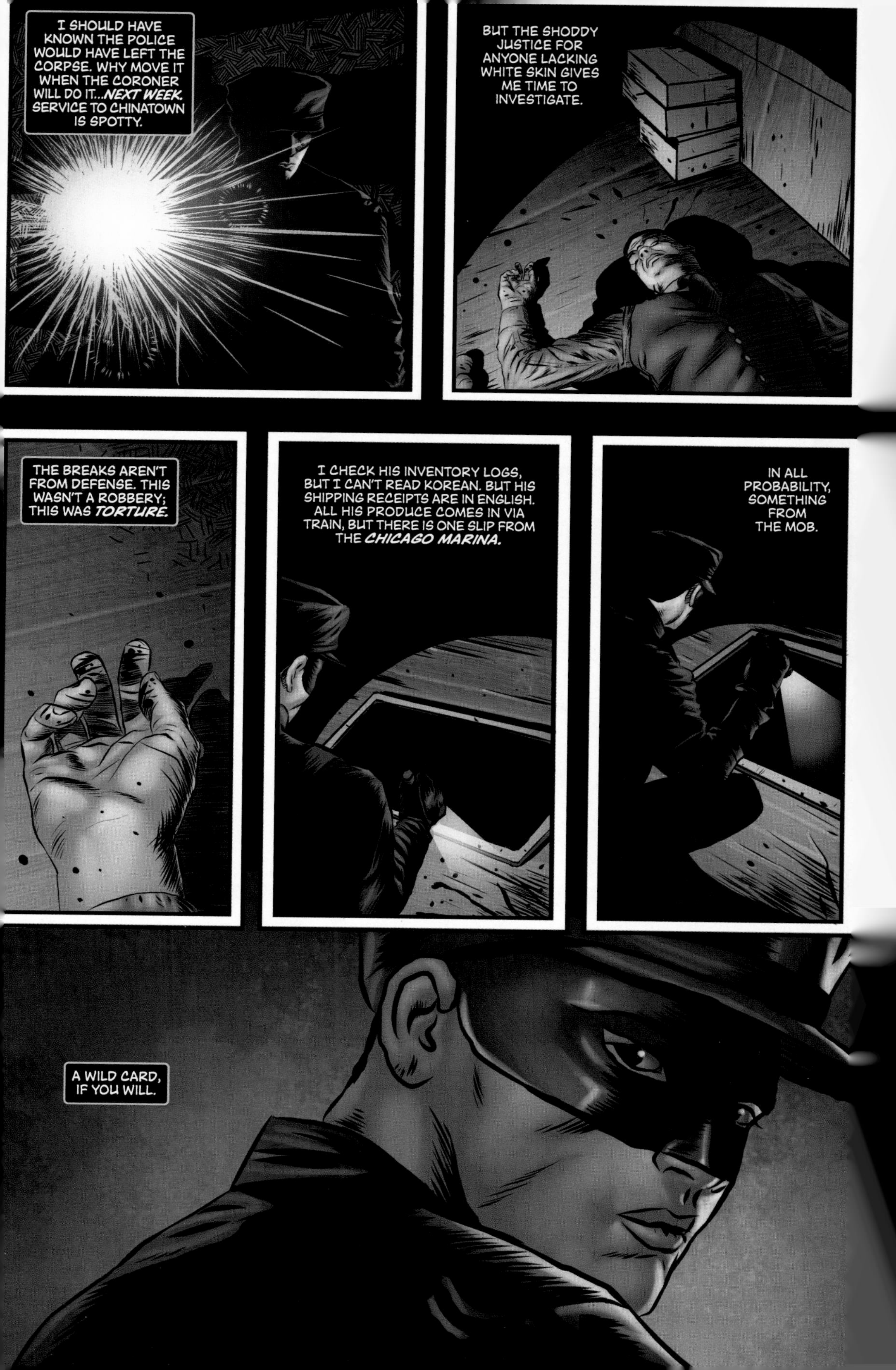
I SHOULD HAVE KNOWN THE POLICE WOULD HAVE LEFT THE CORPSE. WHY MOVE IT WHEN THE CORONER WILL DO IT...NEXT WEEK. SERVICE TO CHINATOWN IS SPOTTY.
BUT THE SHODDY JUSTICE FOR ANYONE LACKING WHITE SKIN GIVES ME TIME TO INVESTIGATE.
THE BREAKS AREN'T FROM DEFENSE. THIS WASN'T A ROBBERY; THIS WAS TORTURE.
I CHECK HIS INVENTORY LOGS, BUT I CAN'T READ KOREAN. BUT HIS SHIPPING RECEIPTS ARE IN ENGLISH. ALL HIS PRODUCE COMES IN VIA TRAIN, BUT THERE IS ONE SLIP FROM THE CHICAGO MARINA.
IN ALL PROBABILITY, SOMETHING FROM THE MOB.
A WILD CARD, IF YOU WILL.

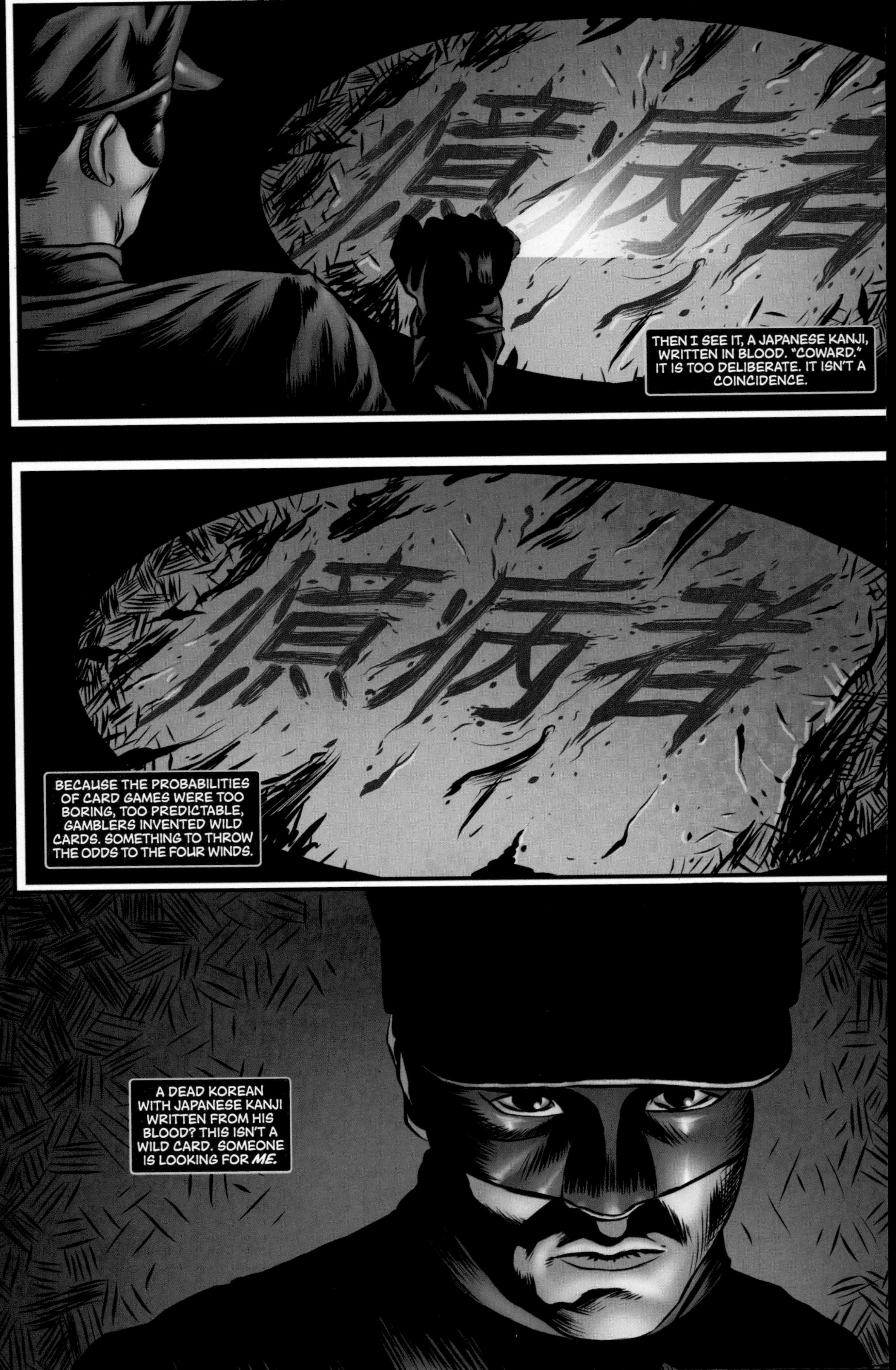
THEN I SEE IT, A JAPANESE KANJI, WRITTEN IN BLOOD. "COWARD." IT IS TOO DELIBERATE. IT ISN'T A COINCIDENCE.
BECAUSE THE PROBABILITIES OF CARD GAMES WERE TOO BORING, TOO PREDICTABLE, GAMBLERS INVENTED WILD CARDS. SOMETHING TO THROW THE ODDS TO THE FOUR WINDS.
A DEAD KOREAN WITH JAPANESE KANJI WRITTEN FROM HIS BLOOD? THIS ISN'T A WILD CARD. SOMEONE IS LOOKING FOR *ME.*

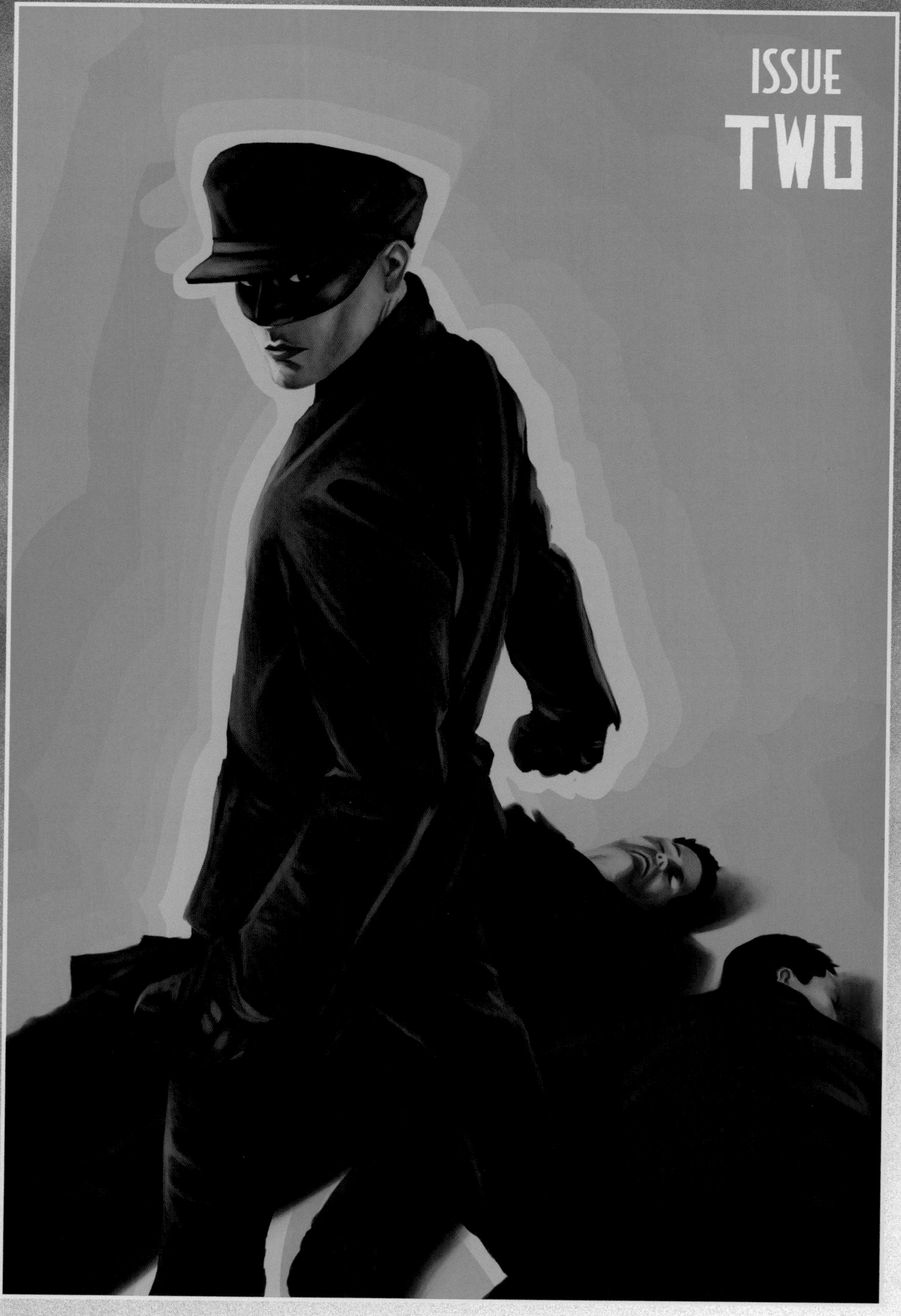
ISSUE
TWO

Issue two cover by **COLTON WORLEY**

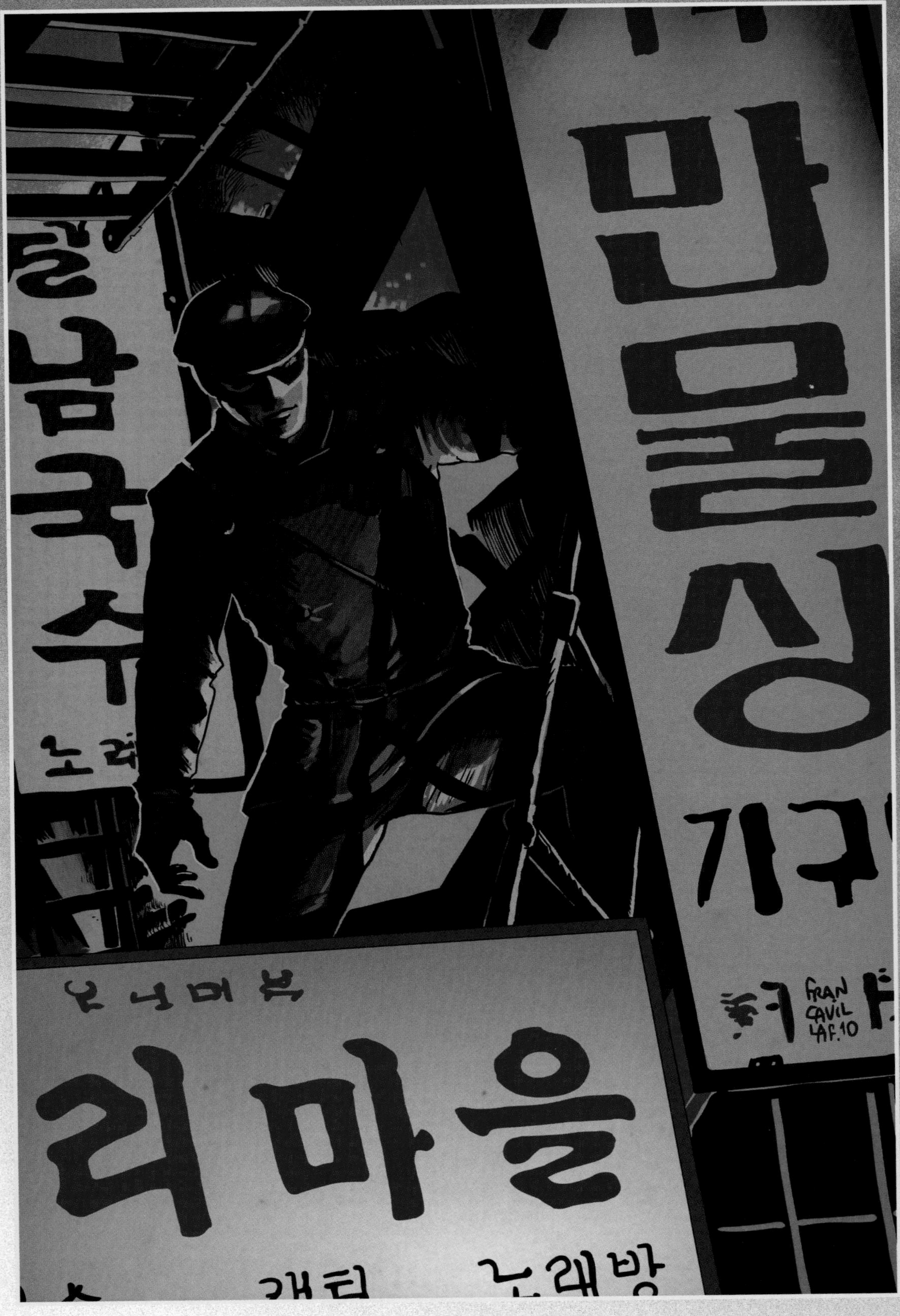
리마을
FRAN
CAVIL
LA F.10

Issue two alternate cover by **FRANCESCO FRANCAVILLA**

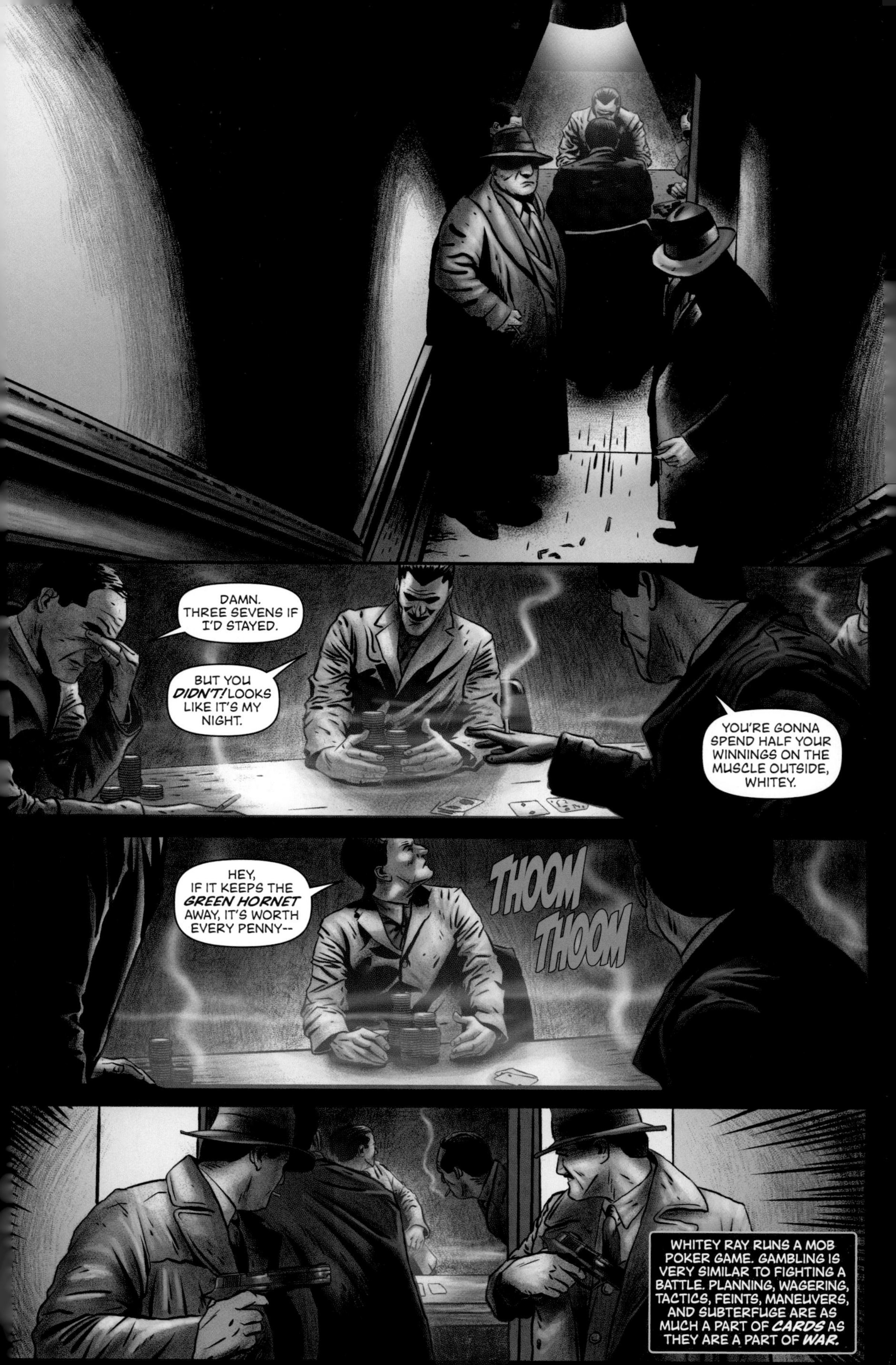
DAMN. THREE SEVENS IF I'D STAYED.
BUT YOU DIDN'T! LOOKS LIKE IT'S MY NIGHT.
YOU'RE GONNA SPEND HALF YOUR WINNINGS ON THE MUSCLE OUTSIDE, WHITEY.
HEY, IF IT KEEPS THE GREEN HORNET AWAY, IT'S WORTH EVERY PENNY--
THOOM THOOM
WHITEY RAY RUNS A MOB POKER GAME. GAMBLING IS VERY SIMILAR TO FIGHTING A BATTLE. PLANNING, WAGERING, TACTICS, FEINTS, MANEUVERS, AND SUBTERFUGE ARE AS MUCH A PART OF CARDS AS THEY ARE A PART OF WAR.

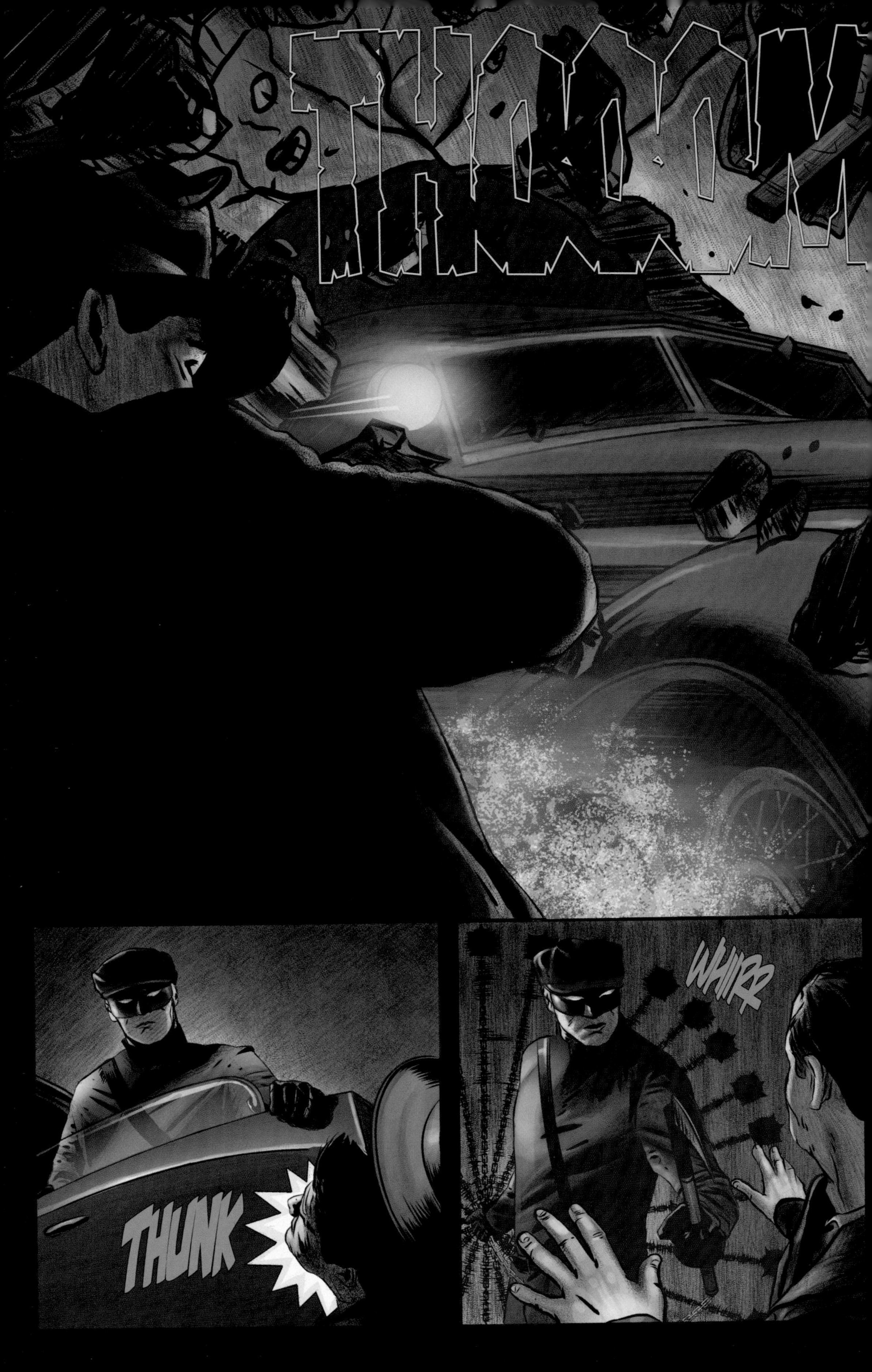
THOOOM
THUNK
WHIIRR

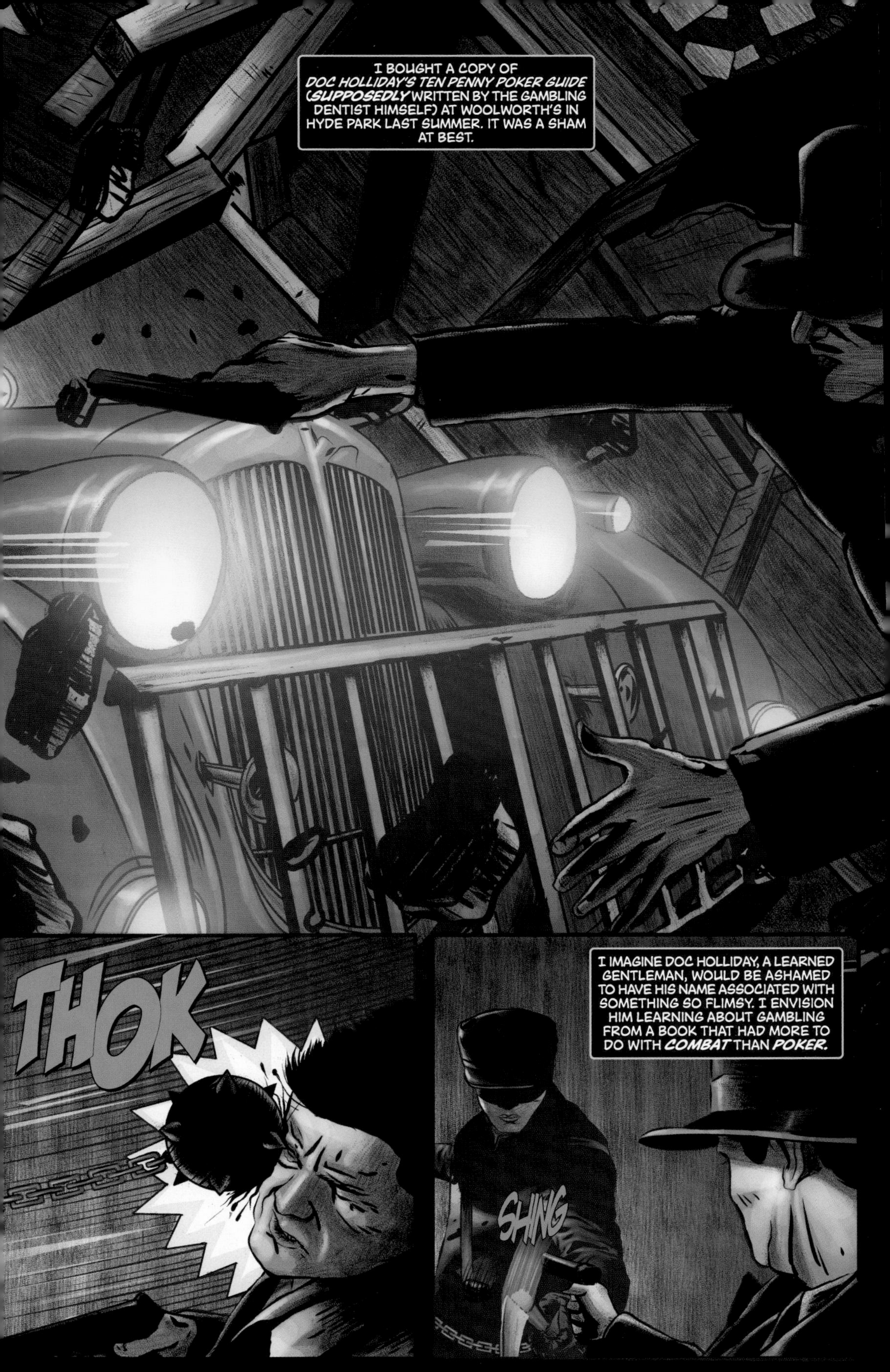
I BOUGHT A COPY OF *DOC HOLLIDAY'S TEN PENNY POKER GUIDE* (***SUPPOSEDLY*** WRITTEN BY THE GAMBLING DENTIST HIMSELF) AT WOOLWORTH'S IN HYDE PARK LAST SUMMER. IT WAS A SHAM AT BEST.
THOK
I IMAGINE DOC HOLLIDAY, A LEARNED GENTLEMAN, WOULD BE ASHAMED TO HAVE HIS NAME ASSOCIATED WITH SOMETHING SO FLIMSY. I ENVISION HIM LEARNING ABOUT GAMBLING FROM A BOOK THAT HAD MORE TO DO WITH ***COMBAT*** THAN ***POKER.***
SHING

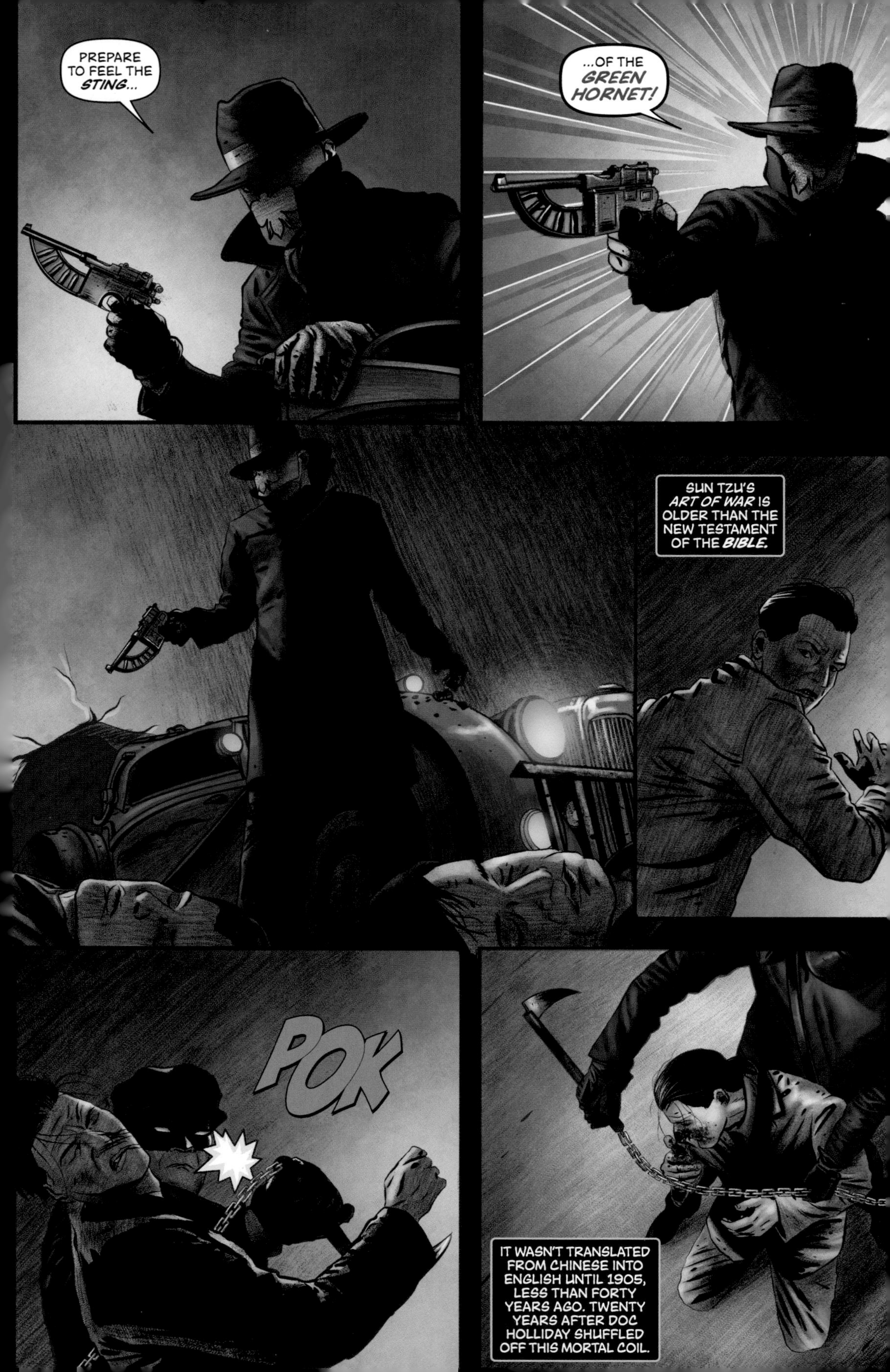
PREPARE TO FEEL THE *STING*...
...OF THE *GREEN HORNET!*
SUN TZU'S *ART OF WAR* IS OLDER THAN THE NEW TESTAMENT OF THE *BIBLE.*
POK
IT WASN'T TRANSLATED FROM CHINESE INTO ENGLISH UNTIL 1905, LESS THAN FORTY YEARS AGO. TWENTY YEARS AFTER DOC HOLLIDAY SHUFFLED OFF THIS MORTAL COIL.

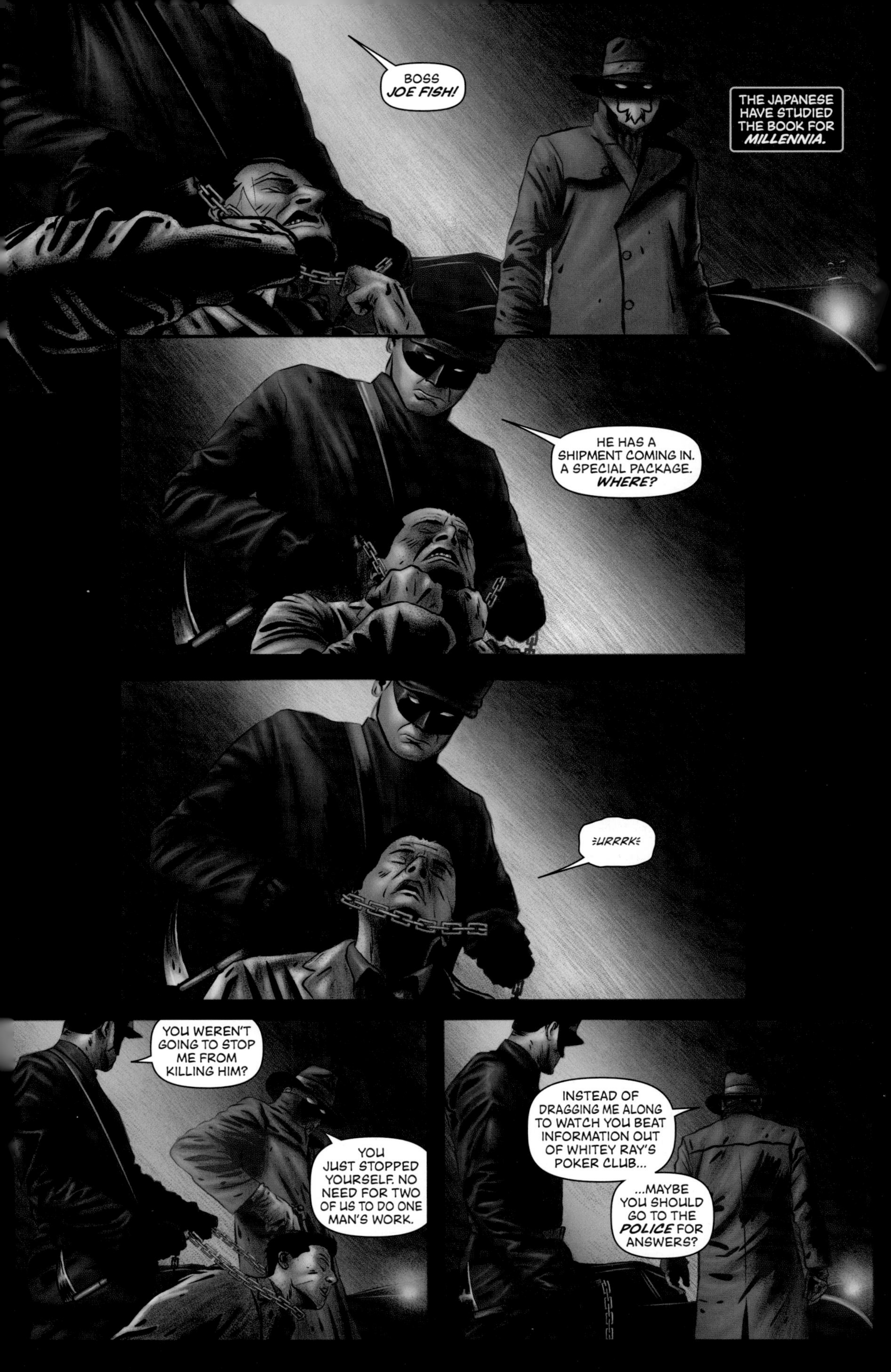
BOSS JOE FISH!
THE JAPANESE HAVE STUDIED THE BOOK FOR MILLENNIA.
HE HAS A SHIPMENT COMING IN. A SPECIAL PACKAGE. WHERE?
URRRK
YOU WEREN'T GOING TO STOP ME FROM KILLING HIM?
YOU JUST STOPPED YOURSELF. NO NEED FOR TWO OF US TO DO ONE MAN'S WORK.
INSTEAD OF DRAGGING ME ALONG TO WATCH YOU BEAT INFORMATION OUT OF WHITEY RAY'S POKER CLUB...
...MAYBE YOU SHOULD GO TO THE POLICE FOR ANSWERS?

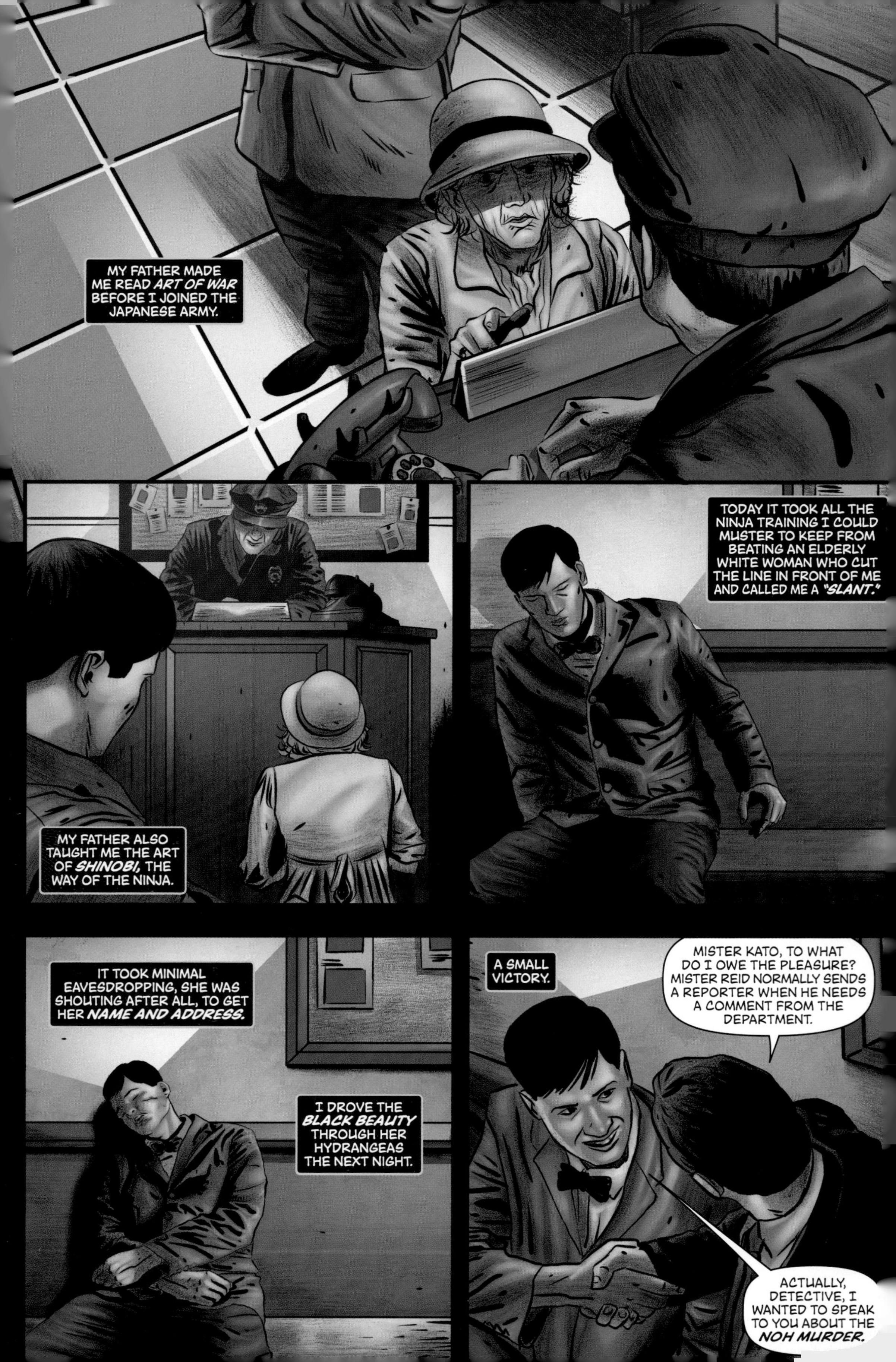
MY FATHER MADE ME READ *ART OF WAR* BEFORE I JOINED THE JAPANESE ARMY.
MY FATHER ALSO TAUGHT ME THE ART OF *SHINOBI,* THE WAY OF THE NINJA.
TODAY IT TOOK ALL THE NINJA TRAINING I COULD MUSTER TO KEEP FROM BEATING AN ELDERLY WHITE WOMAN WHO CUT THE LINE IN FRONT OF ME AND CALLED ME A *"SLANT."*
IT TOOK MINIMAL EAVESDROPPING, SHE WAS SHOUTING AFTER ALL, TO GET HER *NAME AND ADDRESS.*
I DROVE THE *BLACK BEAUTY* THROUGH HER HYDRANGEAS THE NEXT NIGHT.
A SMALL VICTORY.
MISTER KATO, TO WHAT DO I OWE THE PLEASURE? MISTER REID NORMALLY SENDS A REPORTER WHEN HE NEEDS A COMMENT FROM THE DEPARTMENT.
ACTUALLY, DETECTIVE, I WANTED TO SPEAK TO YOU ABOUT THE *NOH MURDER.*

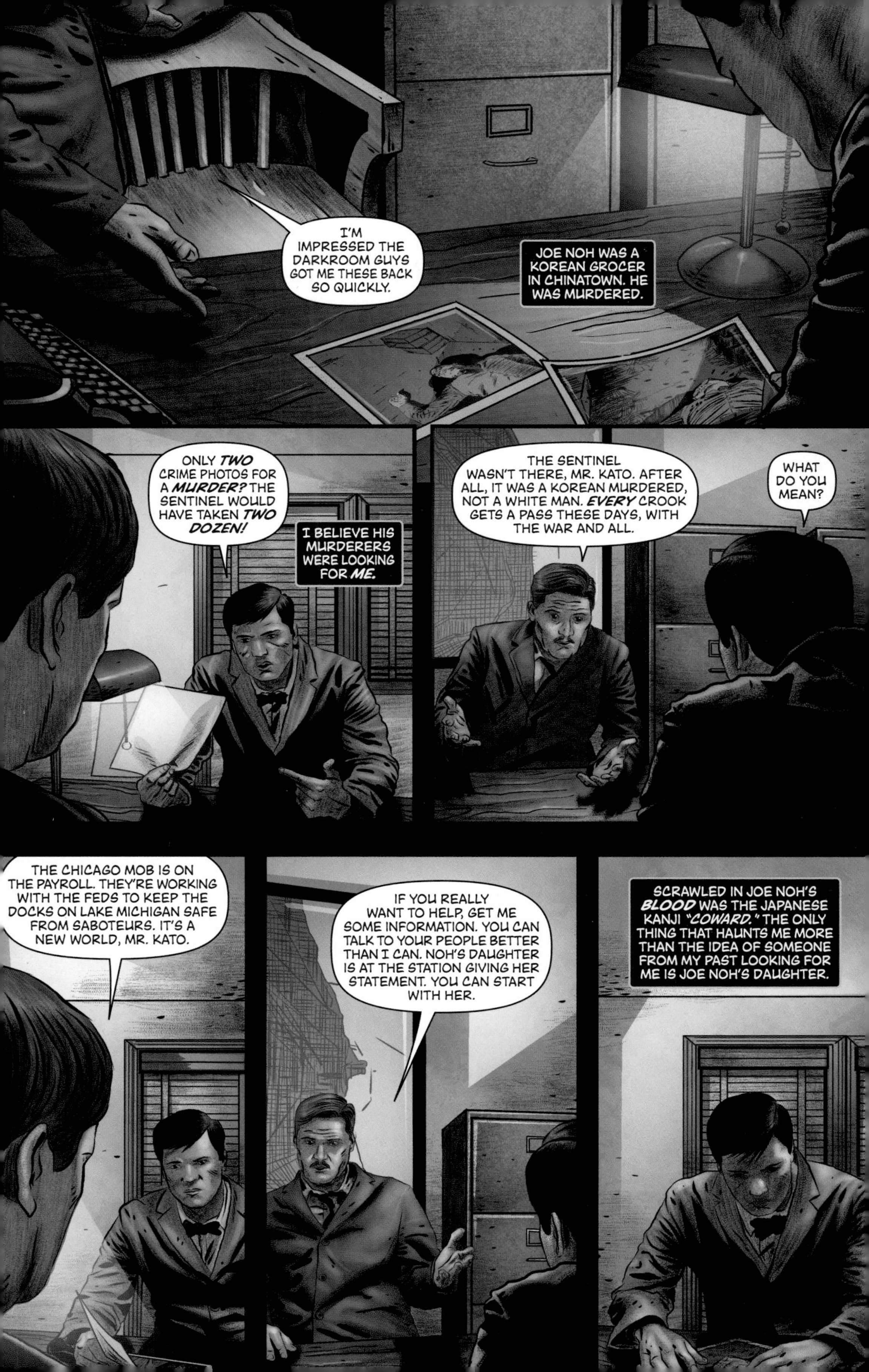
I'M IMPRESSED THE DARKROOM GUYS GOT ME THESE BACK SO QUICKLY.
JOE NOH WAS A KOREAN GROCER IN CHINATOWN. HE WAS MURDERED.
ONLY TWO CRIME PHOTOS FOR A MURDER? THE SENTINEL WOULD HAVE TAKEN TWO DOZEN!
I BELIEVE HIS MURDERERS WERE LOOKING FOR ME.
THE SENTINEL WASN'T THERE, MR. KATO. AFTER ALL, IT WAS A KOREAN MURDERED, NOT A WHITE MAN. EVERY CROOK GETS A PASS THESE DAYS, WITH THE WAR AND ALL.
WHAT DO YOU MEAN?
THE CHICAGO MOB IS ON THE PAYROLL. THEY'RE WORKING WITH THE FEDS TO KEEP THE DOCKS ON LAKE MICHIGAN SAFE FROM SABOTEURS. IT'S A NEW WORLD, MR. KATO.
IF YOU REALLY WANT TO HELP, GET ME SOME INFORMATION. YOU CAN TALK TO YOUR PEOPLE BETTER THAN I CAN. NOH'S DAUGHTER IS AT THE STATION GIVING HER STATEMENT. YOU CAN START WITH HER.
SCRAWLED IN JOE NOH'S BLOOD WAS THE JAPANESE KANJI "COWARD." THE ONLY THING THAT HAUNTS ME MORE THAN THE IDEA OF SOMEONE FROM MY PAST LOOKING FOR ME IS JOE NOH'S DAUGHTER.

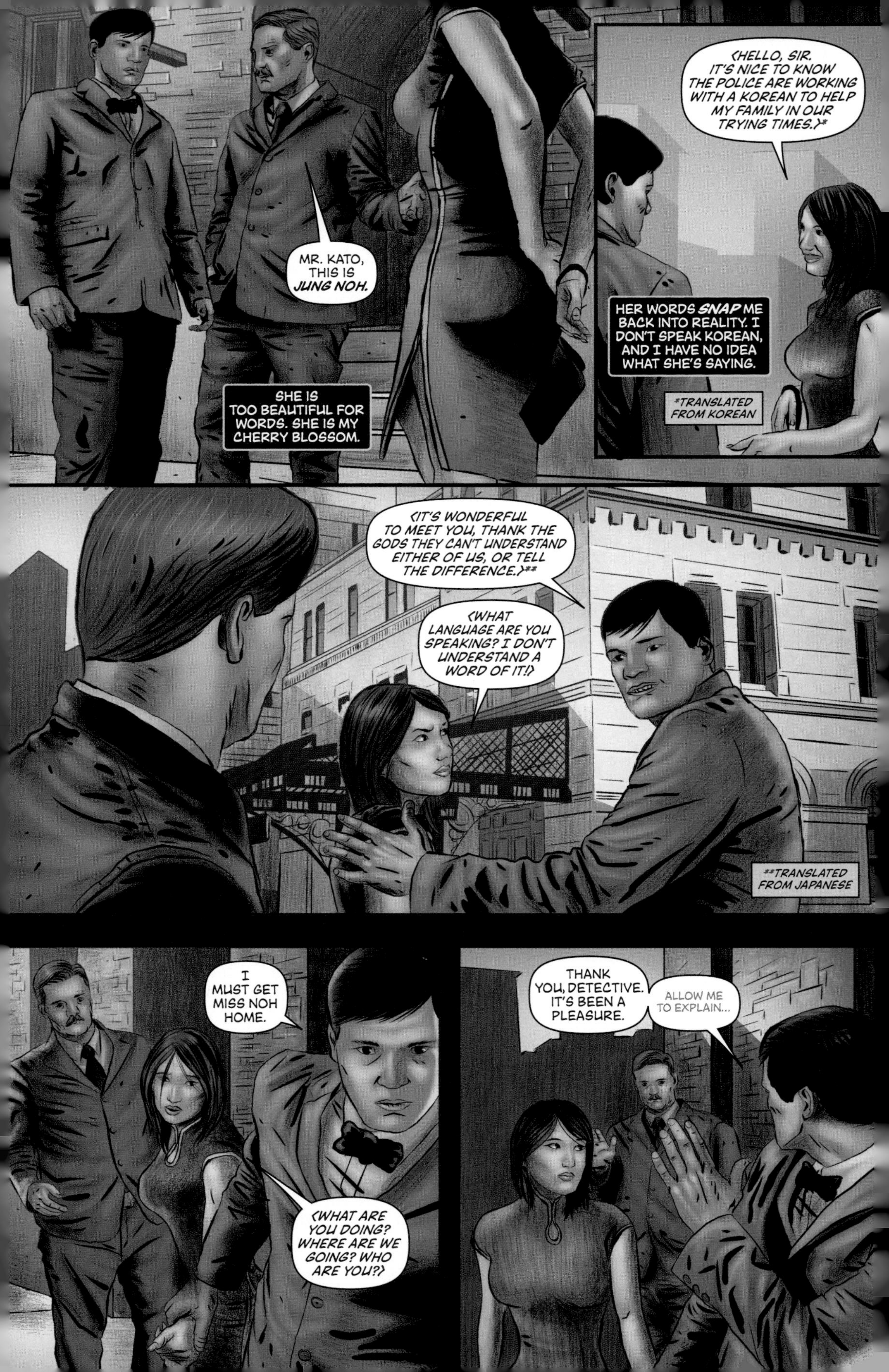
MR. KATO, THIS IS JUNG NOH.
SHE IS TOO BEAUTIFUL FOR WORDS. SHE IS MY CHERRY BLOSSOM.
<HELLO, SIR. IT'S NICE TO KNOW THE POLICE ARE WORKING WITH A KOREAN TO HELP MY FAMILY IN OUR TRYING TIMES.>*
HER WORDS SNAP ME BACK INTO REALITY. I DON'T SPEAK KOREAN, AND I HAVE NO IDEA WHAT SHE'S SAYING.
*TRANSLATED FROM KOREAN
<IT'S WONDERFUL TO MEET YOU, THANK THE GODS THEY CAN'T UNDERSTAND EITHER OF US, OR TELL THE DIFFERENCE.>**
<WHAT LANGUAGE ARE YOU SPEAKING? I DON'T UNDERSTAND A WORD OF IT!>
**TRANSLATED FROM JAPANESE
I MUST GET MISS NOH HOME.
<WHAT ARE YOU DOING? WHERE ARE WE GOING? WHO ARE YOU?>
THANK YOU, DETECTIVE. IT'S BEEN A PLEASURE.
ALLOW ME TO EXPLAIN...

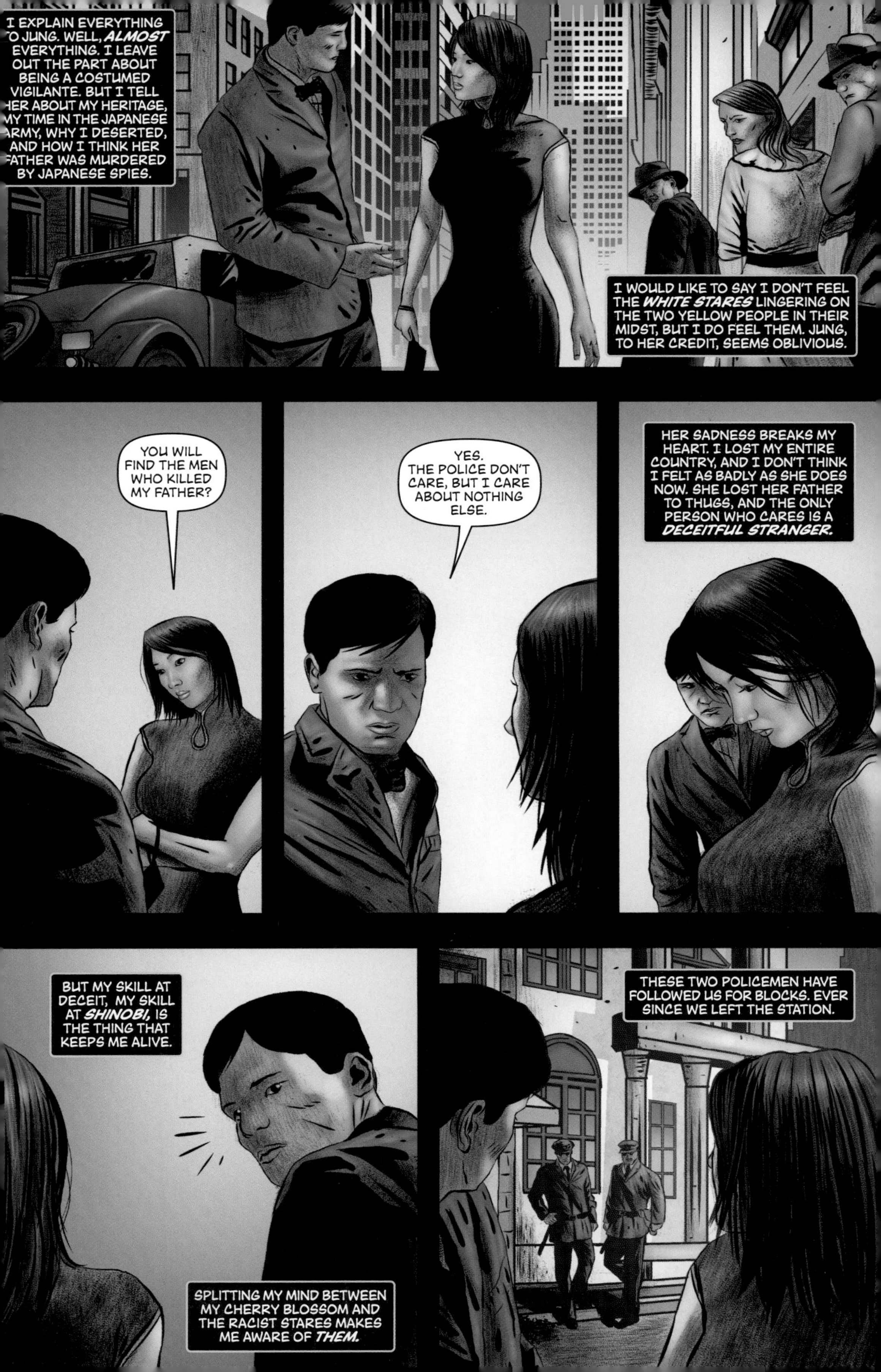

I EXPLAIN EVERYTHING TO JUNG. WELL, *ALMOST* EVERYTHING. I LEAVE OUT THE PART ABOUT BEING A COSTUMED VIGILANTE. BUT I TELL HER ABOUT MY HERITAGE, MY TIME IN THE JAPANESE ARMY, WHY I DESERTED, AND HOW I THINK HER FATHER WAS MURDERED BY JAPANESE SPIES.
I WOULD LIKE TO SAY I DON'T FEEL THE *WHITE STARES* LINGERING ON THE TWO YELLOW PEOPLE IN THEIR MIDST, BUT I DO FEEL THEM. JUNG, TO HER CREDIT, SEEMS OBLIVIOUS.
YOU WILL FIND THE MEN WHO KILLED MY FATHER?
YES. THE POLICE DON'T CARE, BUT I CARE ABOUT NOTHING ELSE.
HER SADNESS BREAKS MY HEART. I LOST MY ENTIRE COUNTRY, AND I DON'T THINK I FELT AS BADLY AS SHE DOES NOW. SHE LOST HER FATHER TO THUGS, AND THE ONLY PERSON WHO CARES IS A *DECEITFUL STRANGER.*
BUT MY SKILL AT DECEIT, MY SKILL AT *SHINOBI,* IS THE THING THAT KEEPS ME ALIVE.
SPLITTING MY MIND BETWEEN MY CHERRY BLOSSOM AND THE RACIST STARES MAKES ME AWARE OF *THEM.*
THESE TWO POLICEMEN HAVE FOLLOWED US FOR BLOCKS. EVER SINCE WE LEFT THE STATION.

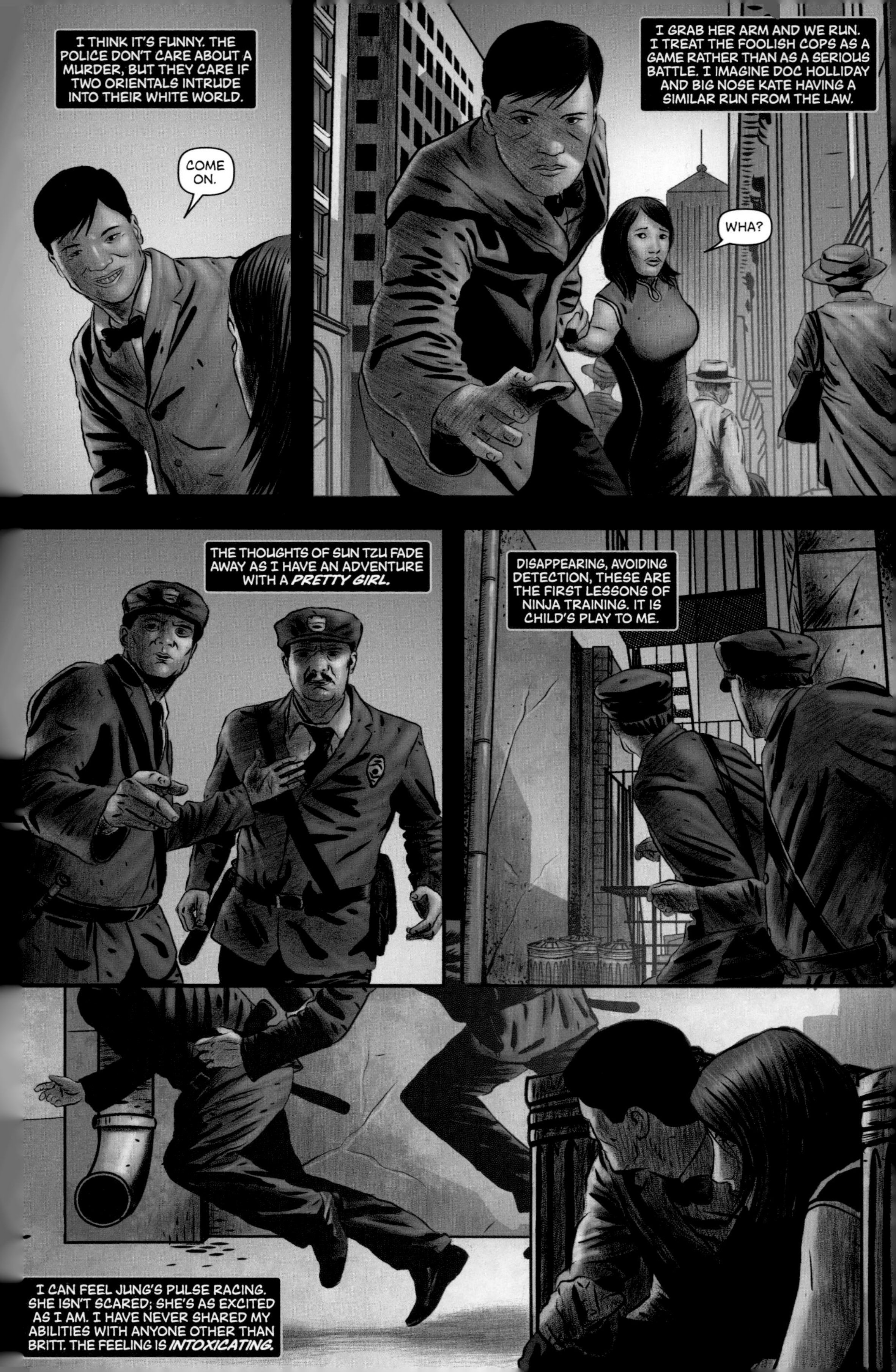
I THINK IT'S FUNNY. THE POLICE DON'T CARE ABOUT A MURDER, BUT THEY CARE IF TWO ORIENTALS INTRUDE INTO THEIR WHITE WORLD.
COME ON.
I GRAB HER ARM AND WE RUN. I TREAT THE FOOLISH COPS AS A GAME RATHER THAN AS A SERIOUS BATTLE. I IMAGINE DOC HOLLIDAY AND BIG NOSE KATE HAVING A SIMILAR RUN FROM THE LAW.
WHA?
THE THOUGHTS OF SUN TZU FADE AWAY AS I HAVE AN ADVENTURE WITH A *PRETTY GIRL.*
DISAPPEARING, AVOIDING DETECTION, THESE ARE THE FIRST LESSONS OF NINJA TRAINING. IT IS CHILD'S PLAY TO ME.
I CAN FEEL JUNG'S PULSE RACING. SHE ISN'T SCARED; SHE'S AS EXCITED AS I AM. I HAVE NEVER SHARED MY ABILITIES WITH ANYONE OTHER THAN BRITT. THE FEELING IS *INTOXICATING.*

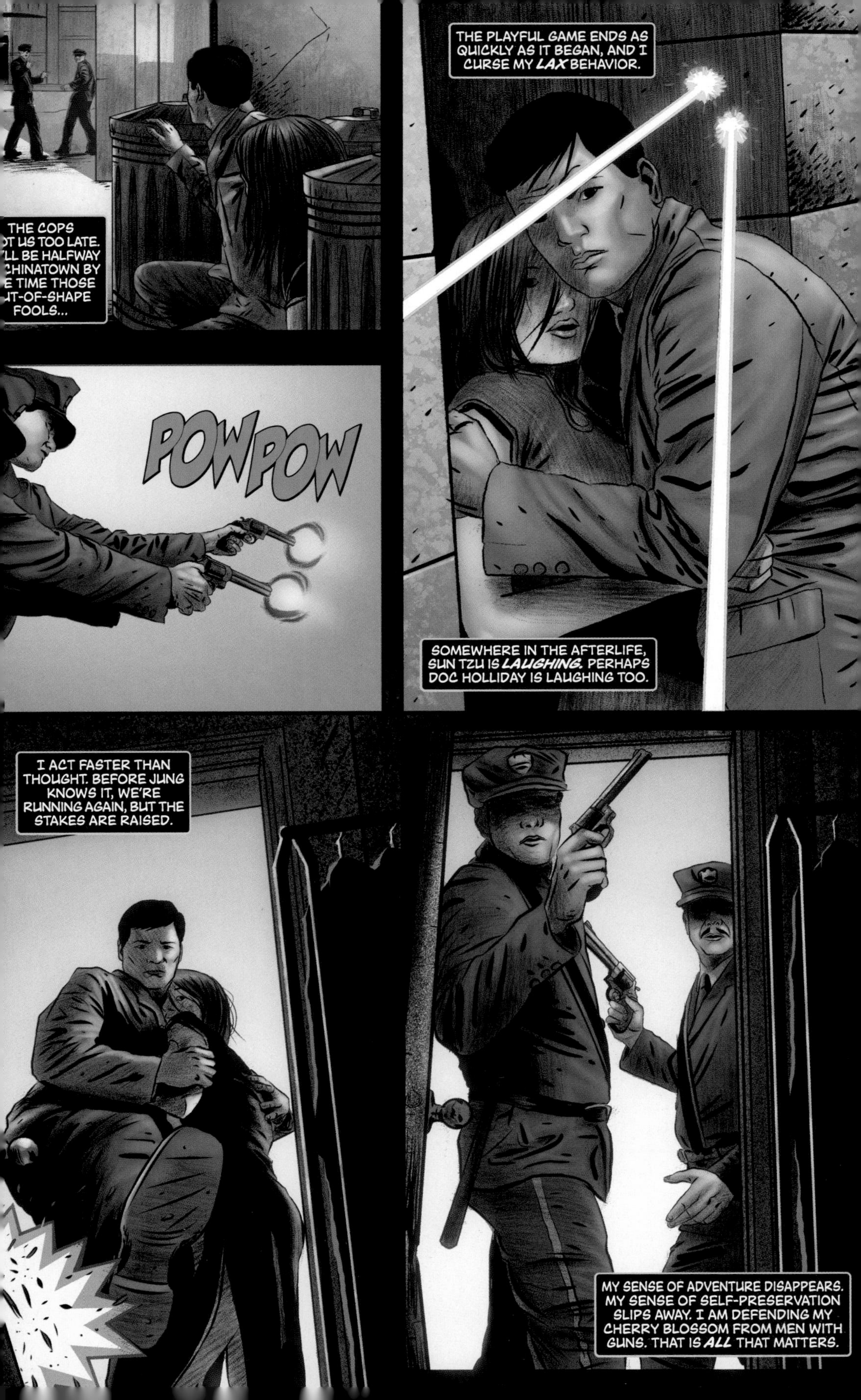
THE COPS
OT US TOO LATE.
'LL BE HALFWAY
CHINATOWN BY
E TIME THOSE
IT-OF-SHAPE
FOOLS...
POW POW
THE PLAYFUL GAME ENDS AS QUICKLY AS IT BEGAN, AND I CURSE MY LAX BEHAVIOR.
SOMEWHERE IN THE AFTERLIFE, SUN TZU IS LAUGHING. PERHAPS DOC HOLLIDAY IS LAUGHING TOO.
I ACT FASTER THAN THOUGHT. BEFORE JUNG KNOWS IT, WE'RE RUNNING AGAIN, BUT THE STAKES ARE RAISED.
MY SENSE OF ADVENTURE DISAPPEARS. MY SENSE OF SELF-PRESERVATION SLIPS AWAY. I AM DEFENDING MY CHERRY BLOSSOM FROM MEN WITH GUNS. THAT IS ALL THAT MATTERS.

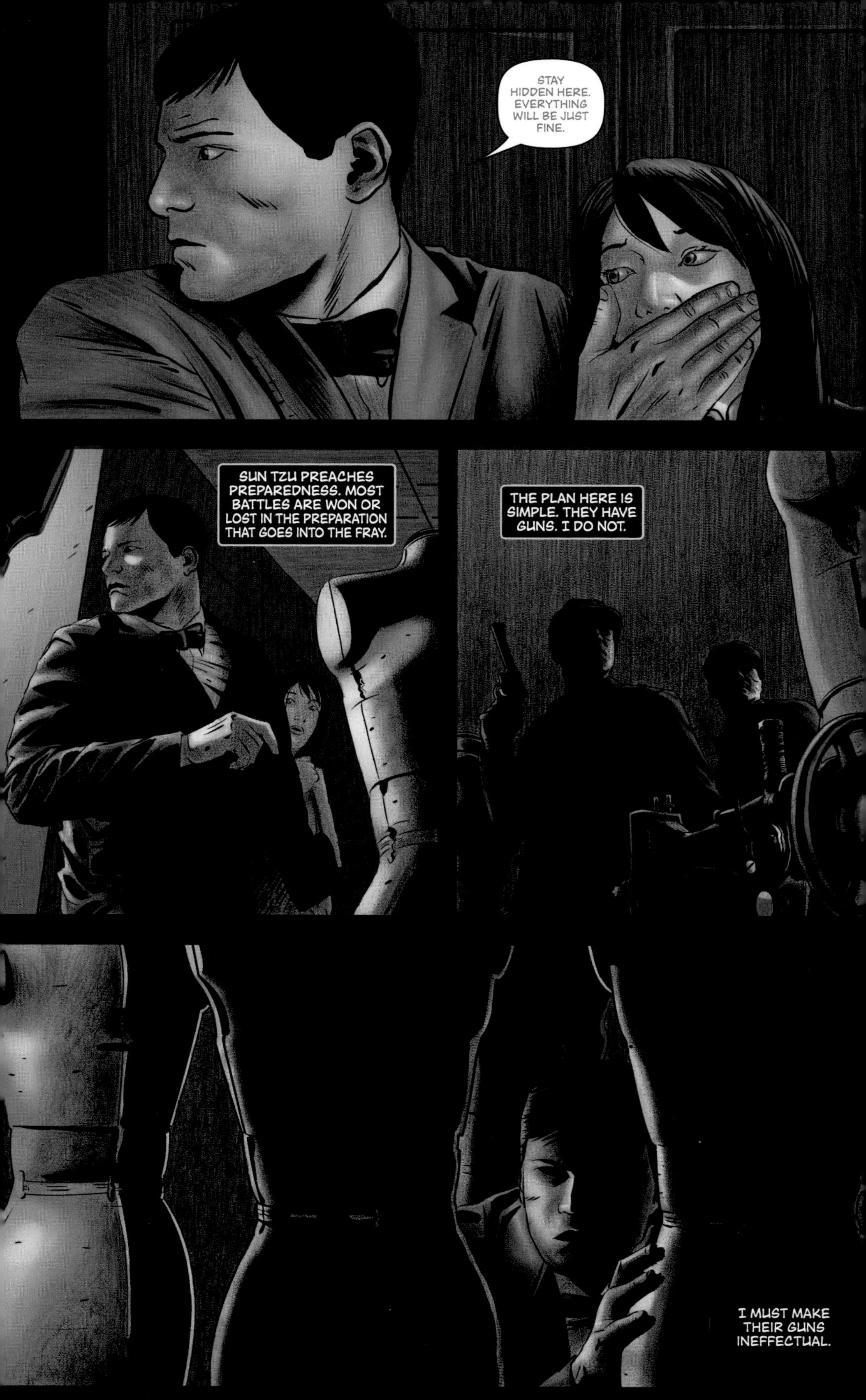
STAY HIDDEN HERE. EVERYTHING WILL BE JUST FINE.
SUN TZU PREACHES PREPAREDNESS. MOST BATTLES ARE WON OR LOST IN THE PREPARATION THAT GOES INTO THE FRAY.
THE PLAN HERE IS SIMPLE. THEY HAVE GUNS. I DO NOT.
I MUST MAKE THEIR GUNS INEFFECTUAL.

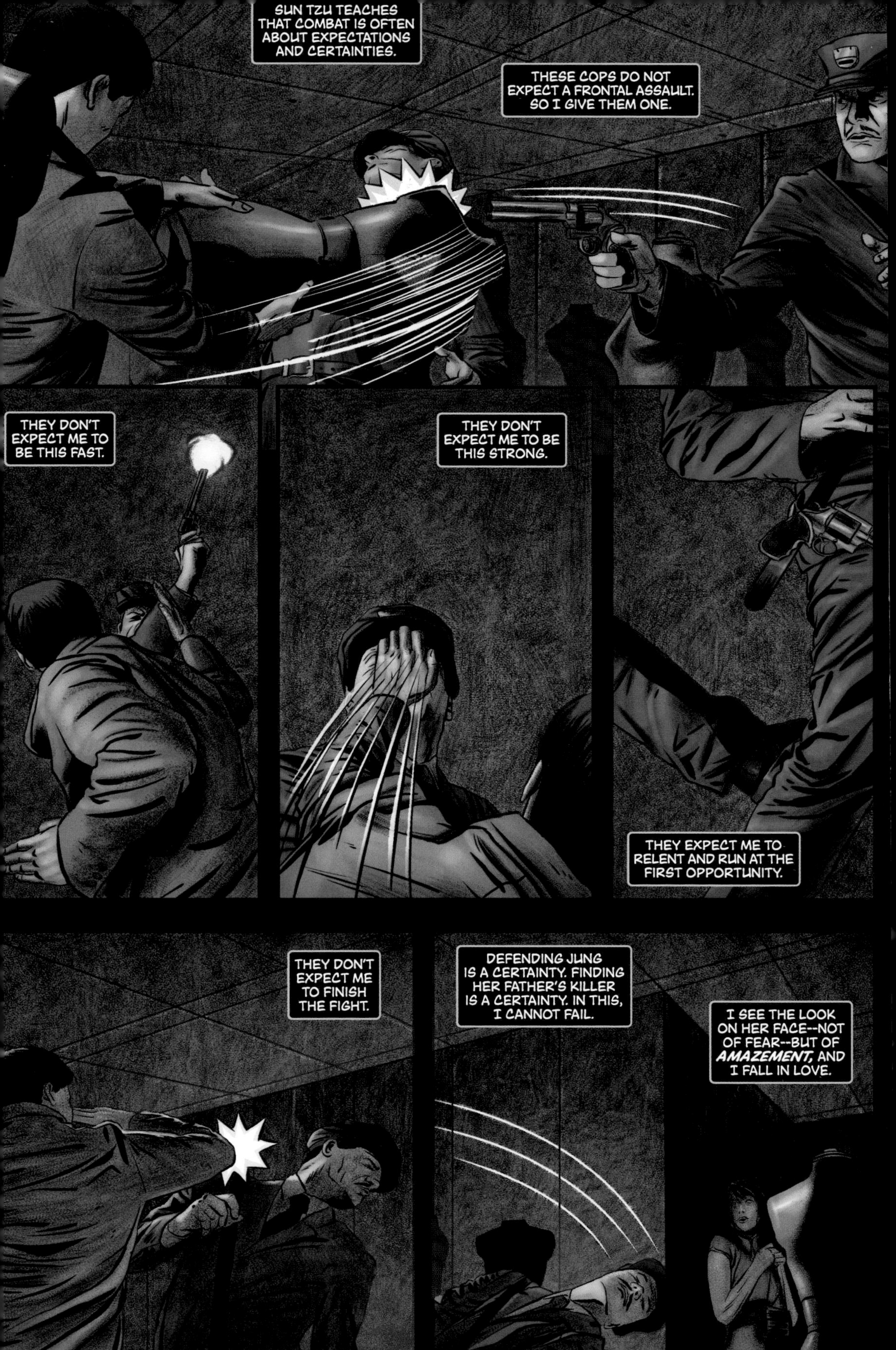
SUN TZU TEACHES THAT COMBAT IS OFTEN ABOUT EXPECTATIONS AND CERTAINTIES.
THESE COPS DO NOT EXPECT A FRONTAL ASSAULT. SO I GIVE THEM ONE.
THEY DON'T EXPECT ME TO BE THIS FAST.
THEY DON'T EXPECT ME TO BE THIS STRONG.
THEY EXPECT ME TO RELENT AND RUN AT THE FIRST OPPORTUNITY.
THEY DON'T EXPECT ME TO FINISH THE FIGHT.
DEFENDING JUNG IS A CERTAINTY. FINDING HER FATHER'S KILLER IS A CERTAINTY. IN THIS, I CANNOT FAIL.
I SEE THE LOOK ON HER FACE--NOT OF FEAR--BUT OF *AMAZEMENT,* AND I FALL IN LOVE.

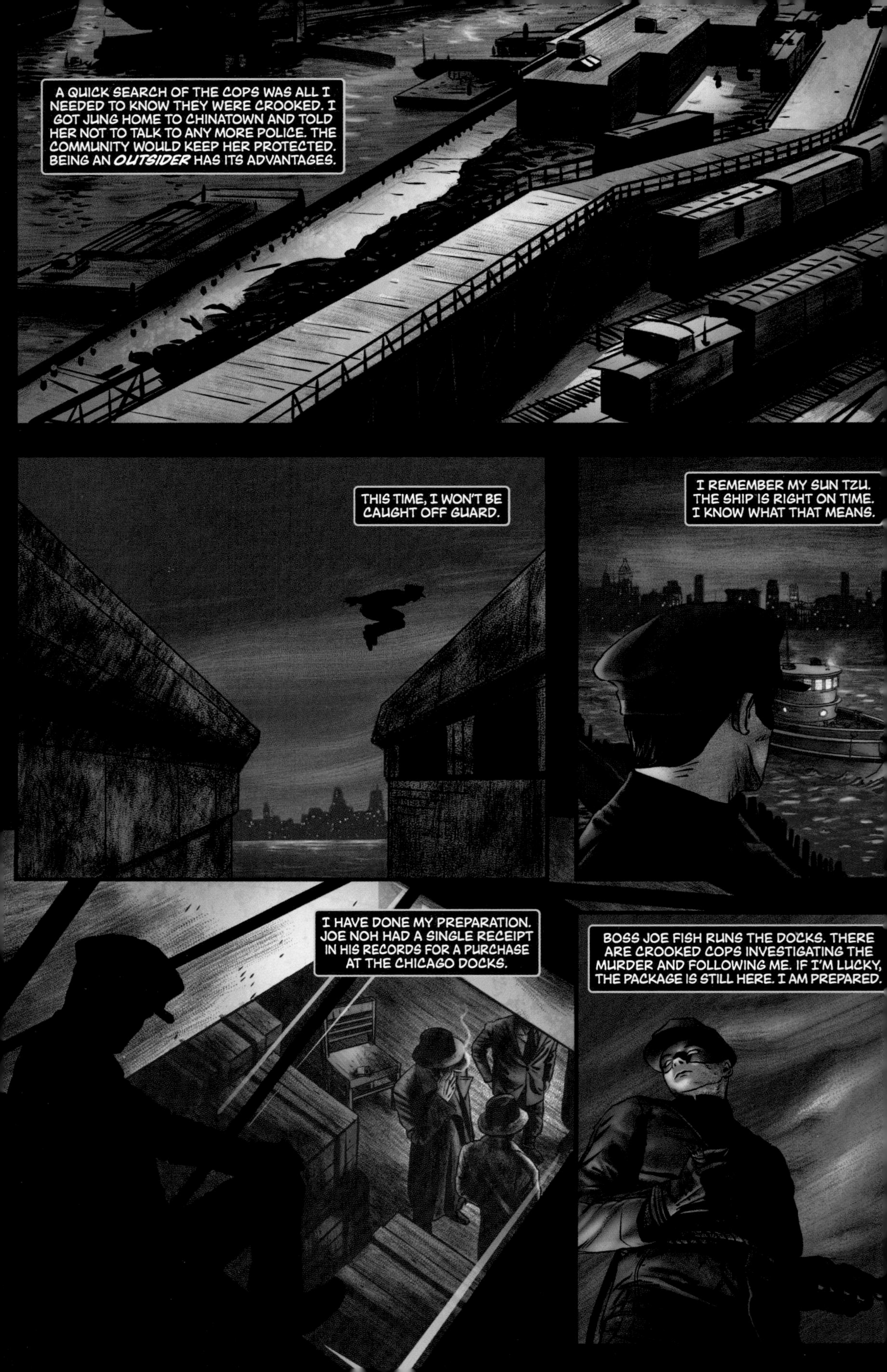
A QUICK SEARCH OF THE COPS WAS ALL I NEEDED TO KNOW THEY WERE CROOKED. I GOT JUNG HOME TO CHINATOWN AND TOLD HER NOT TO TALK TO ANY MORE POLICE. THE COMMUNITY WOULD KEEP HER PROTECTED. BEING AN *OUTSIDER* HAS ITS ADVANTAGES.
THIS TIME, I WON'T BE CAUGHT OFF GUARD.
I REMEMBER MY SUN TZU. THE SHIP IS RIGHT ON TIME. I KNOW WHAT THAT MEANS.
I HAVE DONE MY PREPARATION. JOE NOH HAD A SINGLE RECEIPT IN HIS RECORDS FOR A PURCHASE AT THE CHICAGO DOCKS.
BOSS JOE FISH RUNS THE DOCKS. THERE ARE CROOKED COPS INVESTIGATING THE MURDER AND FOLLOWING ME. IF I'M LUCKY, THE PACKAGE IS STILL HERE. I AM PREPARED.

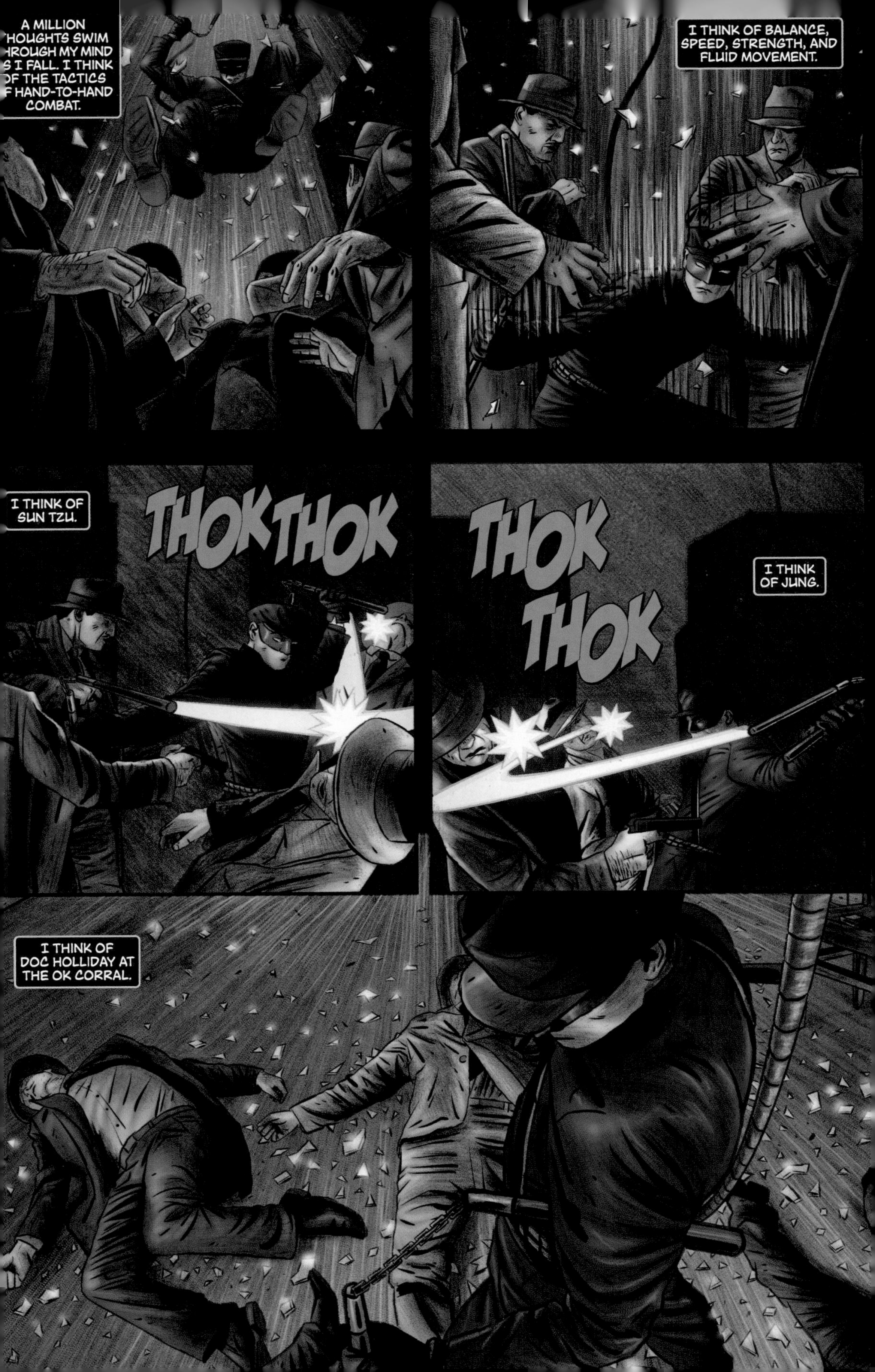
A MILLION THOUGHTS SWIM THROUGH MY MIND AS I FALL. I THINK OF THE TACTICS OF HAND-TO-HAND COMBAT.
I THINK OF BALANCE, SPEED, STRENGTH, AND FLUID MOVEMENT.
I THINK OF SUN TZU.
THOK THOK
THOK
THOK
I THINK OF JUNG.
I THINK OF DOC HOLLIDAY AT THE OK CORRAL.

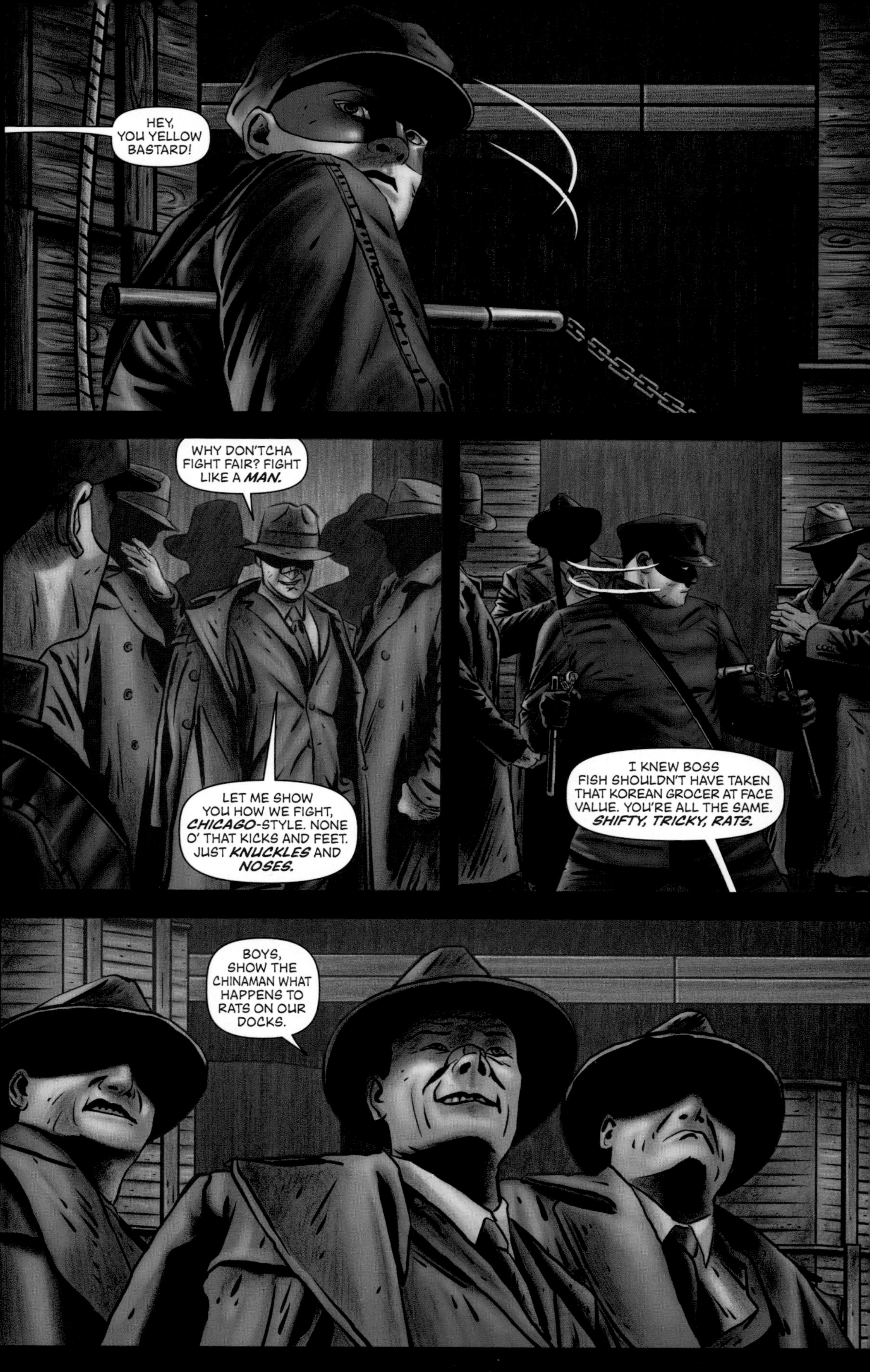
HEY, YOU YELLOW BASTARD!
WHY DON'TCHA FIGHT FAIR? FIGHT LIKE A *MAN.*
LET ME SHOW YOU HOW WE FIGHT, *CHICAGO*-STYLE. NONE O' THAT KICKS AND FEET. JUST *KNUCKLES* AND *NOSES.*
I KNEW BOSS FISH SHOULDN'T HAVE TAKEN THAT KOREAN GROCER AT FACE VALUE. YOU'RE ALL THE SAME. *SHIFTY, TRICKY, RATS.*
BOYS, SHOW THE CHINAMAN WHAT HAPPENS TO RATS ON OUR DOCKS.

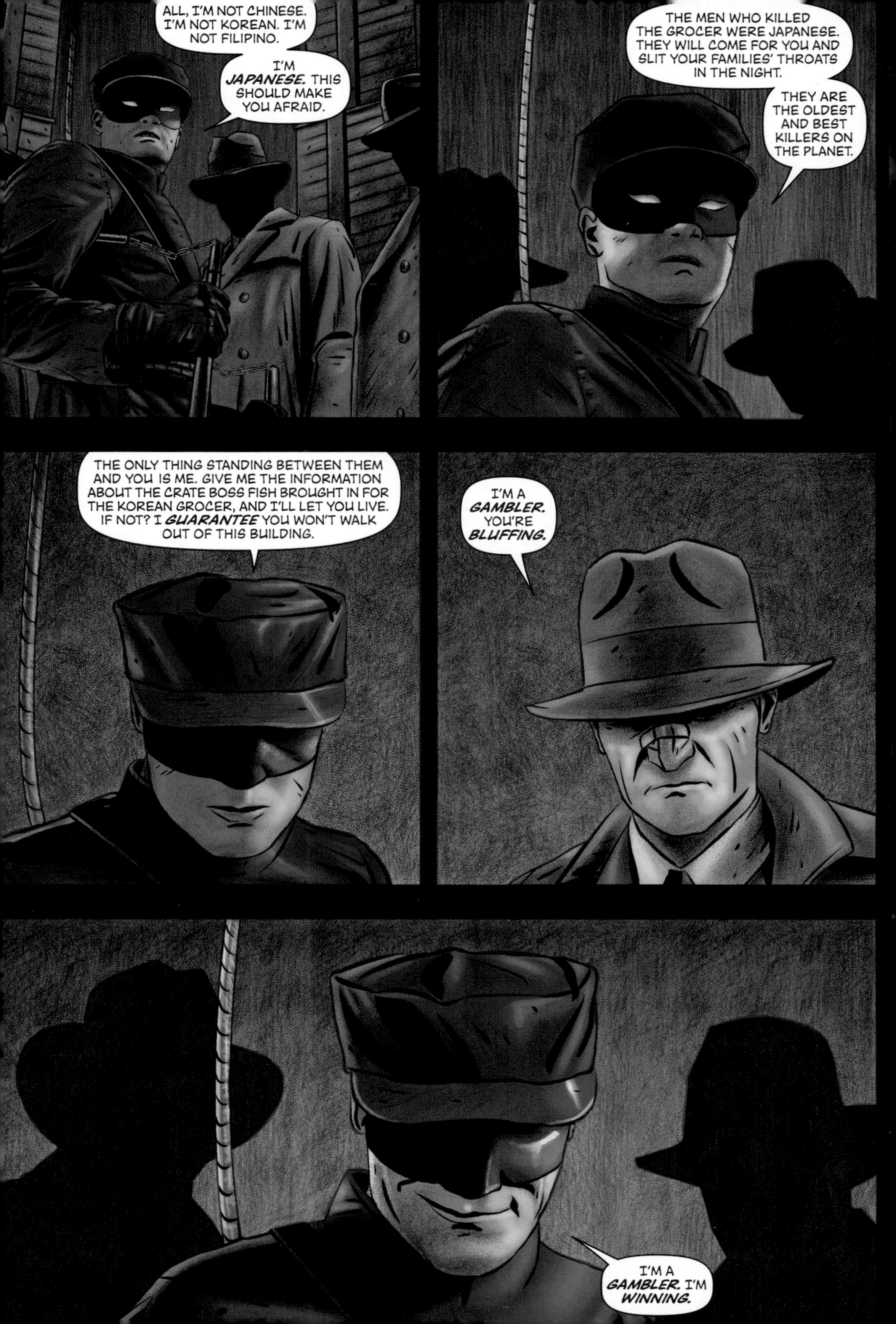
ALL, I'M NOT CHINESE. I'M NOT KOREAN. I'M NOT FILIPINO.
I'M JAPANESE. THIS SHOULD MAKE YOU AFRAID.
THE MEN WHO KILLED THE GROCER WERE JAPANESE. THEY WILL COME FOR YOU AND SLIT YOUR FAMILIES' THROATS IN THE NIGHT.
THEY ARE THE OLDEST AND BEST KILLERS ON THE PLANET.
THE ONLY THING STANDING BETWEEN THEM AND YOU IS ME. GIVE ME THE INFORMATION ABOUT THE CRATE BOSS FISH BROUGHT IN FOR THE KOREAN GROCER, AND I'LL LET YOU LIVE. IF NOT? I GUARANTEE YOU WON'T WALK OUT OF THIS BUILDING.
I'M A GAMBLER. YOU'RE BLUFFING.
I'M A GAMBLER. I'M WINNING.

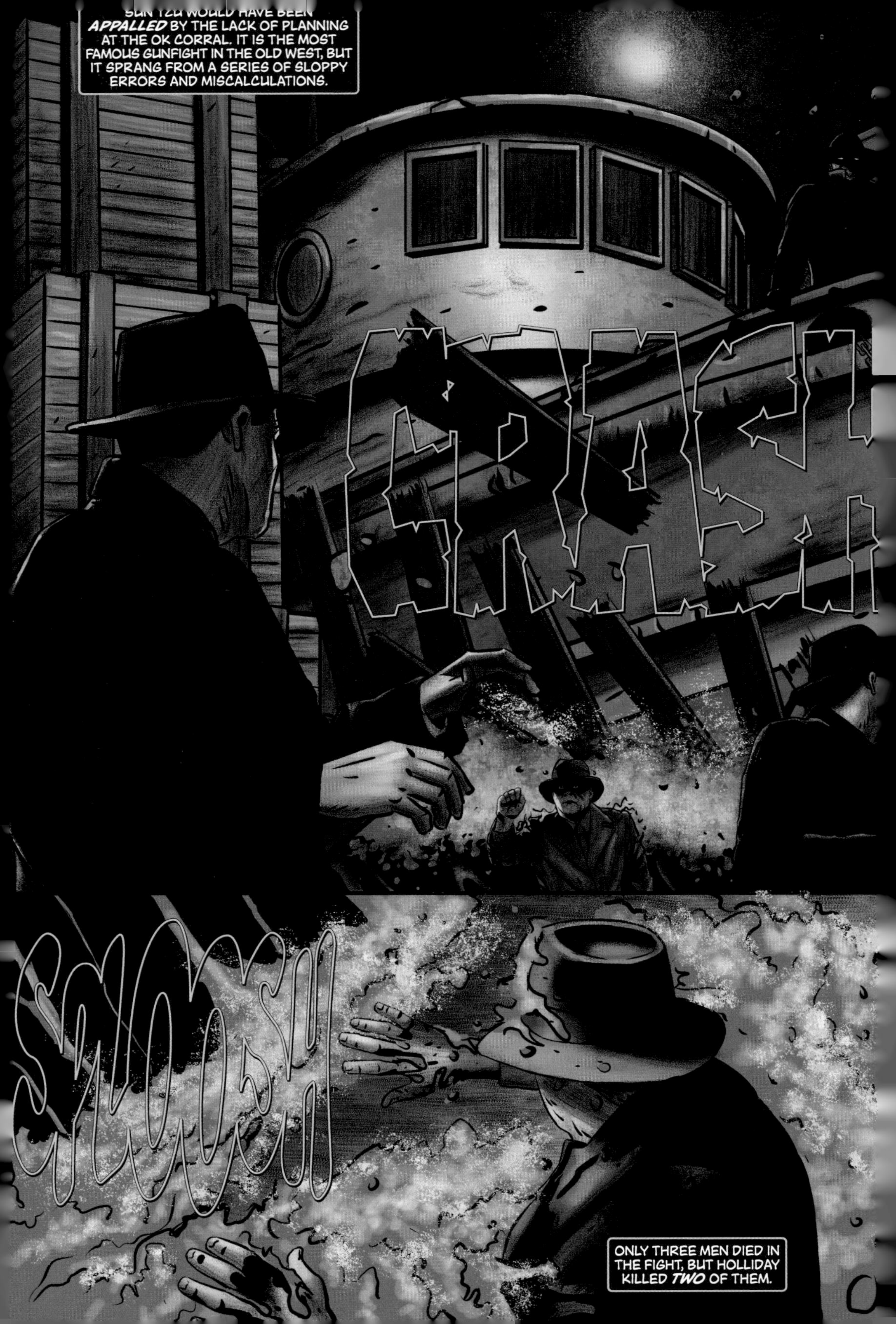
SUN TZU WOULD HAVE BEEN *APPALLED* BY THE LACK OF PLANNING AT THE OK CORRAL. IT IS THE MOST FAMOUS GUNFIGHT IN THE OLD WEST, BUT IT SPRANG FROM A SERIES OF SLOPPY ERRORS AND MISCALCULATIONS.
CRASH
SPLOOSH
ONLY THREE MEN DIED IN THE FIGHT, BUT HOLLIDAY KILLED *TWO* OF THEM.

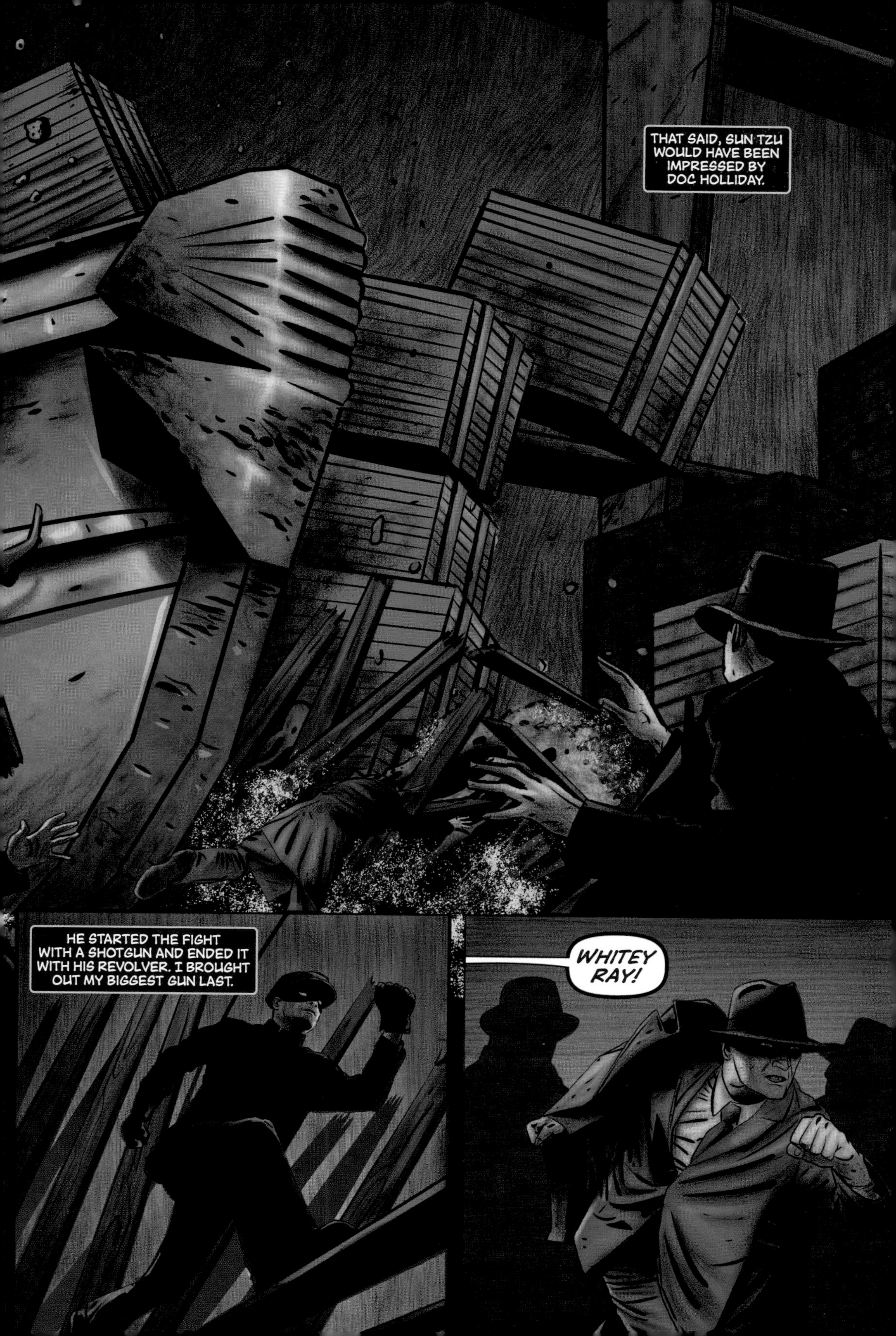
THAT SAID, SUN TZU WOULD HAVE BEEN IMPRESSED BY DOC HOLLIDAY.
HE STARTED THE FIGHT WITH A SHOTGUN AND ENDED IT WITH HIS REVOLVER. I BROUGHT OUT MY BIGGEST GUN LAST.
WHITEY RAY!

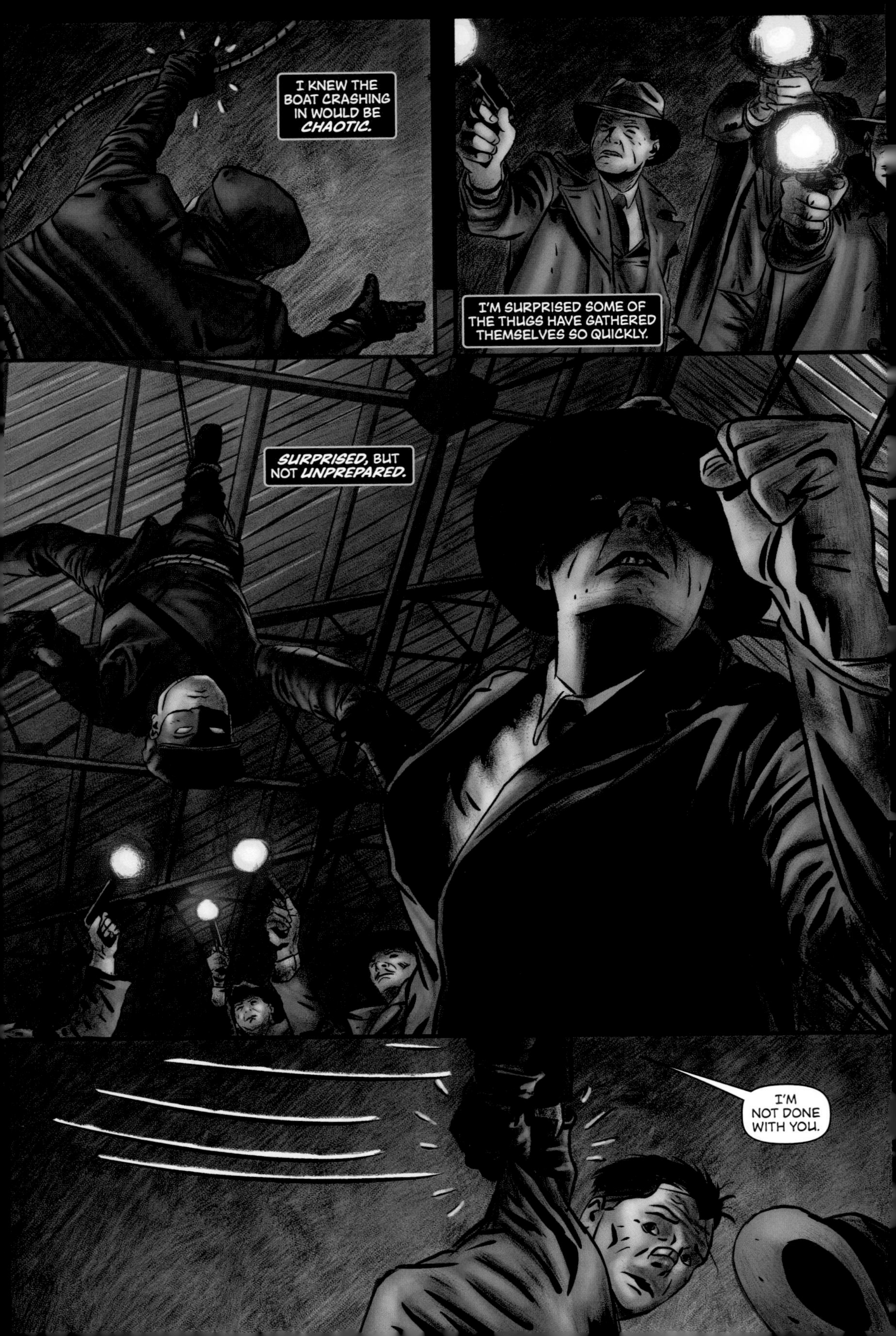
I KNEW THE BOAT CRASHING IN WOULD BE *CHAOTIC.*
I'M SURPRISED SOME OF THE THUGS HAVE GATHERED THEMSELVES SO QUICKLY.
SURPRISED, BUT NOT *UNPREPARED.*
I'M NOT DONE WITH YOU.

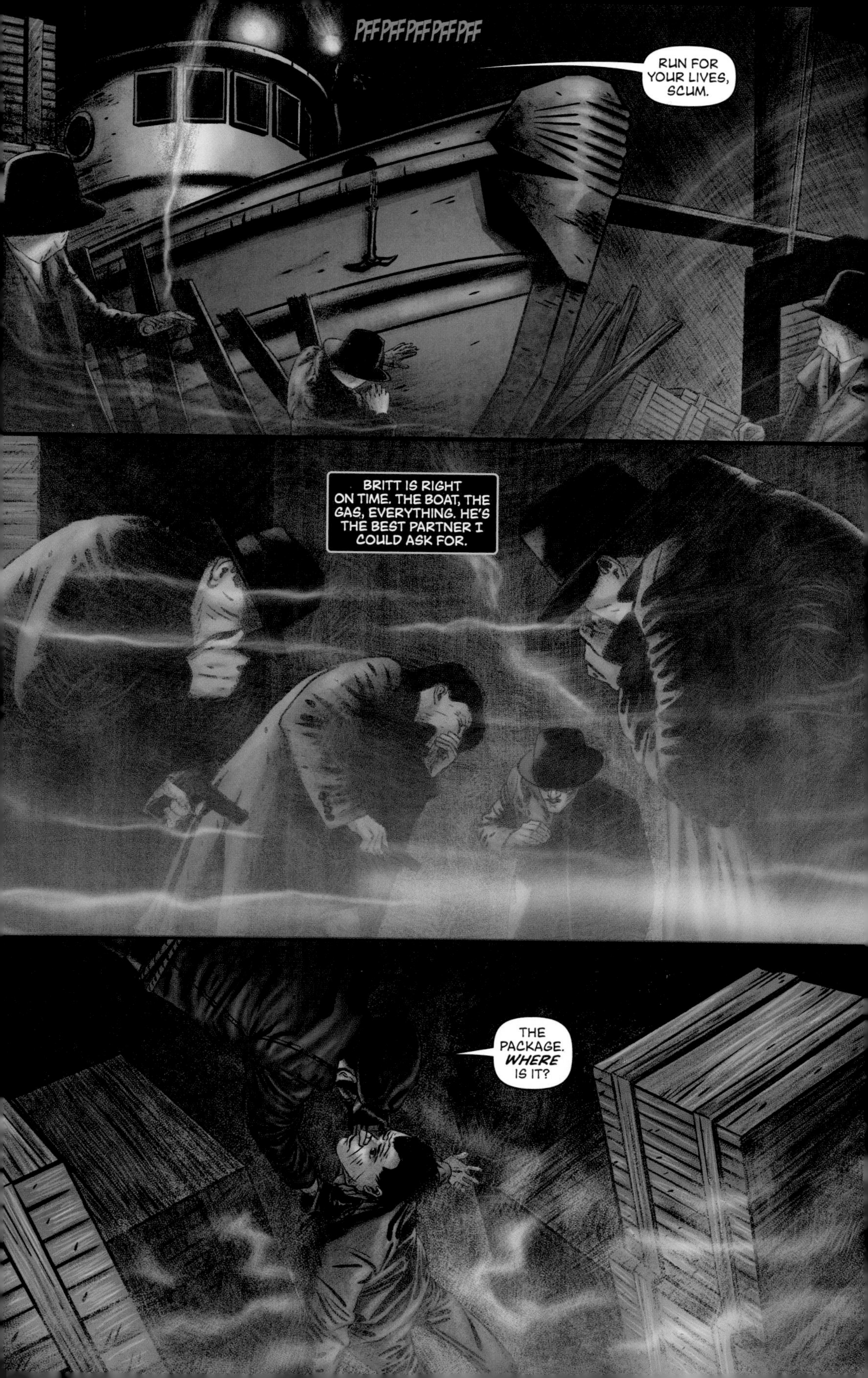
PFF PFF PFF PFF PFF
RUN FOR YOUR LIVES, SCUM.
BRITT IS RIGHT ON TIME. THE BOAT, THE GAS, EVERYTHING. HE'S THE BEST PARTNER I COULD ASK FOR.
THE PACKAGE. *WHERE* IS IT?

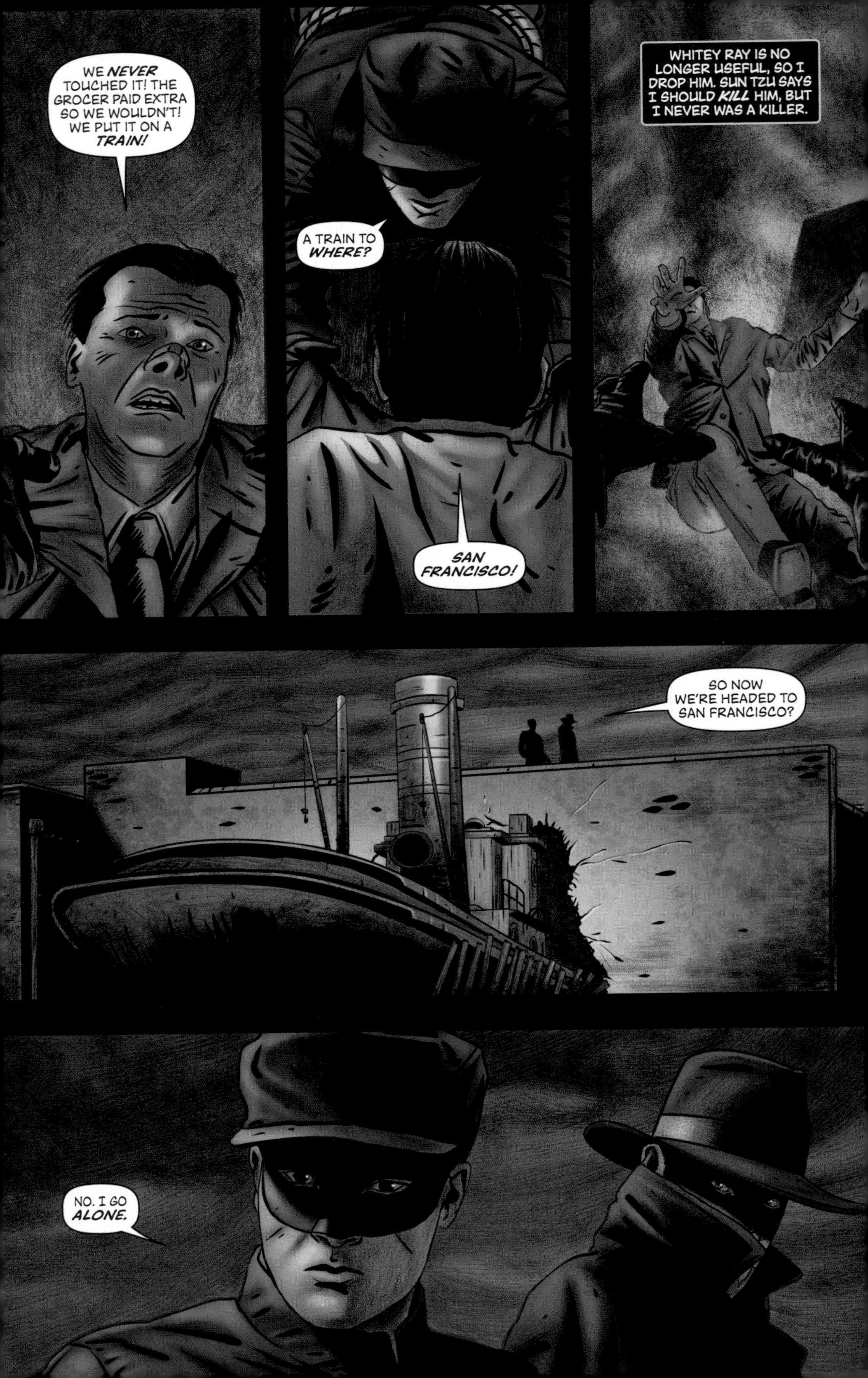
WE NEVER TOUCHED IT! THE GROCER PAID EXTRA SO WE WOULDN'T! WE PUT IT ON A TRAIN!
A TRAIN TO WHERE?
SAN FRANCISCO!
WHITEY RAY IS NO LONGER USEFUL, SO I DROP HIM. SUN TZU SAYS I SHOULD KILL HIM, BUT I NEVER WAS A KILLER.
SO NOW WE'RE HEADED TO SAN FRANCISCO?
NO. I GO ALONE.

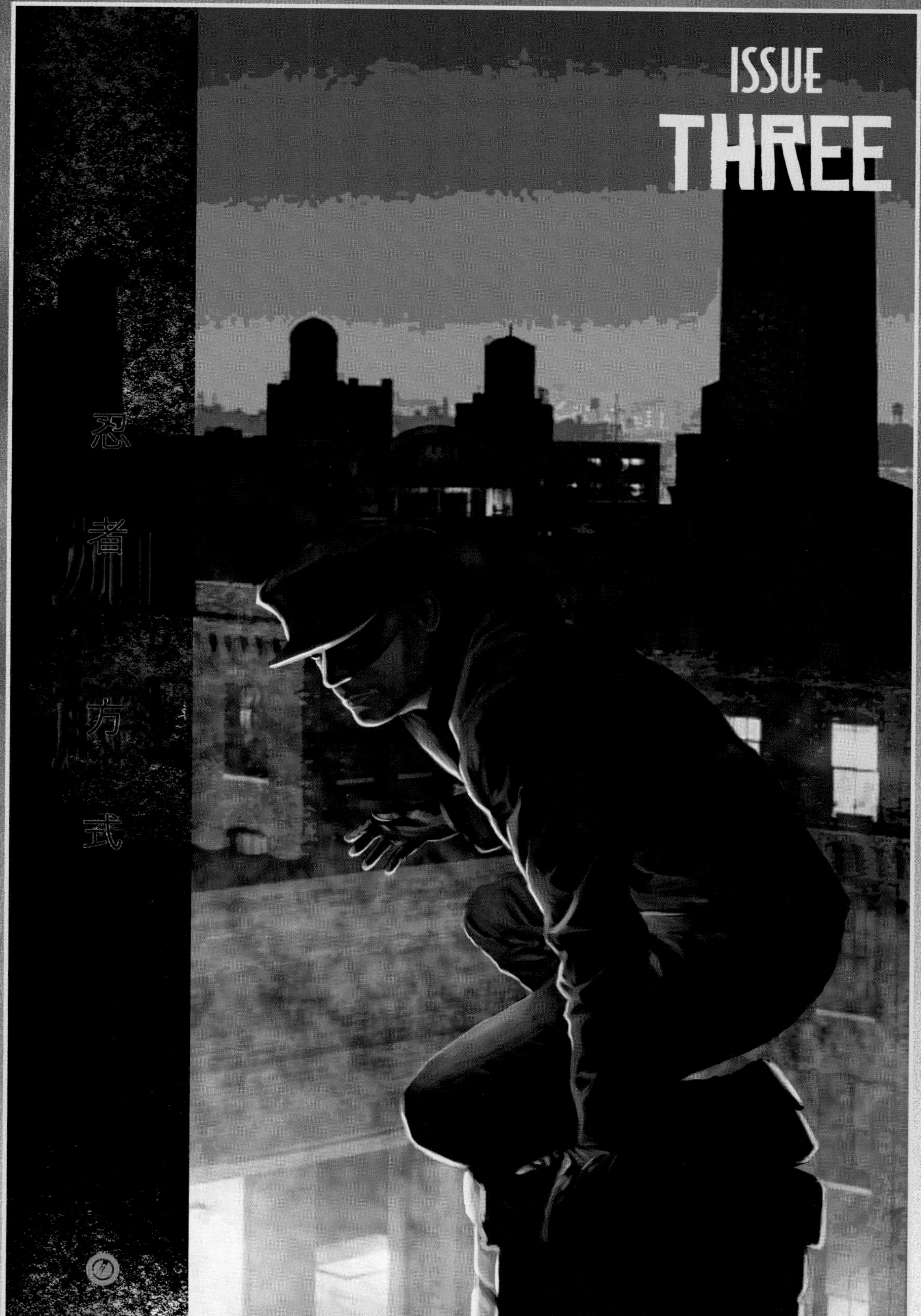
ISSUE
THREE
忍
者
方
式

Issue three cover by **COLTON WORLEY**

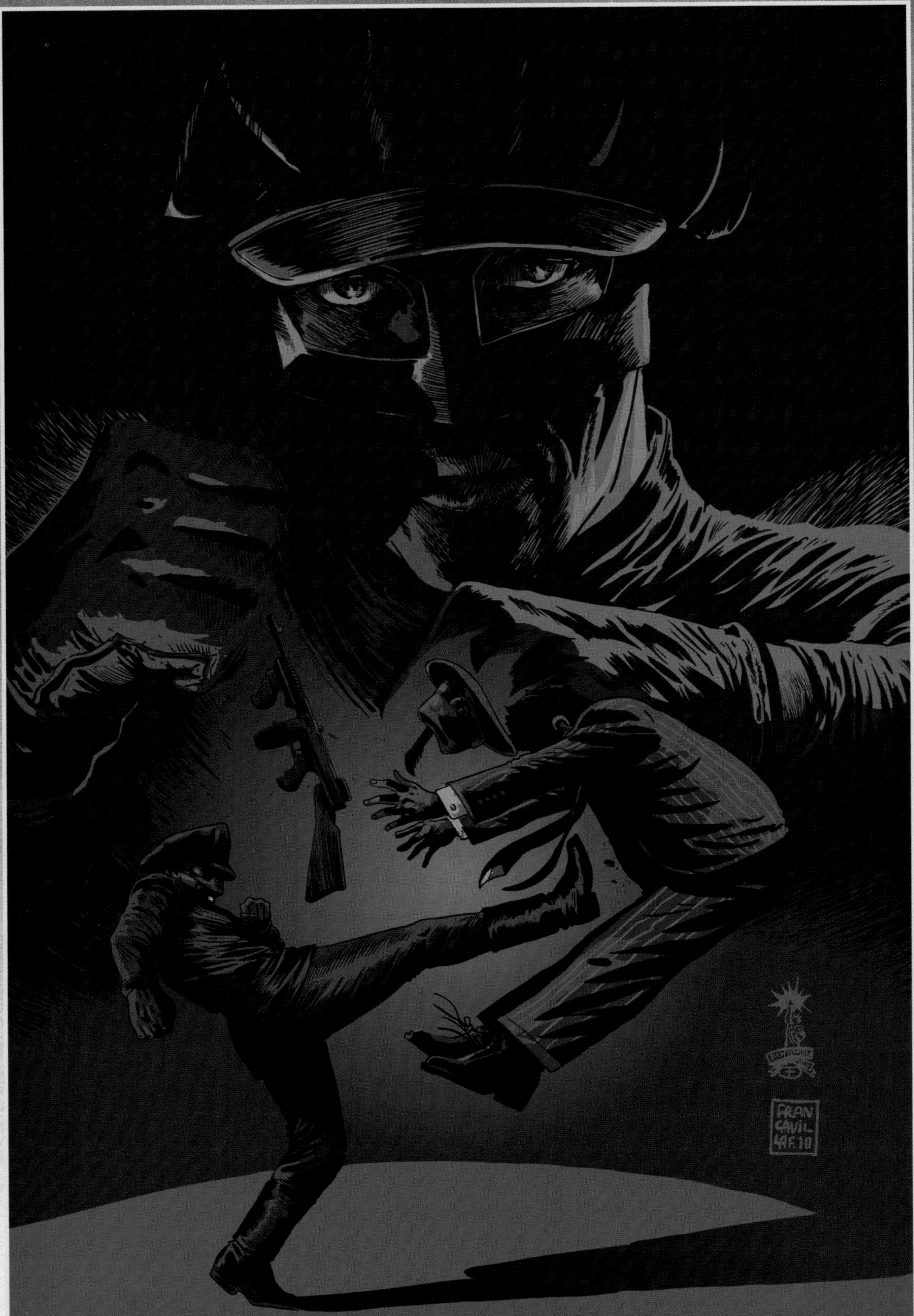

Issue three alternate cover by **FRANCESCO FRANCAVILLA**

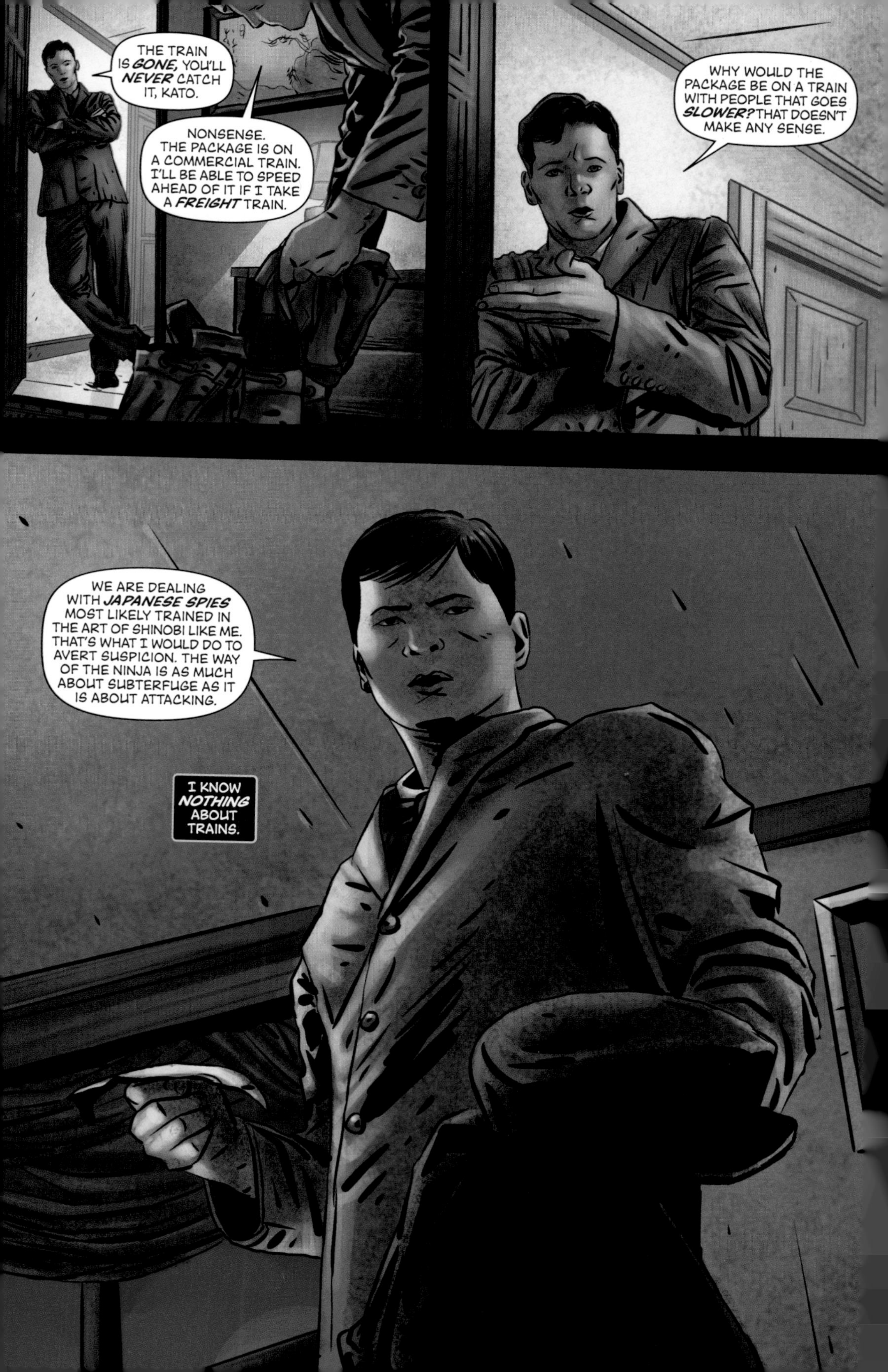
THE TRAIN IS GONE, YOU'LL NEVER CATCH IT, KATO.
NONSENSE. THE PACKAGE IS ON A COMMERCIAL TRAIN. I'LL BE ABLE TO SPEED AHEAD OF IT IF I TAKE A FREIGHT TRAIN.
WHY WOULD THE PACKAGE BE ON A TRAIN WITH PEOPLE THAT GOES SLOWER? THAT DOESN'T MAKE ANY SENSE.
WE ARE DEALING WITH JAPANESE SPIES MOST LIKELY TRAINED IN THE ART OF SHINOBI LIKE ME. THAT'S WHAT I WOULD DO TO AVERT SUSPICION. THE WAY OF THE NINJA IS AS MUCH ABOUT SUBTERFUGE AS IT IS ABOUT ATTACKING.
I KNOW NOTHING ABOUT TRAINS.

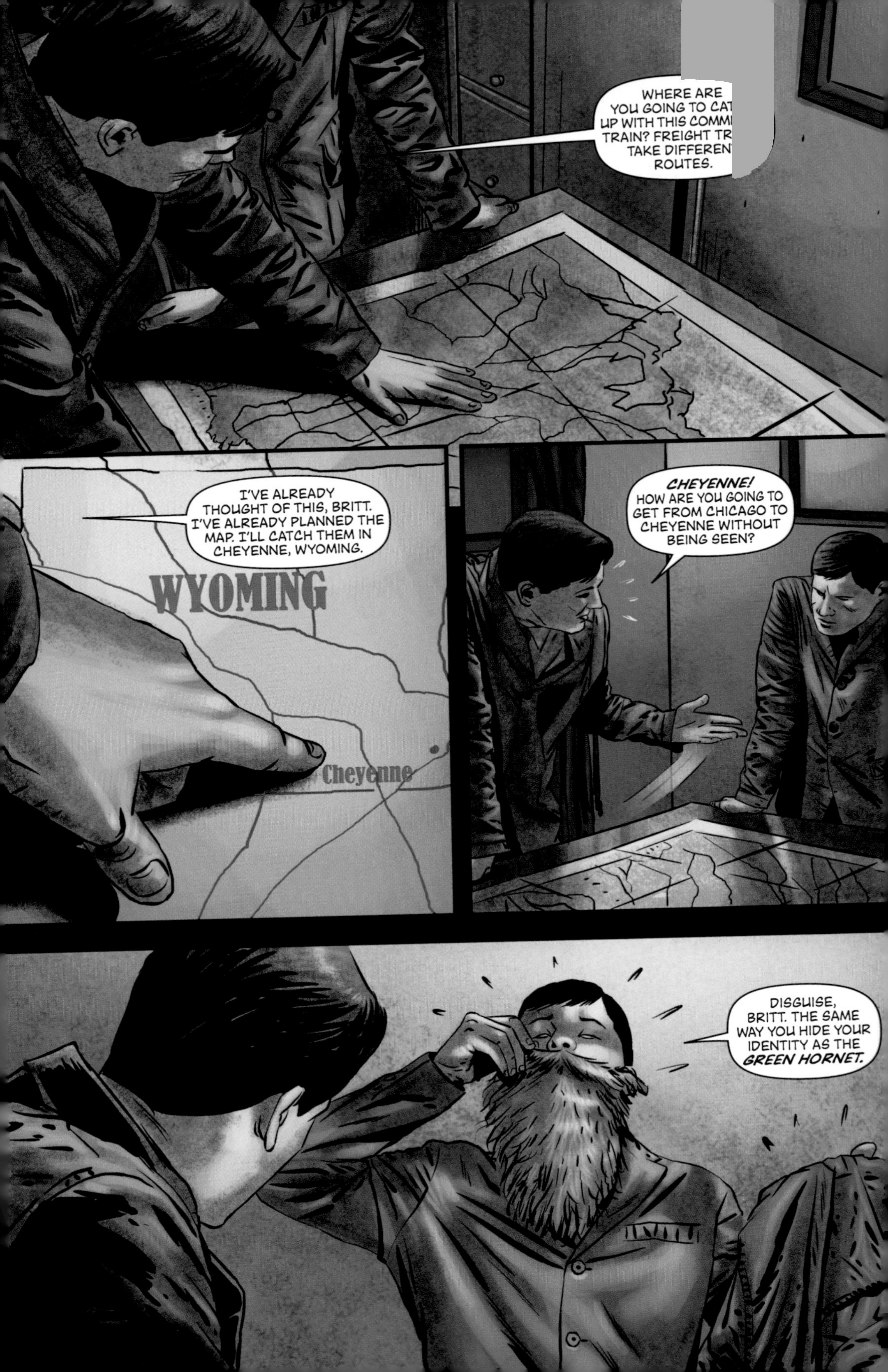
WHERE ARE YOU GOING TO CAT UP WITH THIS COMM TRAIN? FREIGHT TR TAKE DIFFEREN ROUTES.
I'VE ALREADY THOUGHT OF THIS, BRITT. I'VE ALREADY PLANNED THE MAP. I'LL CATCH THEM IN CHEYENNE, WYOMING.
WYOMING
Cheyenne
CHEYENNE! HOW ARE YOU GOING TO GET FROM CHICAGO TO CHEYENNE WITHOUT BEING SEEN?
DISGUISE, BRITT. THE SAME WAY YOU HIDE YOUR IDENTITY AS THE GREEN HORNET.

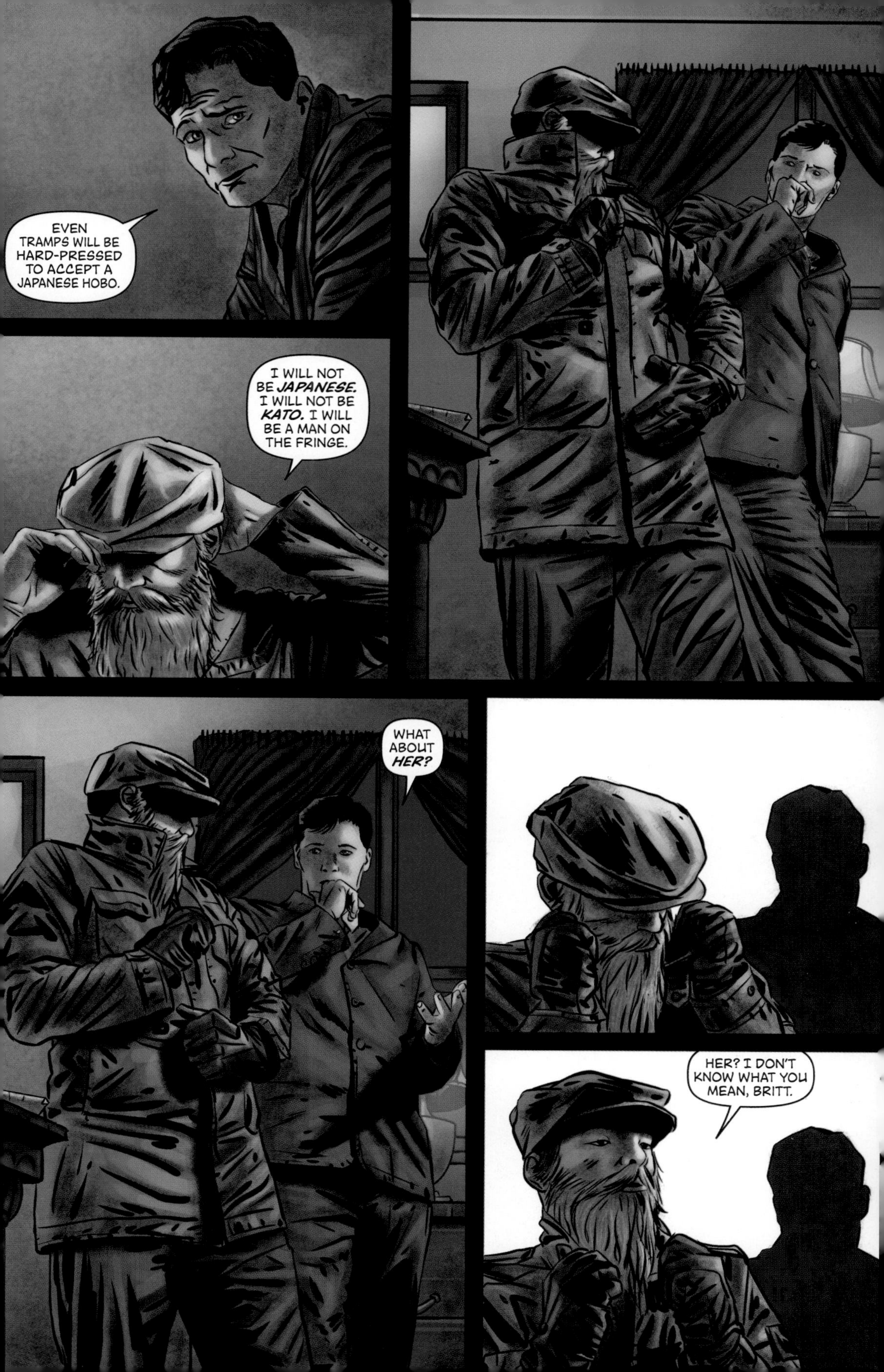
EVEN TRAMPS WILL BE HARD-PRESSED TO ACCEPT A JAPANESE HOBO.
I WILL NOT BE *JAPANESE.* I WILL NOT BE *KATO.* I WILL BE A MAN ON THE FRINGE.
WHAT ABOUT *HER?*
HER? I DON'T KNOW WHAT YOU MEAN, BRITT.

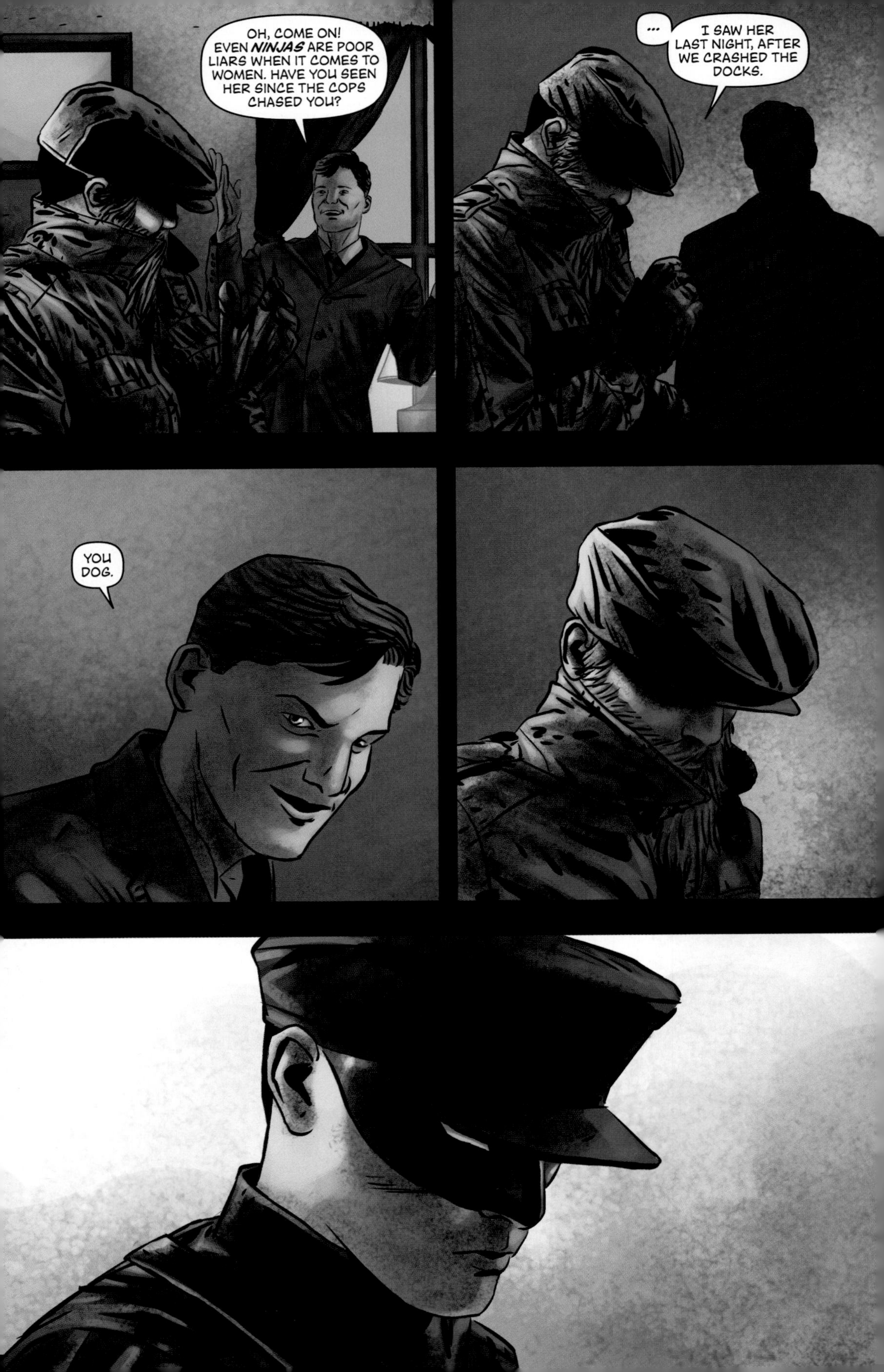
OH, COME ON! EVEN NINJAS ARE POOR LIARS WHEN IT COMES TO WOMEN. HAVE YOU SEEN HER SINCE THE COPS CHASED YOU?
...
I SAW HER LAST NIGHT, AFTER WE CRASHED THE DOCKS.
YOU DOG.

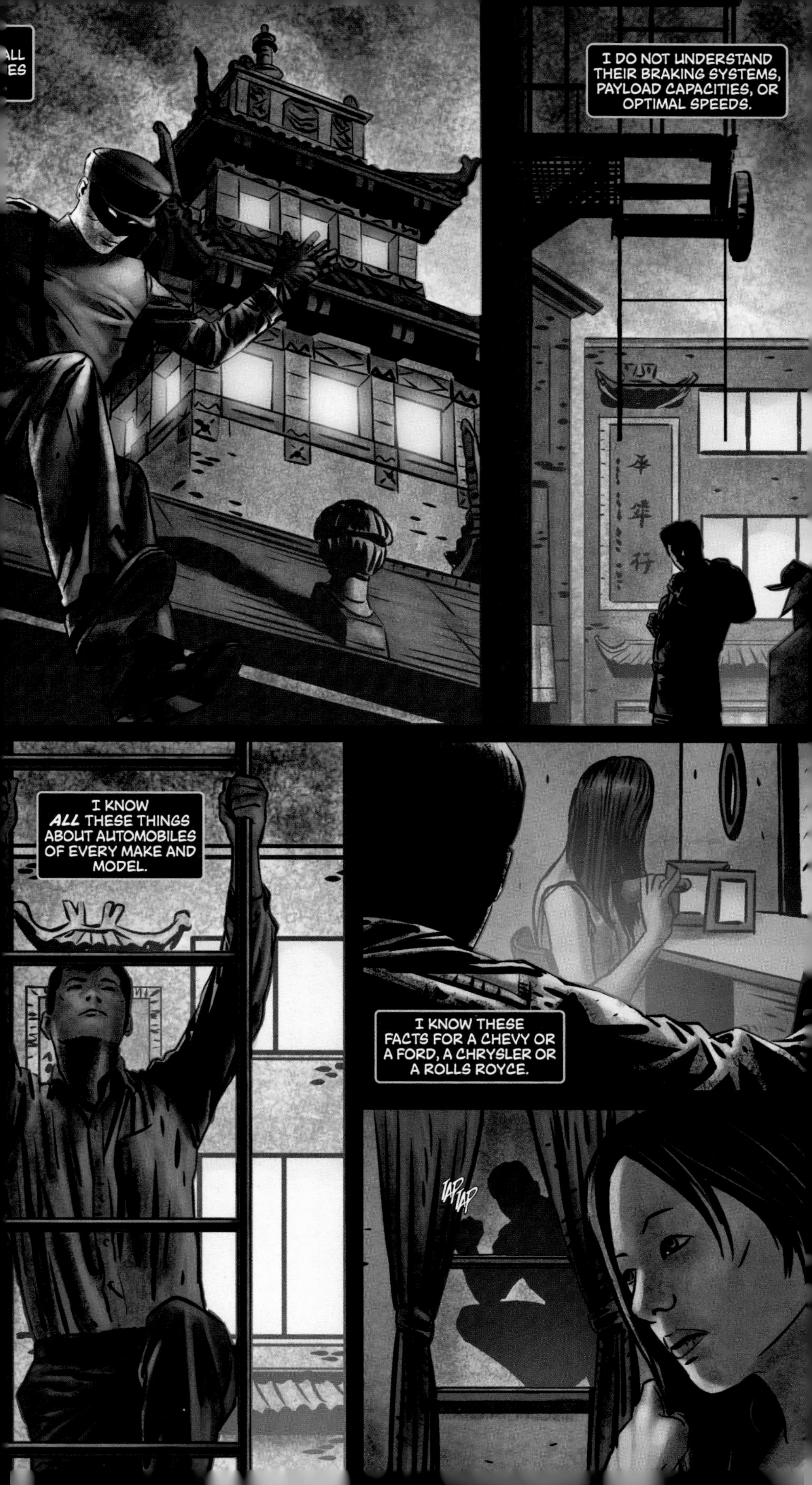
I DO NOT UNDERSTAND THEIR BRAKING SYSTEMS, PAYLOAD CAPACITIES, OR OPTIMAL SPEEDS.
I KNOW *ALL* THESE THINGS ABOUT AUTOMOBILES OF EVERY MAKE AND MODEL.
I KNOW THESE FACTS FOR A CHEVY OR A FORD, A CHRYSLER OR A ROLLS ROYCE.
TAP TAP

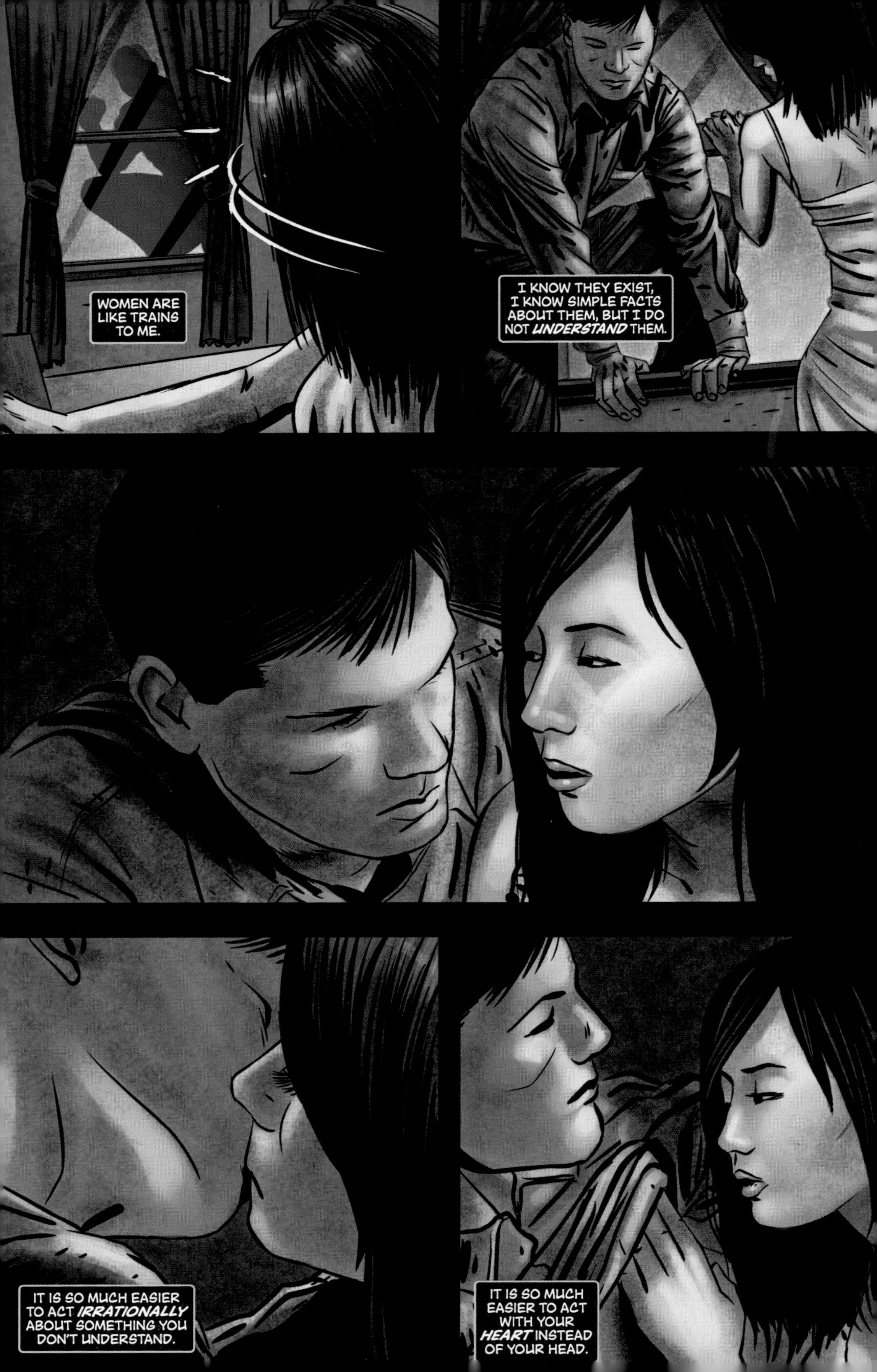
WOMEN ARE LIKE TRAINS TO ME.
I KNOW THEY EXIST, I KNOW SIMPLE FACTS ABOUT THEM, BUT I DO NOT *UNDERSTAND* THEM.
IT IS SO MUCH EASIER TO ACT *IRRATIONALLY* ABOUT SOMETHING YOU DON'T UNDERSTAND.
IT IS SO MUCH EASIER TO ACT WITH YOUR *HEART* INSTEAD OF YOUR HEAD.

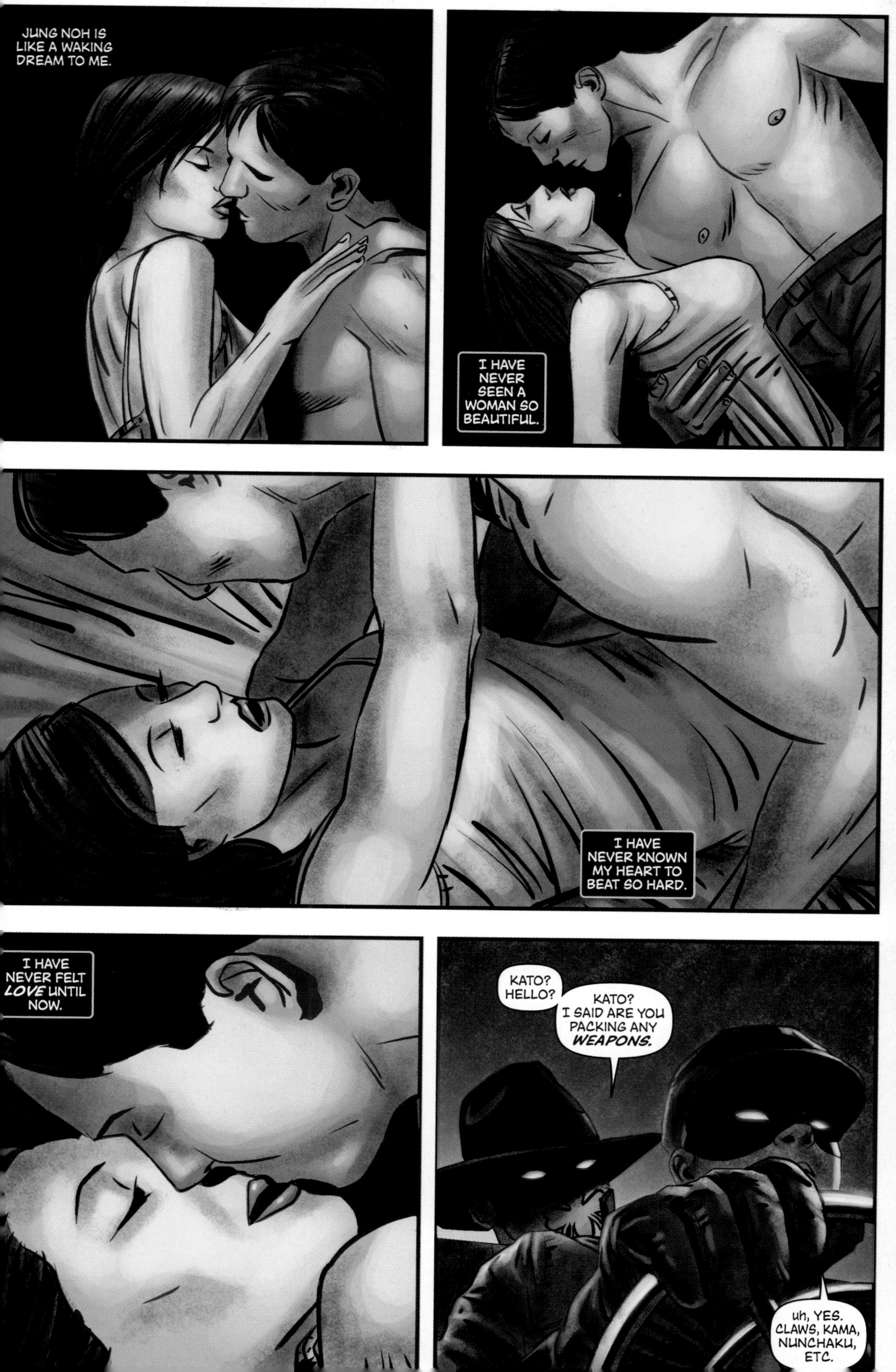
JUNG NOH IS LIKE A WAKING DREAM TO ME.
I HAVE NEVER SEEN A WOMAN SO BEAUTIFUL.
I HAVE NEVER KNOWN MY HEART TO BEAT SO HARD.
I HAVE NEVER FELT *LOVE* UNTIL NOW.
KATO? HELLO?
KATO? I SAID ARE YOU PACKING ANY *WEAPONS.*
uh, YES. CLAWS, KAMA, NUNCHAKU, ETC.

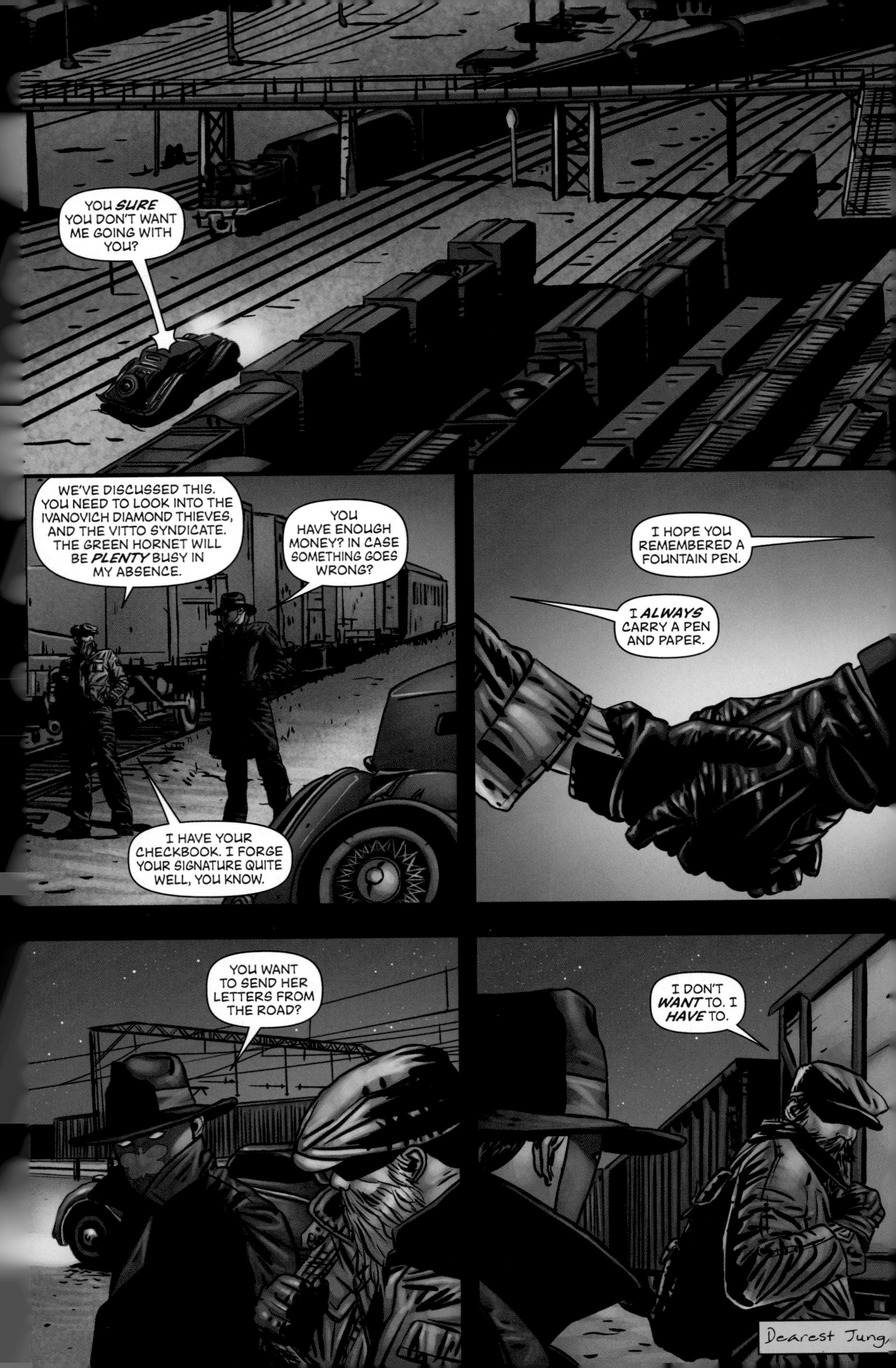
YOU SURE YOU DON'T WANT ME GOING WITH YOU?
WE'VE DISCUSSED THIS. YOU NEED TO LOOK INTO THE IVANOVICH DIAMOND THIEVES, AND THE VITTO SYNDICATE. THE GREEN HORNET WILL BE PLENTY BUSY IN MY ABSENCE.
YOU HAVE ENOUGH MONEY? IN CASE SOMETHING GOES WRONG?
I HAVE YOUR CHECKBOOK. I FORGE YOUR SIGNATURE QUITE WELL, YOU KNOW.
I HOPE YOU REMEMBERED A FOUNTAIN PEN.
I ALWAYS CARRY A PEN AND PAPER.
YOU WANT TO SEND HER LETTERS FROM THE ROAD?
I DON'T WANT TO. I HAVE TO.
Dearest Jung,

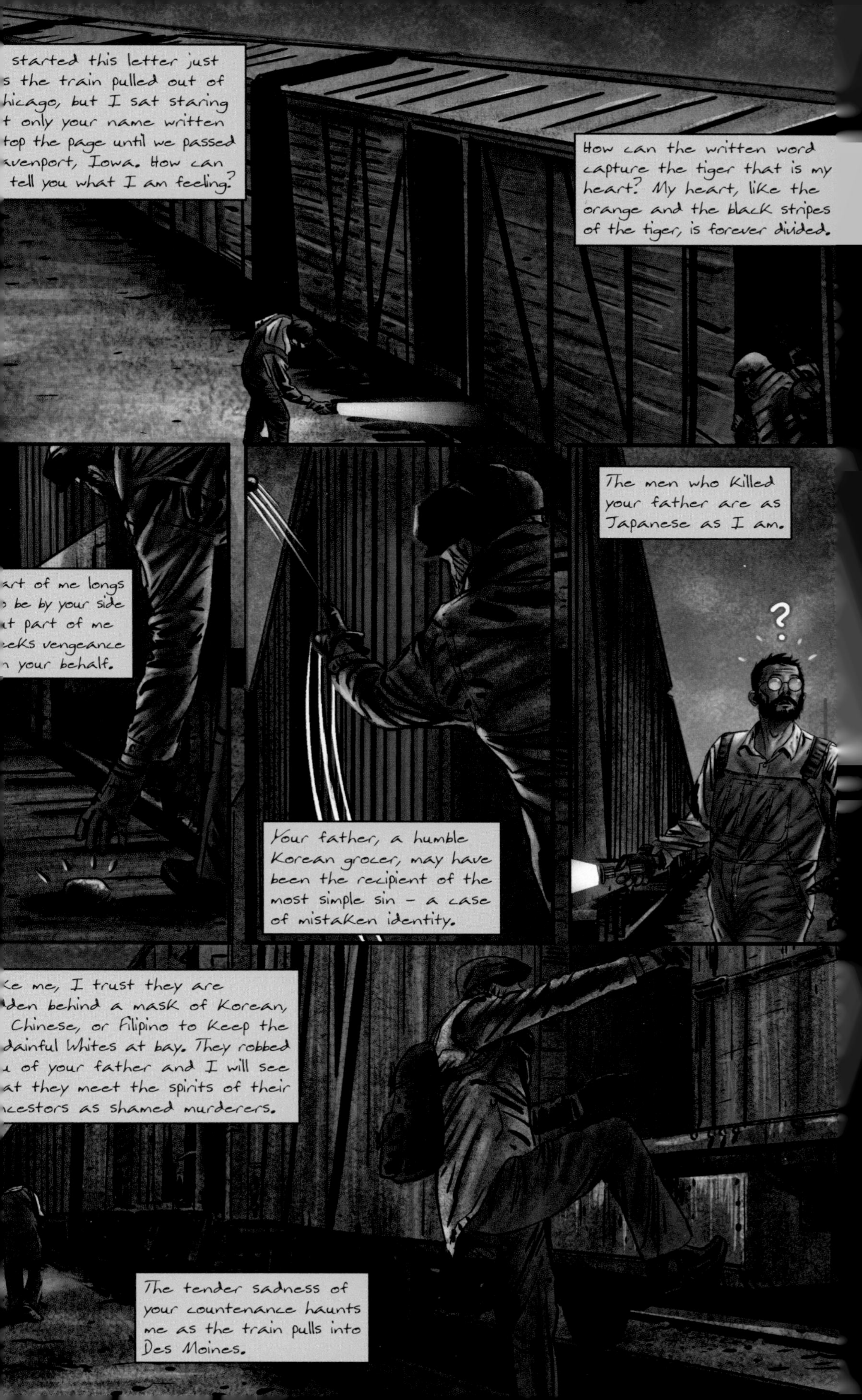
started this letter just
s the train pulled out of
hicago, but I sat staring
t only your name written
top the page until we passed
avenport, Iowa. How can
tell you what I am feeling?
How can the written word capture the tiger that is my heart? My heart, like the orange and the black stripes of the tiger, is forever divided.
art of me longs
be by your side
t part of me
eeks vengeance
n your behalf.
Your father, a humble Korean grocer, may have been the recipient of the most simple sin – a case of mistaken identity.
The men who killed your father are as Japanese as I am.
?
ke me, I trust they are
den behind a mask of Korean,
Chinese, or Filipino to keep the
dainful Whites at bay. They robbed
u of your father and I will see
at they meet the spirits of their
cestors as shamed murderers.
The tender sadness of your countenance haunts me as the train pulls into Des Moines.

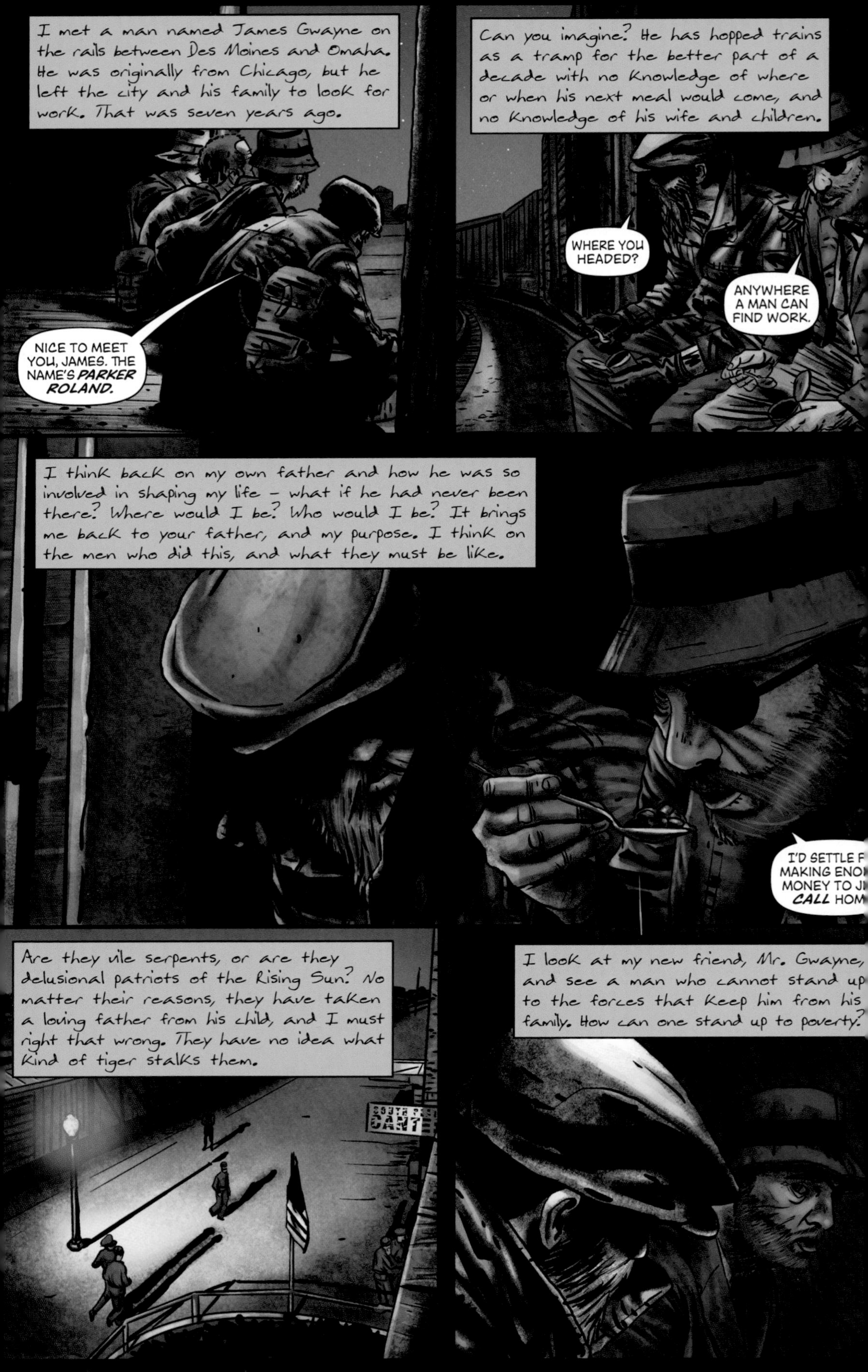
I met a man named James Gwayne on the rails between Des Moines and Omaha. He was originally from Chicago, but he left the city and his family to look for work. That was seven years ago.
NICE TO MEET YOU, JAMES. THE NAME'S *PARKER ROLAND.*
Can you imagine? He has hopped trains as a tramp for the better part of a decade with no knowledge of where or when his next meal would come, and no knowledge of his wife and children.
WHERE YOU HEADED?
ANYWHERE A MAN CAN FIND WORK.
I think back on my own father and how he was so involved in shaping my life – what if he had never been there? Where would I be? Who would I be? It brings me back to your father, and my purpose. I think on the men who did this, and what they must be like.
I'D SETTLE F MAKING ENO MONEY TO J *CALL* HOM
Are they vile serpents, or are they delusional patriots of the Rising Sun? No matter their reasons, they have taken a loving father from his child, and I must right that wrong. They have no idea what kind of tiger stalks them.
I look at my new friend, Mr. Gwayne, and see a man who cannot stand up to the forces that keep him from his family. How can one stand up to poverty?

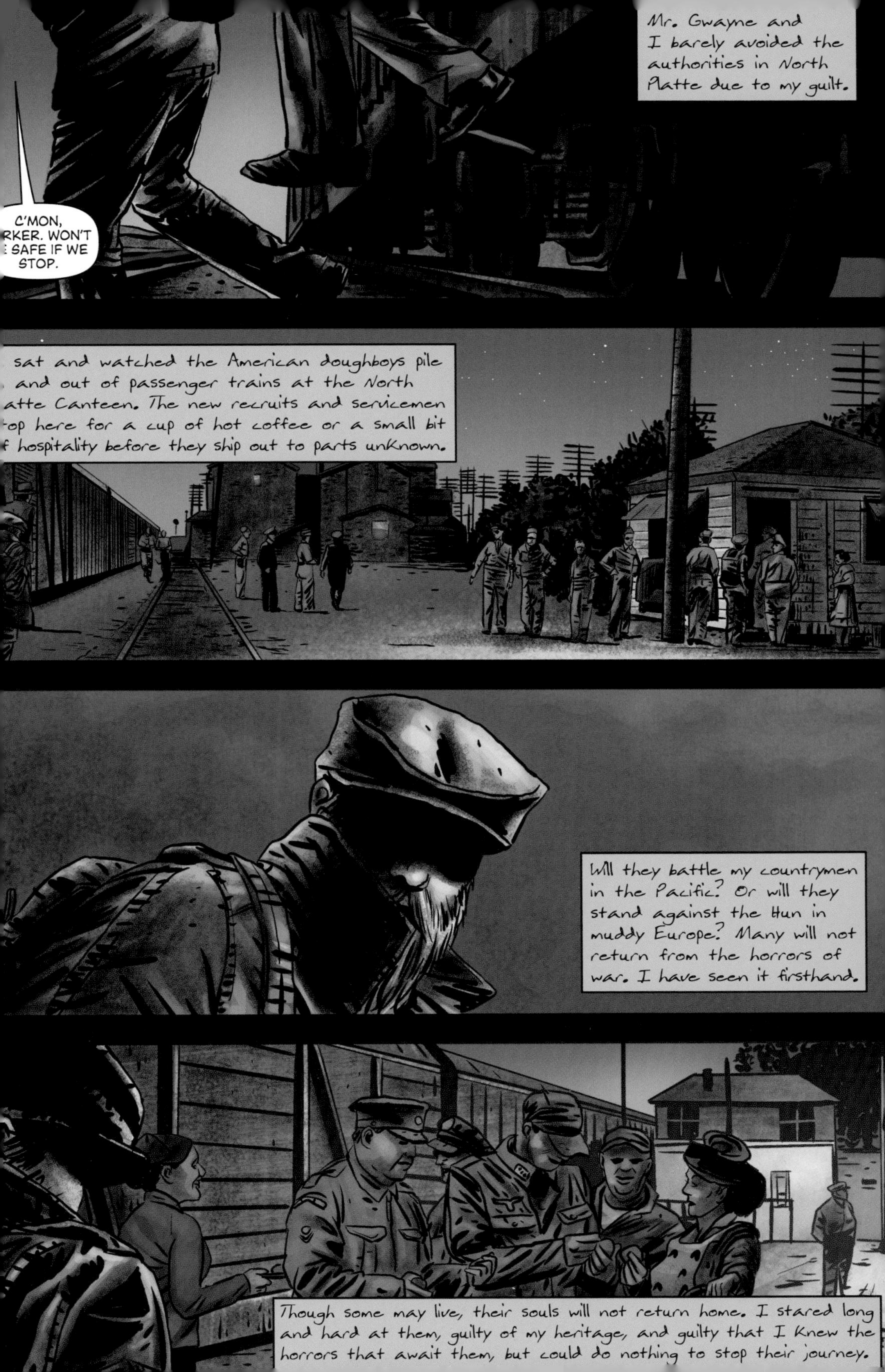
Mr. Gwayne and I barely avoided the authorities in North Platte due to my guilt.
C'MON, RKER. WON'T E SAFE IF WE STOP.
sat and watched the American doughboys pile and out of passenger trains at the North atte Canteen. The new recruits and servicemen top here for a cup of hot coffee or a small bit f hospitality before they ship out to parts unknown.
Will they battle my countrymen in the Pacific? Or will they stand against the Hun in muddy Europe? Many will not return from the horrors of war. I have seen it firsthand.
Though some may live, their souls will not return home. I stared long and hard at them, guilty of my heritage, and guilty that I knew the horrors that await them, but could do nothing to stop their journey.

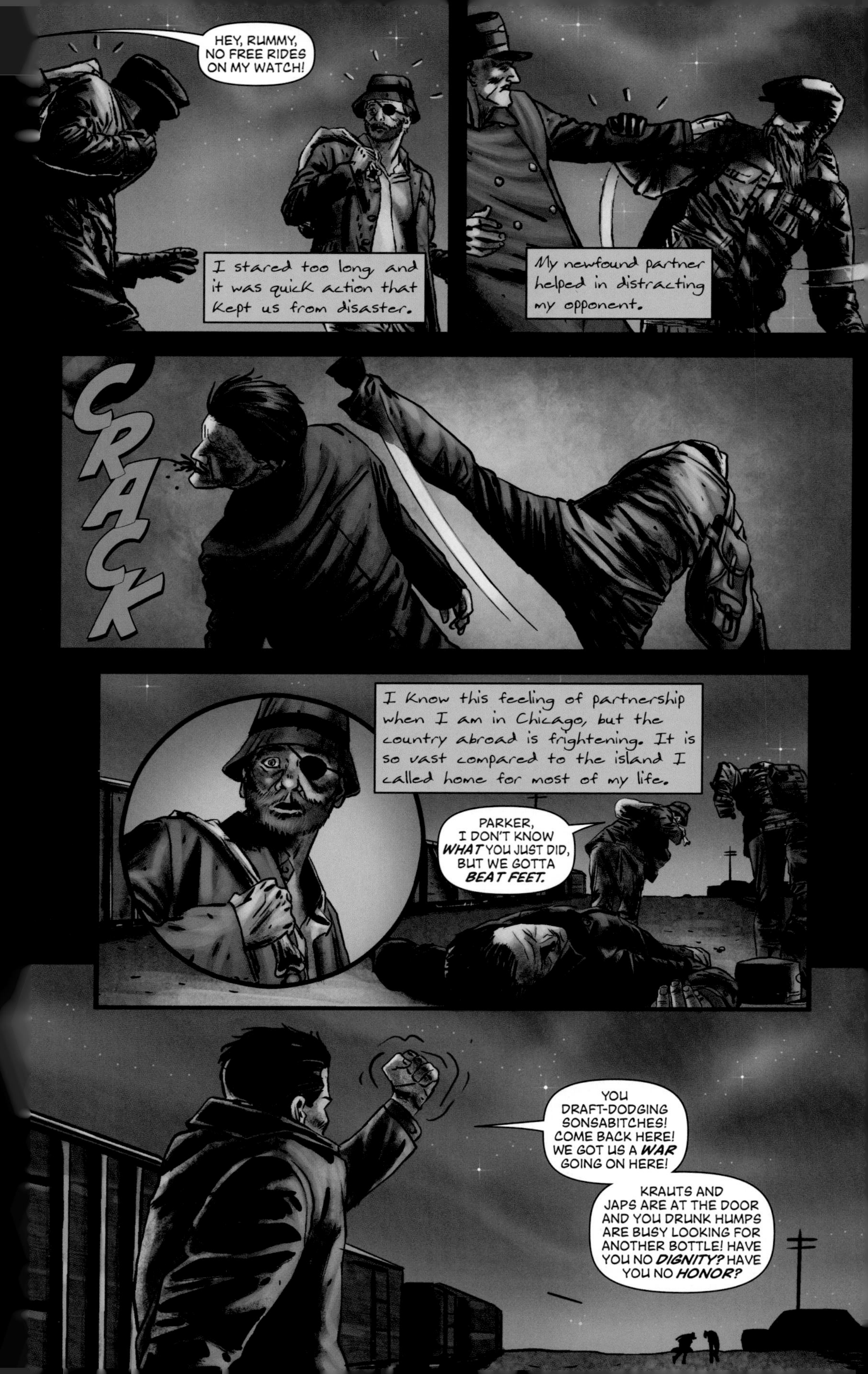
HEY, RUMMY, NO FREE RIDES ON MY WATCH!
I stared too long and it was quick action that kept us from disaster.
My newfound partner helped in distracting my opponent.
CRACK
I know this feeling of partnership when I am in Chicago, but the country abroad is frightening. It is so vast compared to the island I called home for most of my life.
PARKER, I DON'T KNOW WHAT YOU JUST DID, BUT WE GOTTA BEAT FEET.
YOU DRAFT-DODGING SONSABITCHES! COME BACK HERE! WE GOT US A WAR GOING ON HERE!
KRAUTS AND JAPS ARE AT THE DOOR AND YOU DRUNK HUMPS ARE BUSY LOOKING FOR ANOTHER BOTTLE! HAVE YOU NO DIGNITY? HAVE YOU NO HONOR?

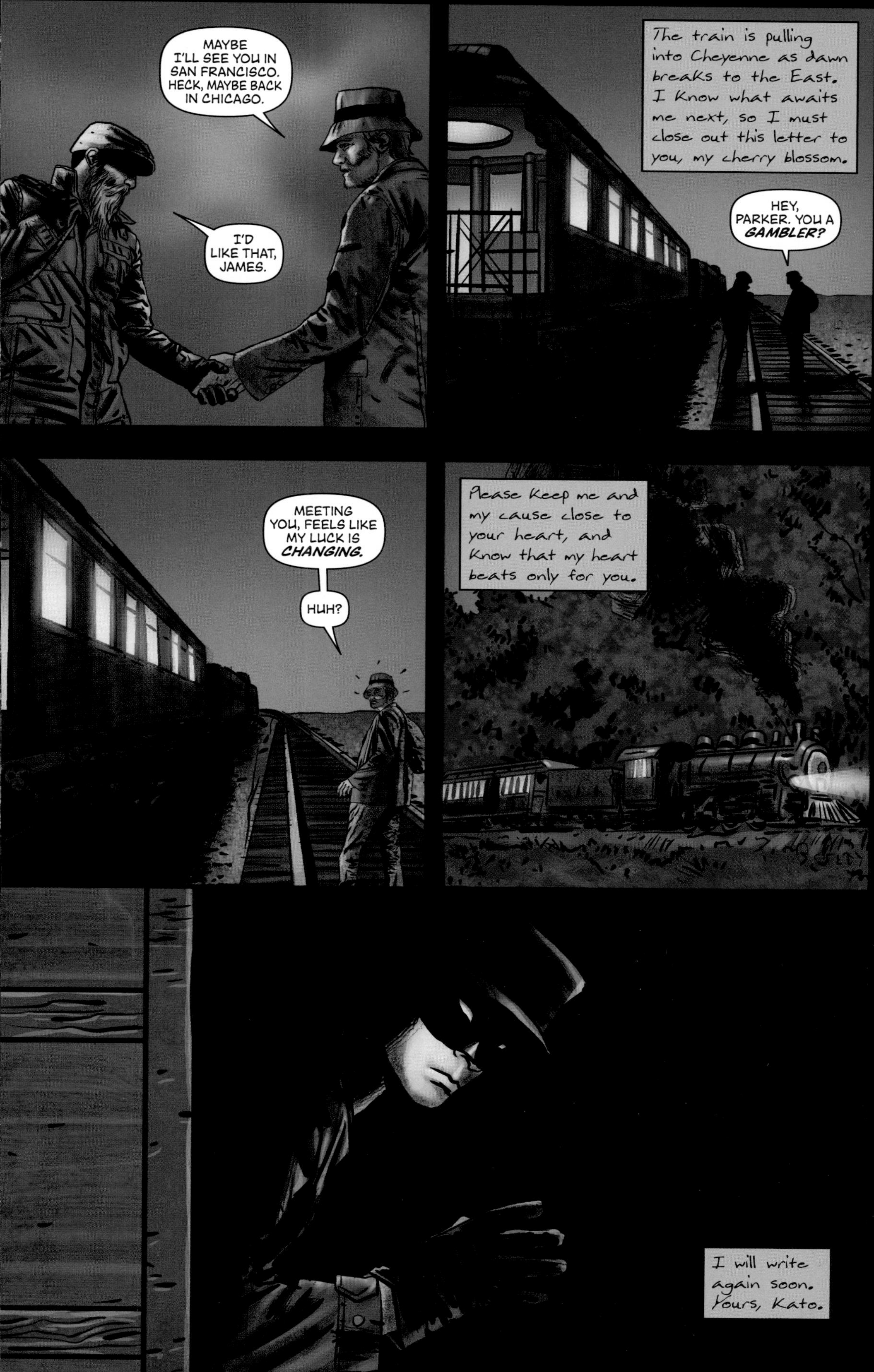
MAYBE I'LL SEE YOU IN SAN FRANCISCO. HECK, MAYBE BACK IN CHICAGO.
I'D LIKE THAT, JAMES.
The train is pulling into Cheyenne as dawn breaks to the East. I know what awaits me next, so I must close out this letter to you, my cherry blossom.
HEY, PARKER. YOU A GAMBLER?
MEETING YOU, FEELS LIKE MY LUCK IS CHANGING.
HUH?
Please keep me and my cause close to your heart, and know that my heart beats only for you.
I will write again soon. Yours, Kato.

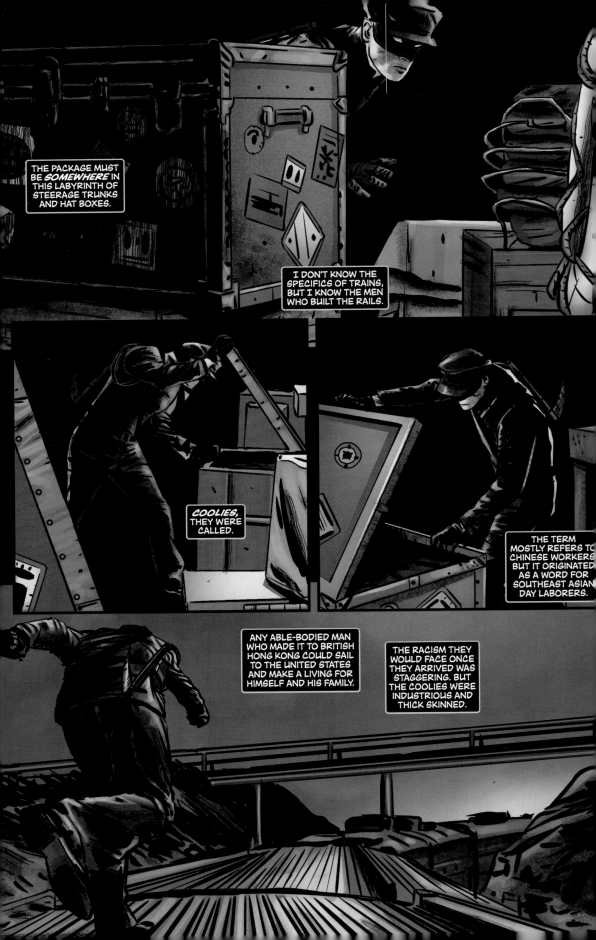

THE PACKAGE MUST BE **SOMEWHERE** IN THIS LABYRINTH OF STEERAGE TRUNKS AND HAT BOXES.

I DON'T KNOW THE SPECIFICS OF TRAINS, BUT I KNOW THE MEN WHO BUILT THE RAILS.

COOLIES, THEY WERE CALLED.

THE TERM MOSTLY REFERS TO CHINESE WORKERS, BUT IT ORIGINATED AS A WORD FOR SOUTHEAST ASIAN DAY LABORERS.

ANY ABLE-BODIED MAN WHO MADE IT TO BRITISH HONG KONG COULD SAIL TO THE UNITED STATES AND MAKE A LIVING FOR HIMSELF AND HIS FAMILY.

THE RACISM THEY WOULD FACE ONCE THEY ARRIVED WAS STAGGERING. BUT THE COOLIES WERE INDUSTRIOUS AND THICK SKINNED.

COOLIES COULD ENDURE *ANYTHING* TO ESCAPE THE POVERTY OF THEIR HOMES.

EVEN LYNCHING AND MURDER WERE BETTER THAN *STARVING.*

SPEAK OF THE DEVIL, SOME OF THE GREATEST RACISTS ON THE PLANET REAR THEIR UGLY HEADS. *NAZIS.*

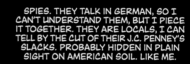

SPIES. THEY TALK IN GERMAN, SO I CAN'T UNDERSTAND THEM, BUT I PIECE IT TOGETHER. THEY ARE LOCALS, I CAN TELL BY THE CUT OF THEIR J.C. PENNEY'S SLACKS. PROBABLY HIDDEN IN PLAIN SIGHT ON AMERICAN SOIL. LIKE ME.

I MAKE OUT THE KANJI ON THE PACKAGE. *"KATANA."* THE AXIS POWERS ARE WORKING TOGETHER, SWAPPING IDEAS OR WEAPONS OR BOTH.

THIS IS BIGGER THAN I THOUGHT. BIGGER THAN *ME.*

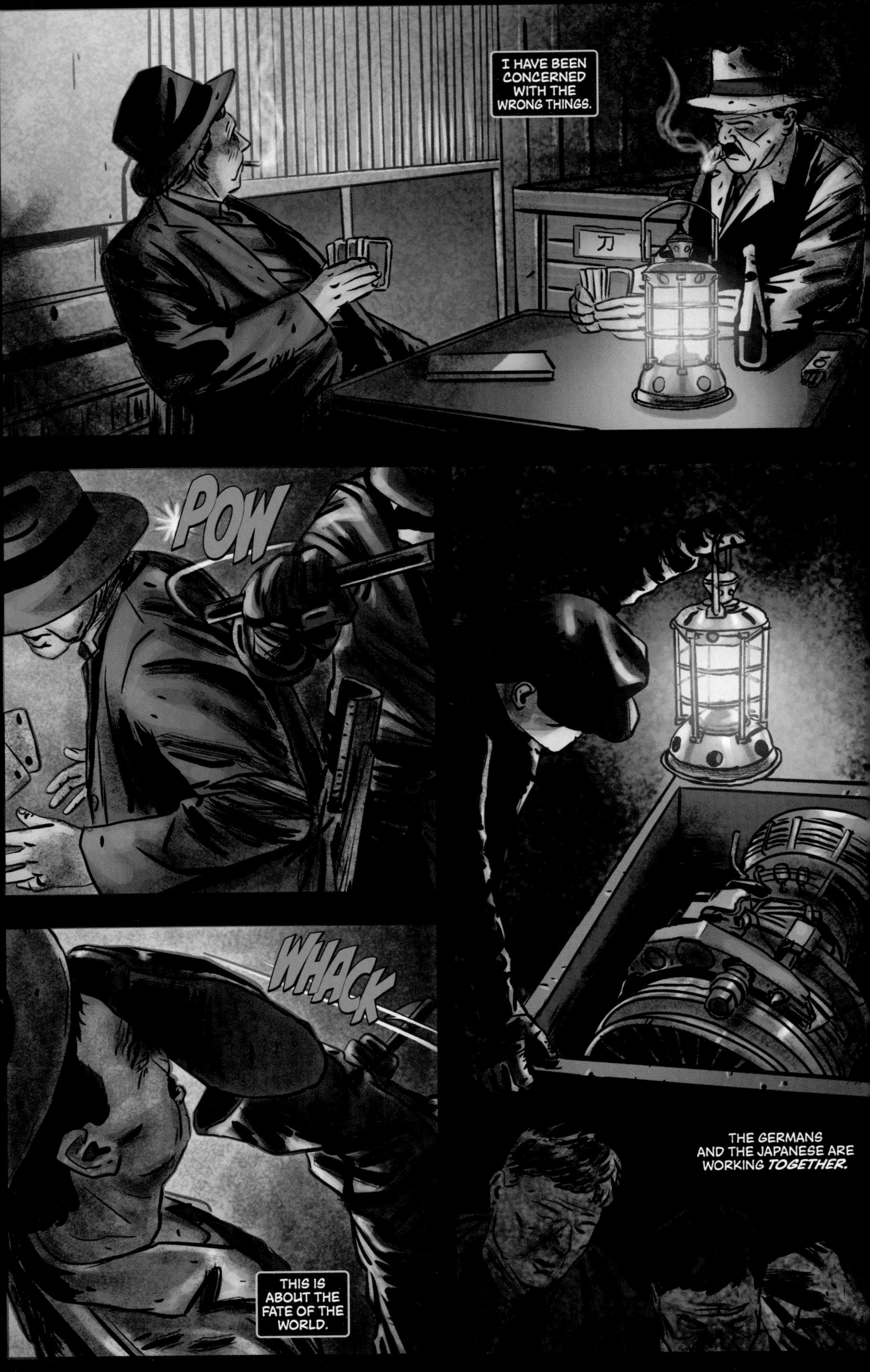
I HAVE BEEN CONCERNED WITH THE WRONG THINGS.
刀
POW
WHACK
THE GERMANS AND THE JAPANESE ARE WORKING *TOGETHER.*
THIS IS ABOUT THE FATE OF THE WORLD.

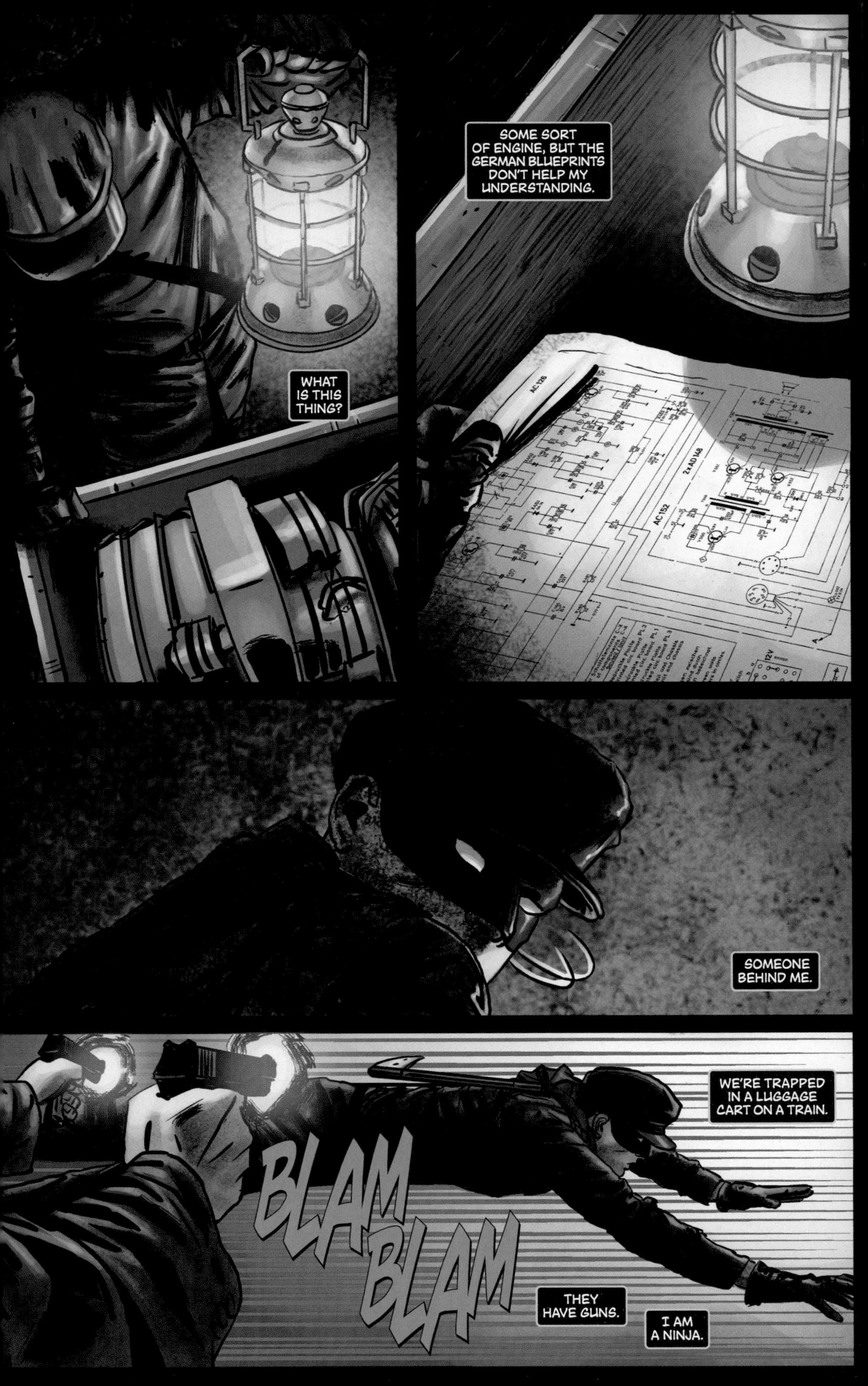
WHAT IS THIS THING?
SOME SORT OF ENGINE, BUT THE GERMAN BLUEPRINTS DON'T HELP MY UNDERSTANDING.
SOMEONE BEHIND ME.
WE'RE TRAPPED IN A LUGGAGE CART ON A TRAIN.
BLAM
BLAM
THEY HAVE GUNS.
I AM A NINJA.

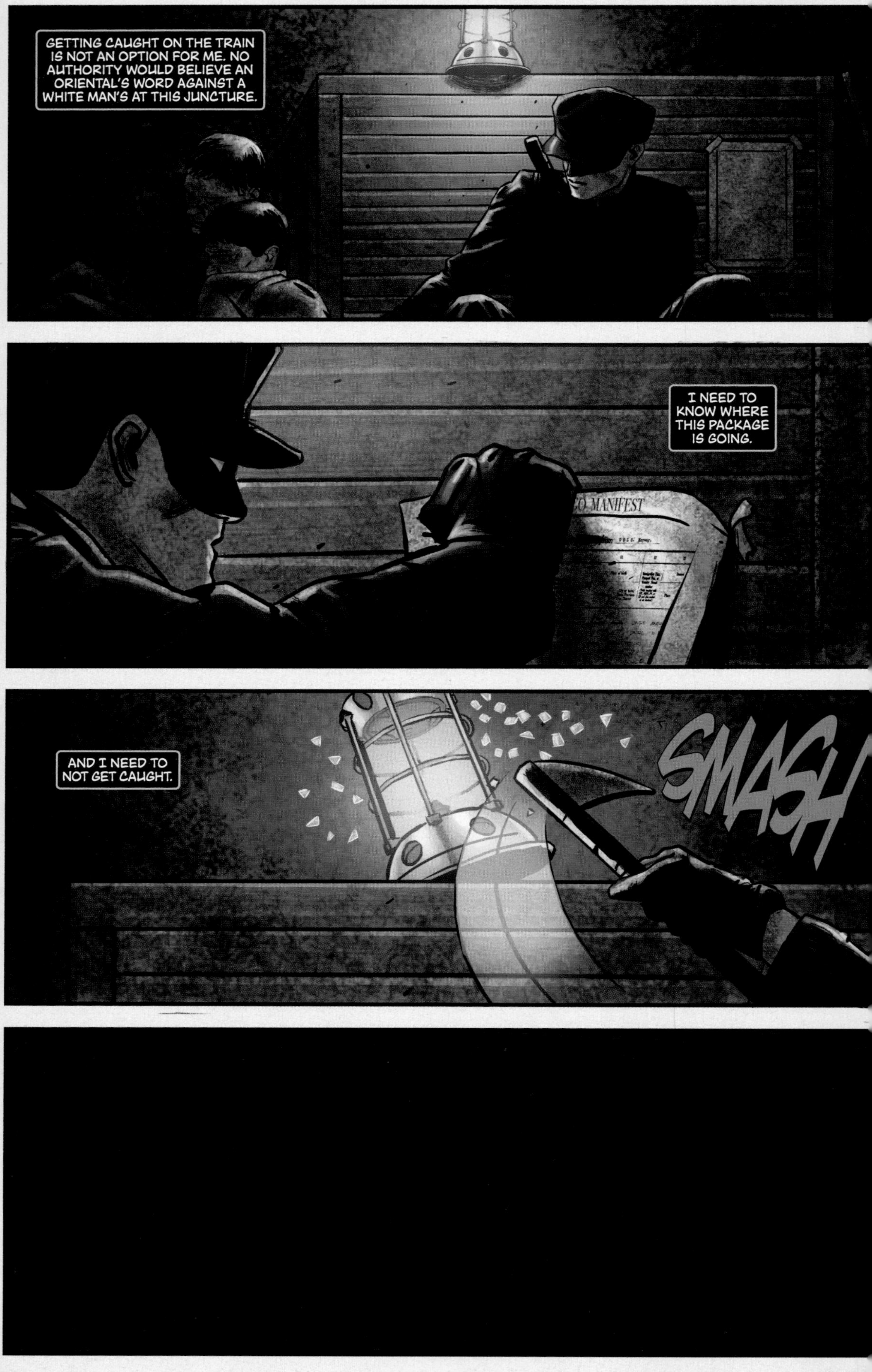
GETTING CAUGHT ON THE TRAIN IS NOT AN OPTION FOR ME. NO AUTHORITY WOULD BELIEVE AN ORIENTAL'S WORD AGAINST A WHITE MAN'S AT THIS JUNCTURE.
I NEED TO KNOW WHERE THIS PACKAGE IS GOING.
AND I NEED TO NOT GET CAUGHT.
SMASH

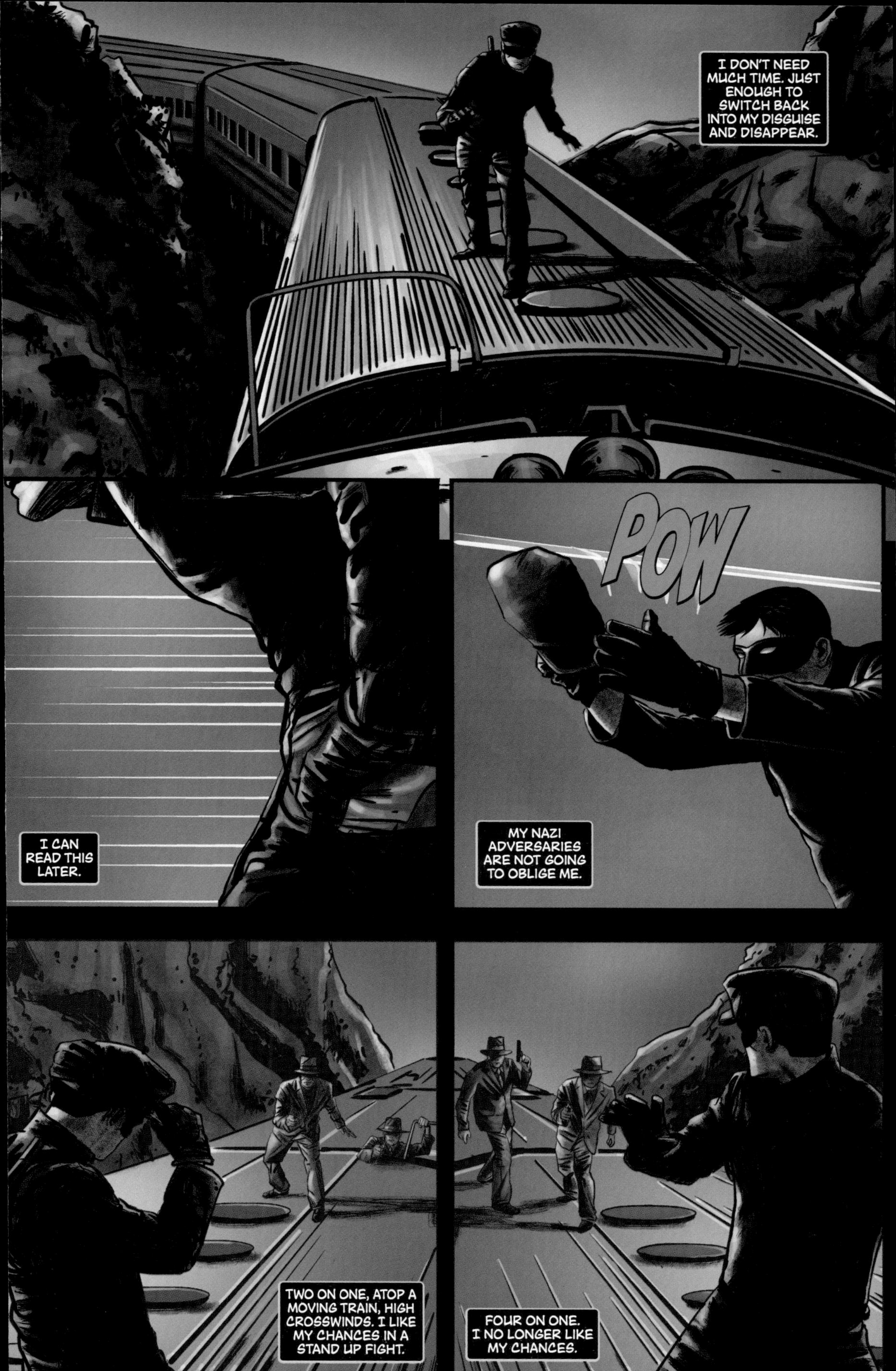
I DON'T NEED MUCH TIME. JUST ENOUGH TO SWITCH BACK INTO MY DISGUISE AND DISAPPEAR.
I CAN READ THIS LATER.
POW
MY NAZI ADVERSARIES ARE NOT GOING TO OBLIGE ME.
TWO ON ONE, ATOP A MOVING TRAIN, HIGH CROSSWINDS. I LIKE MY CHANCES IN A STAND UP FIGHT.
FOUR ON ONE. I NO LONGER LIKE MY CHANCES.

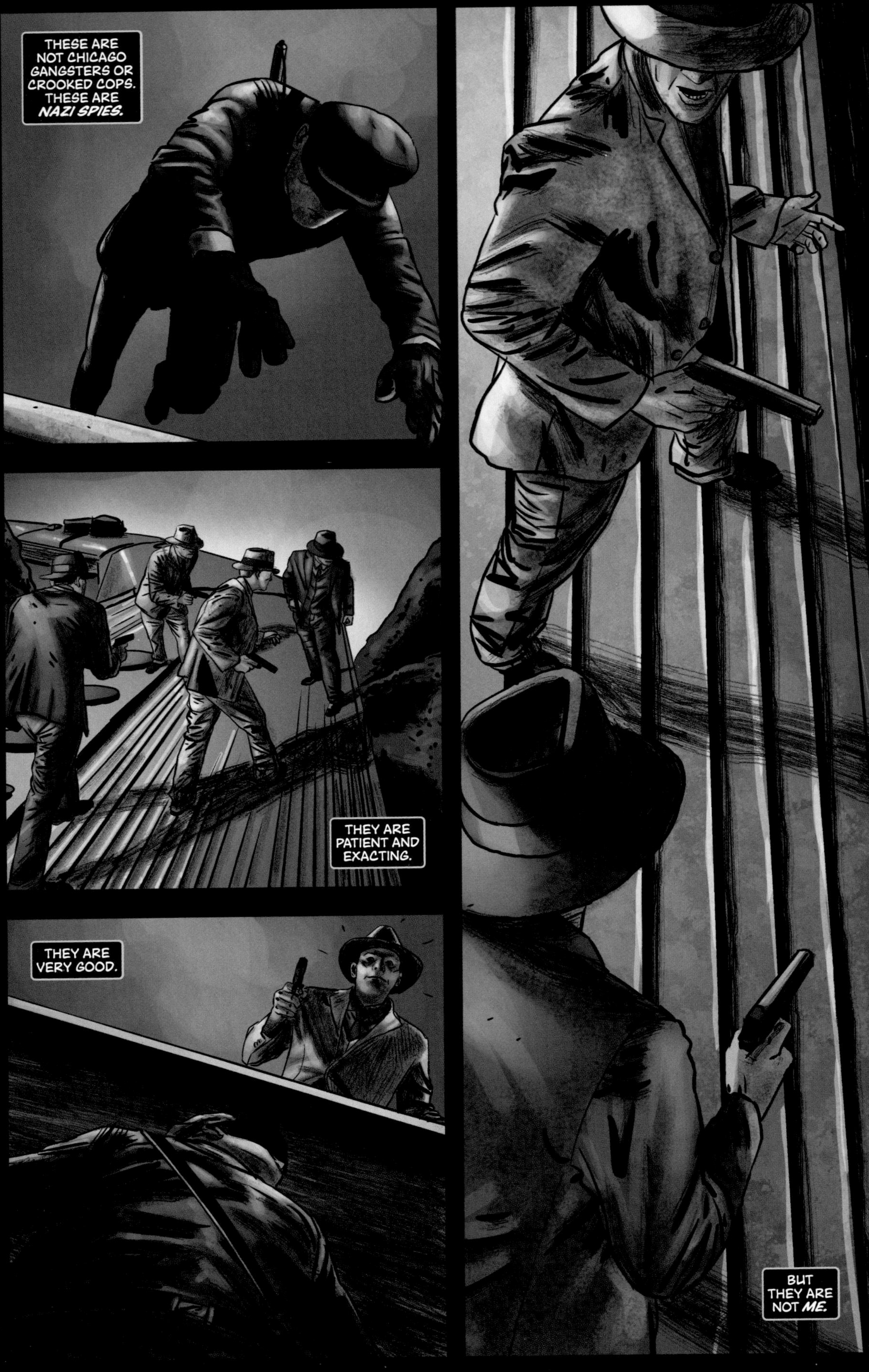
THESE ARE NOT CHICAGO GANGSTERS OR CROOKED COPS. THESE ARE *NAZI SPIES.*
THEY ARE PATIENT AND EXACTING.
THEY ARE VERY GOOD.
BUT THEY ARE NOT *ME.*

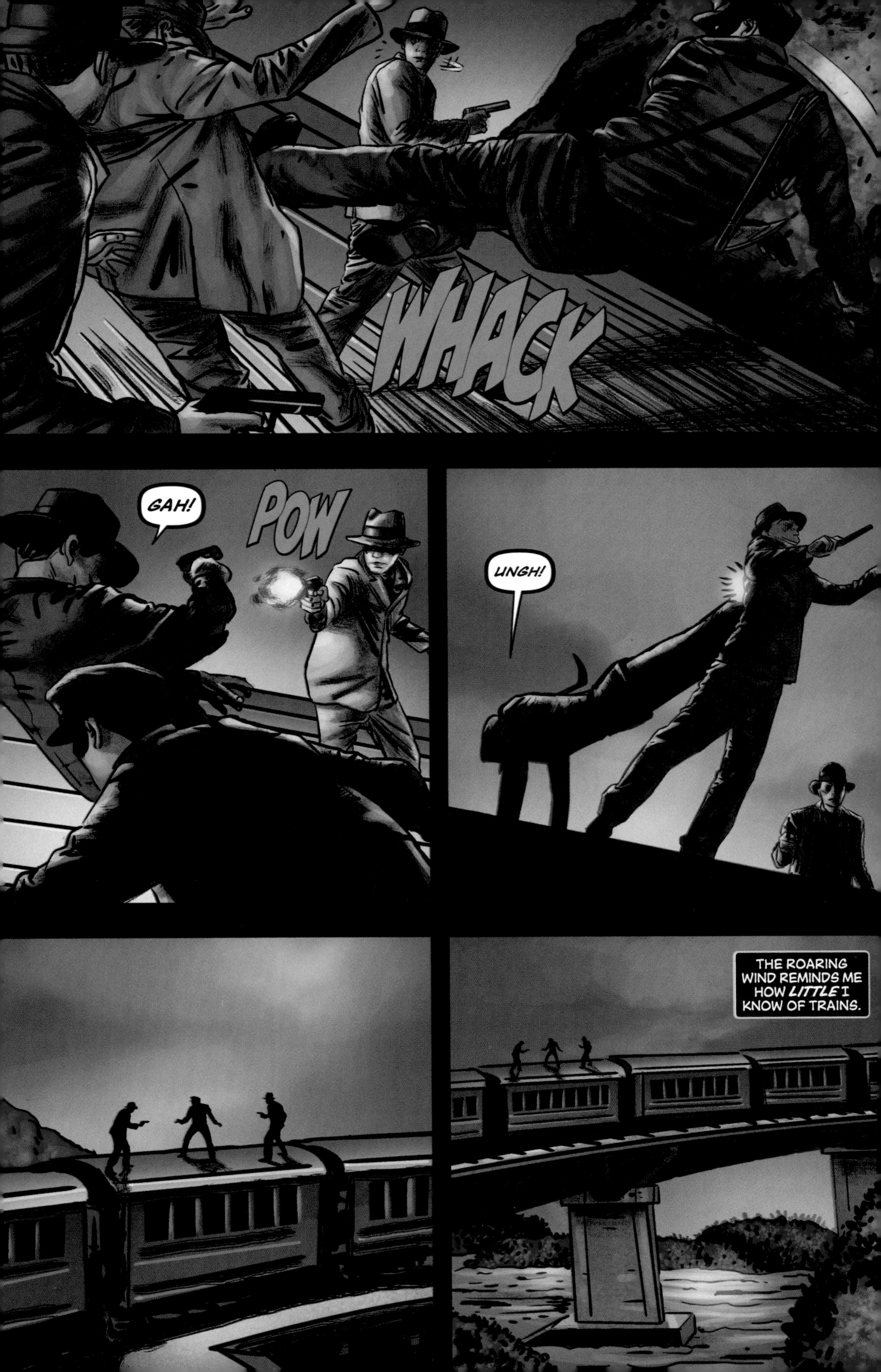
WHACK
GAH!
POW
UNGH!
THE ROARING WIND REMINDS ME HOW *LITTLE* I KNOW OF TRAINS.

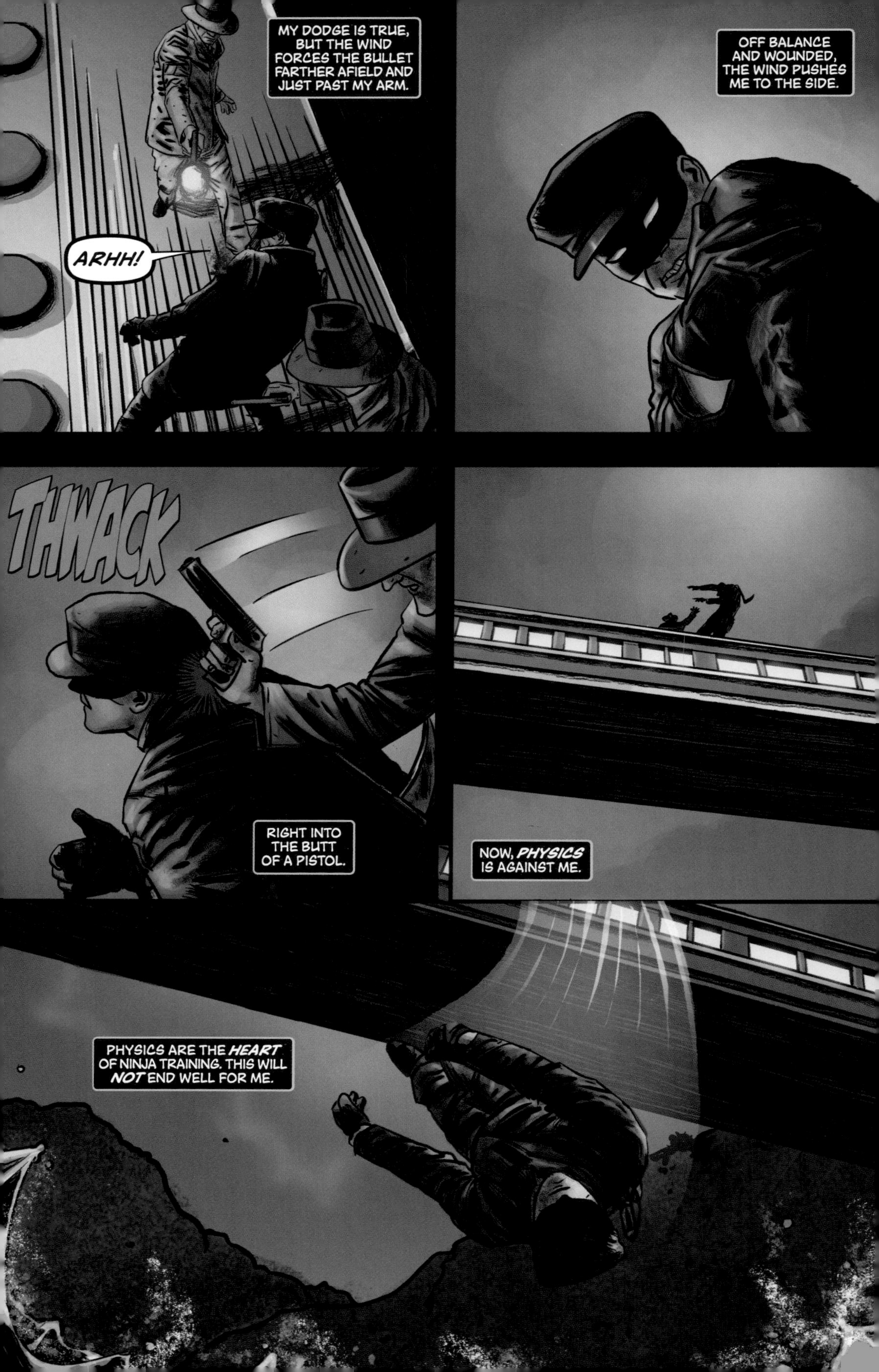
MY DODGE IS TRUE, BUT THE WIND FORCES THE BULLET FARTHER AFIELD AND JUST PAST MY ARM.
ARHH!
OFF BALANCE AND WOUNDED, THE WIND PUSHES ME TO THE SIDE.
THWACK
RIGHT INTO THE BUTT OF A PISTOL.
NOW, *PHYSICS* IS AGAINST ME.
PHYSICS ARE THE *HEART* OF NINJA TRAINING. THIS WILL *NOT* END WELL FOR ME.

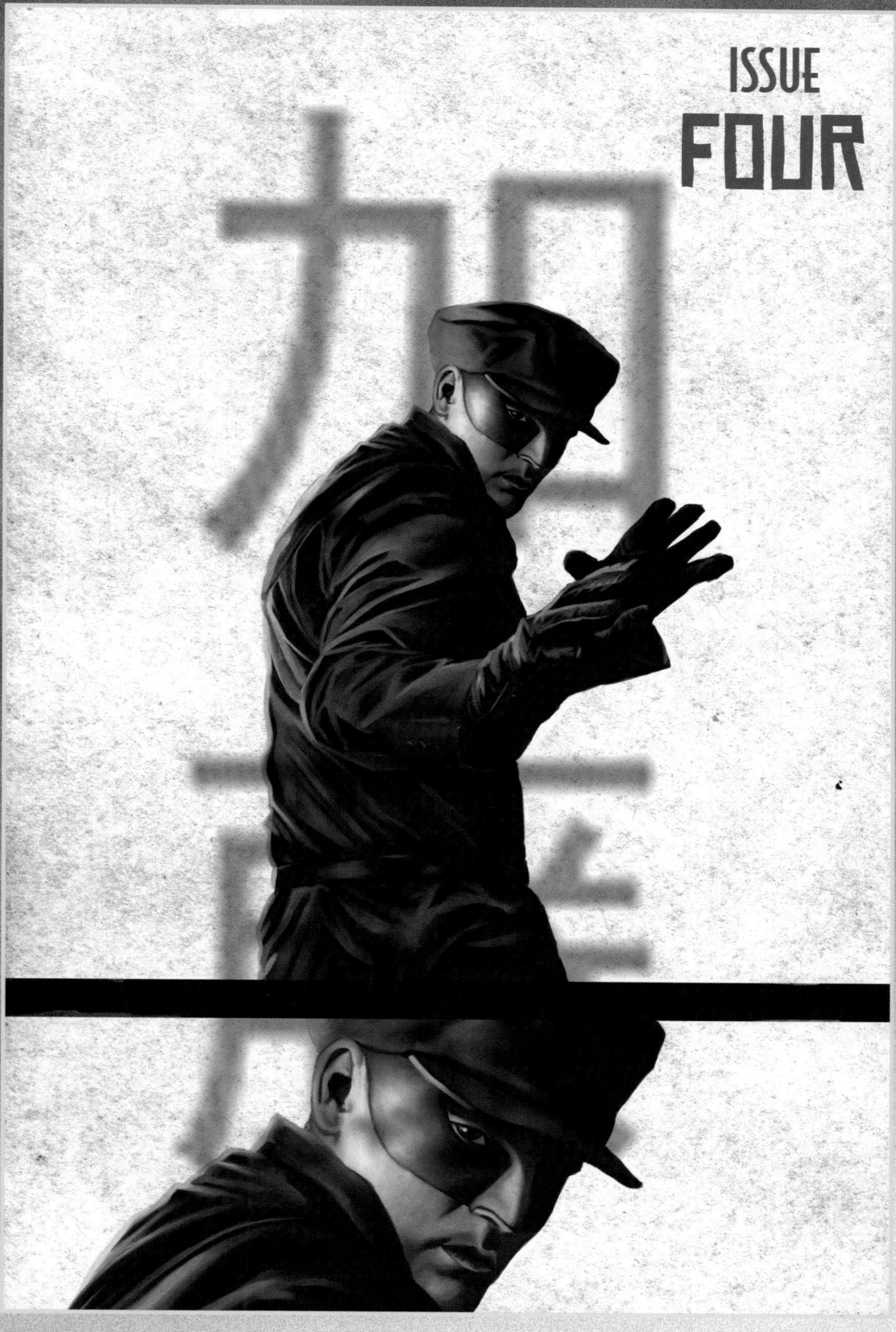
ISSUE
FOUR

Issue four cover by **COLTON WORLEY**

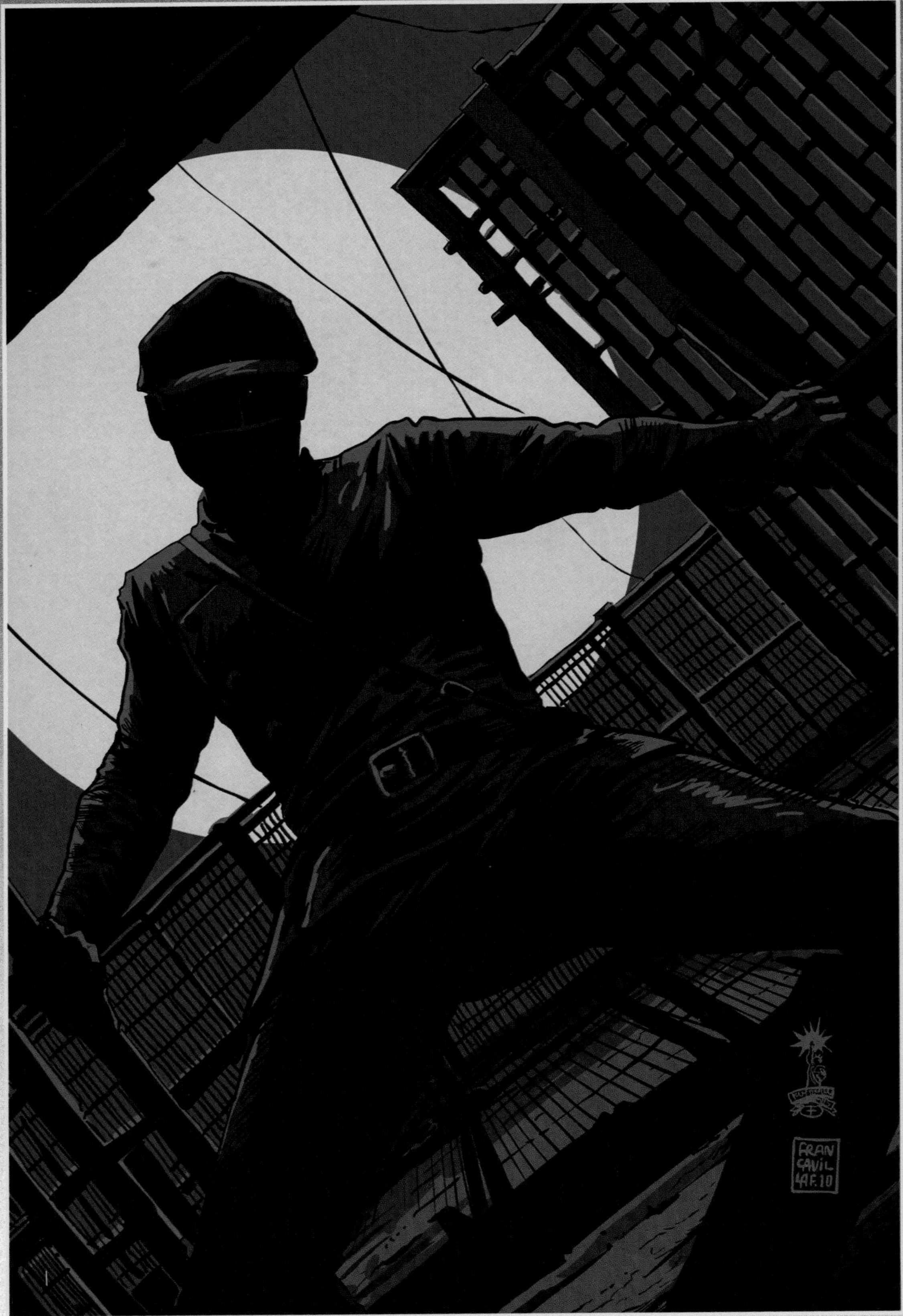

Issue four alternate cover by **FRANCESCO FRANCAVILLA**

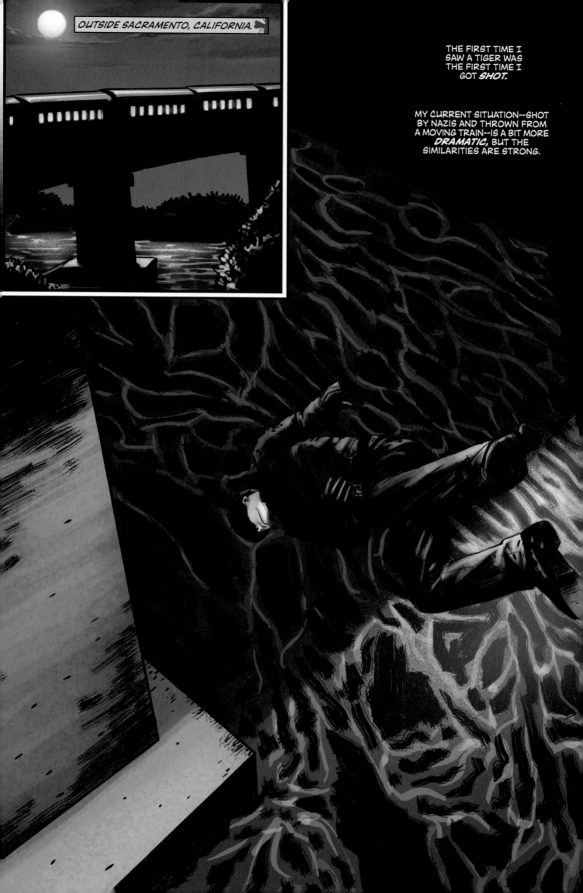

OUTSIDE SACRAMENTO, CALIFORNIA.

THE FIRST TIME I SAW A TIGER WAS THE FIRST TIME I GOT *SHOT*.

MY CURRENT SITUATION--SHOT BY NAZIS AND THROWN FROM A MOVING TRAIN--IS A BIT MORE *DRAMATIC,* BUT THE SIMILARITIES ARE STRONG.

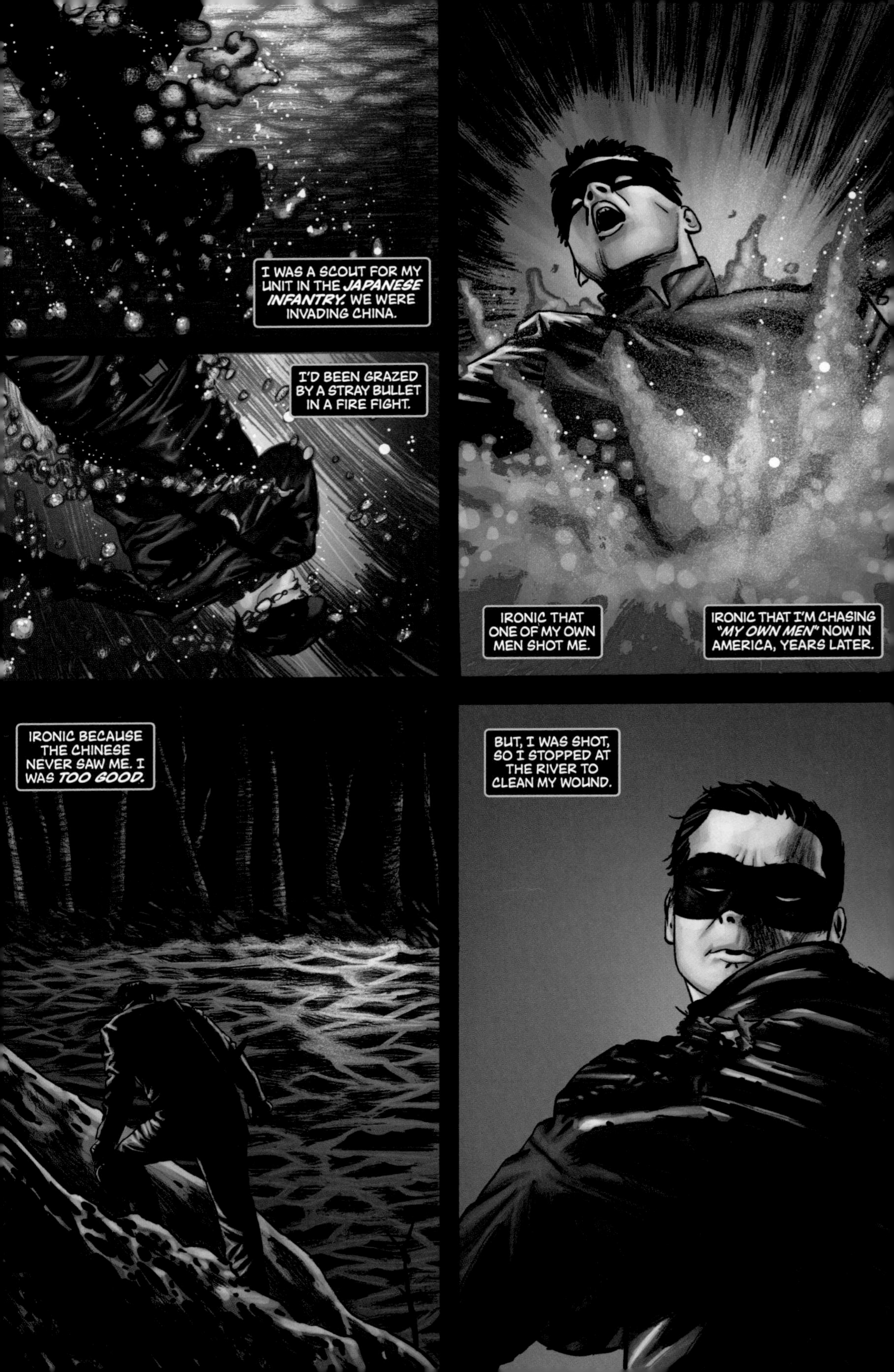
I WAS A SCOUT FOR MY UNIT IN THE *JAPANESE INFANTRY.* WE WERE INVADING CHINA.
I'D BEEN GRAZED BY A STRAY BULLET IN A FIRE FIGHT.
IRONIC THAT ONE OF MY OWN MEN SHOT ME.
IRONIC THAT I'M CHASING *"MY OWN MEN"* NOW IN AMERICA, YEARS LATER.
IRONIC BECAUSE THE CHINESE NEVER SAW ME. I WAS *TOO GOOD.*
BUT, I WAS SHOT, SO I STOPPED AT THE RIVER TO CLEAN MY WOUND.

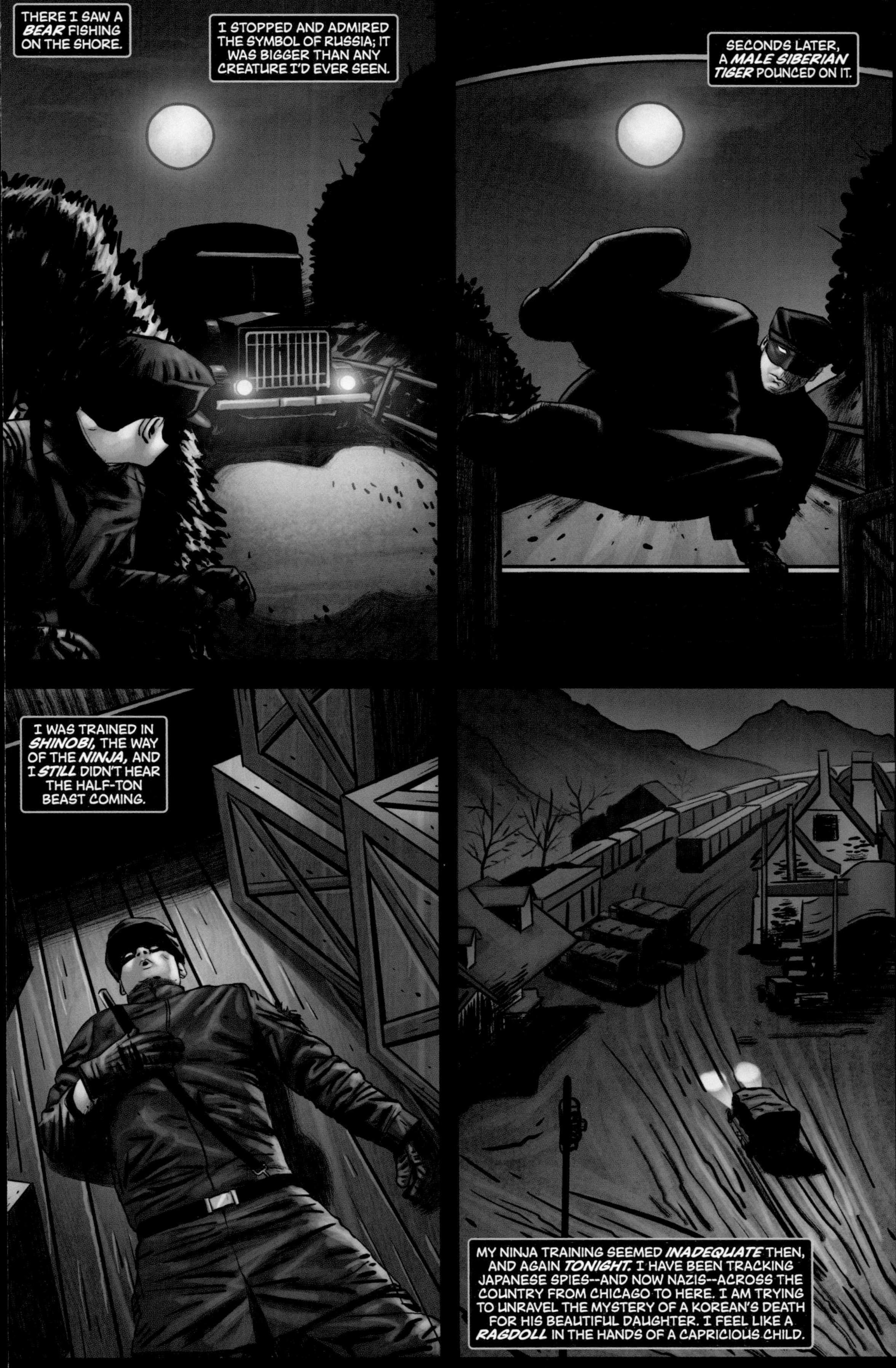
THERE I SAW A BEAR FISHING ON THE SHORE.
I STOPPED AND ADMIRED THE SYMBOL OF RUSSIA; IT WAS BIGGER THAN ANY CREATURE I'D EVER SEEN.
SECONDS LATER, A MALE SIBERIAN TIGER POUNCED ON IT.
I WAS TRAINED IN SHINOBI, THE WAY OF THE NINJA, AND I STILL DIDN'T HEAR THE HALF-TON BEAST COMING.
MY NINJA TRAINING SEEMED INADEQUATE THEN, AND AGAIN TONIGHT. I HAVE BEEN TRACKING JAPANESE SPIES--AND NOW NAZIS--ACROSS THE COUNTRY FROM CHICAGO TO HERE. I AM TRYING TO UNRAVEL THE MYSTERY OF A KOREAN'S DEATH FOR HIS BEAUTIFUL DAUGHTER. I FEEL LIKE A RAGDOLL IN THE HANDS OF A CAPRICIOUS CHILD.

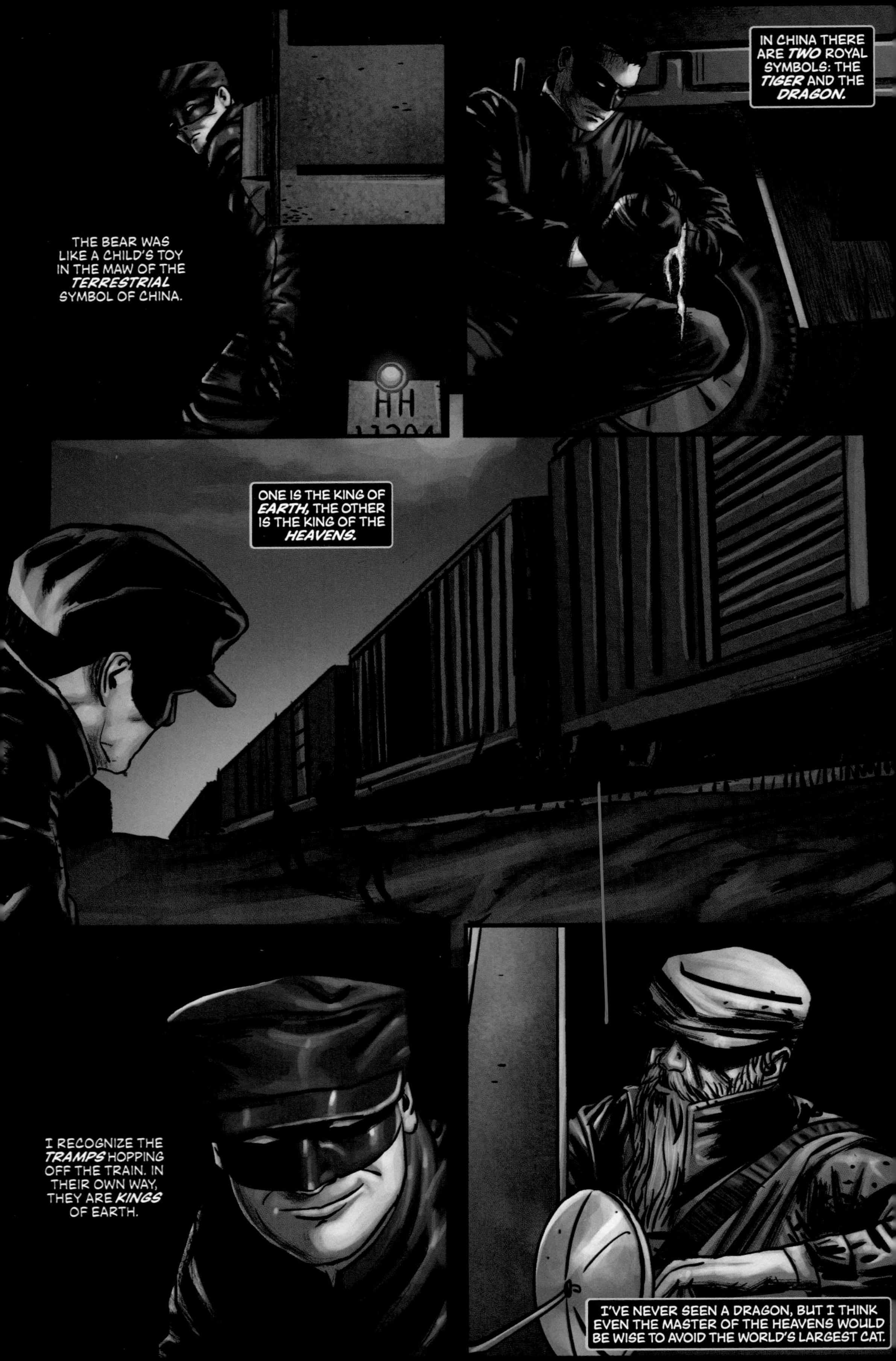
THE BEAR WAS LIKE A CHILD'S TOY IN THE MAW OF THE *TERRESTRIAL* SYMBOL OF CHINA.
HH
IN CHINA THERE ARE *TWO* ROYAL SYMBOLS: THE *TIGER* AND THE *DRAGON.*
ONE IS THE KING OF *EARTH,* THE OTHER IS THE KING OF THE *HEAVENS.*
I RECOGNIZE THE *TRAMPS* HOPPING OFF THE TRAIN. IN THEIR OWN WAY, THEY ARE *KINGS* OF EARTH.
I'VE NEVER SEEN A DRAGON, BUT I THINK EVEN THE MASTER OF THE HEAVENS WOULD BE WISE TO AVOID THE WORLD'S LARGEST CAT.

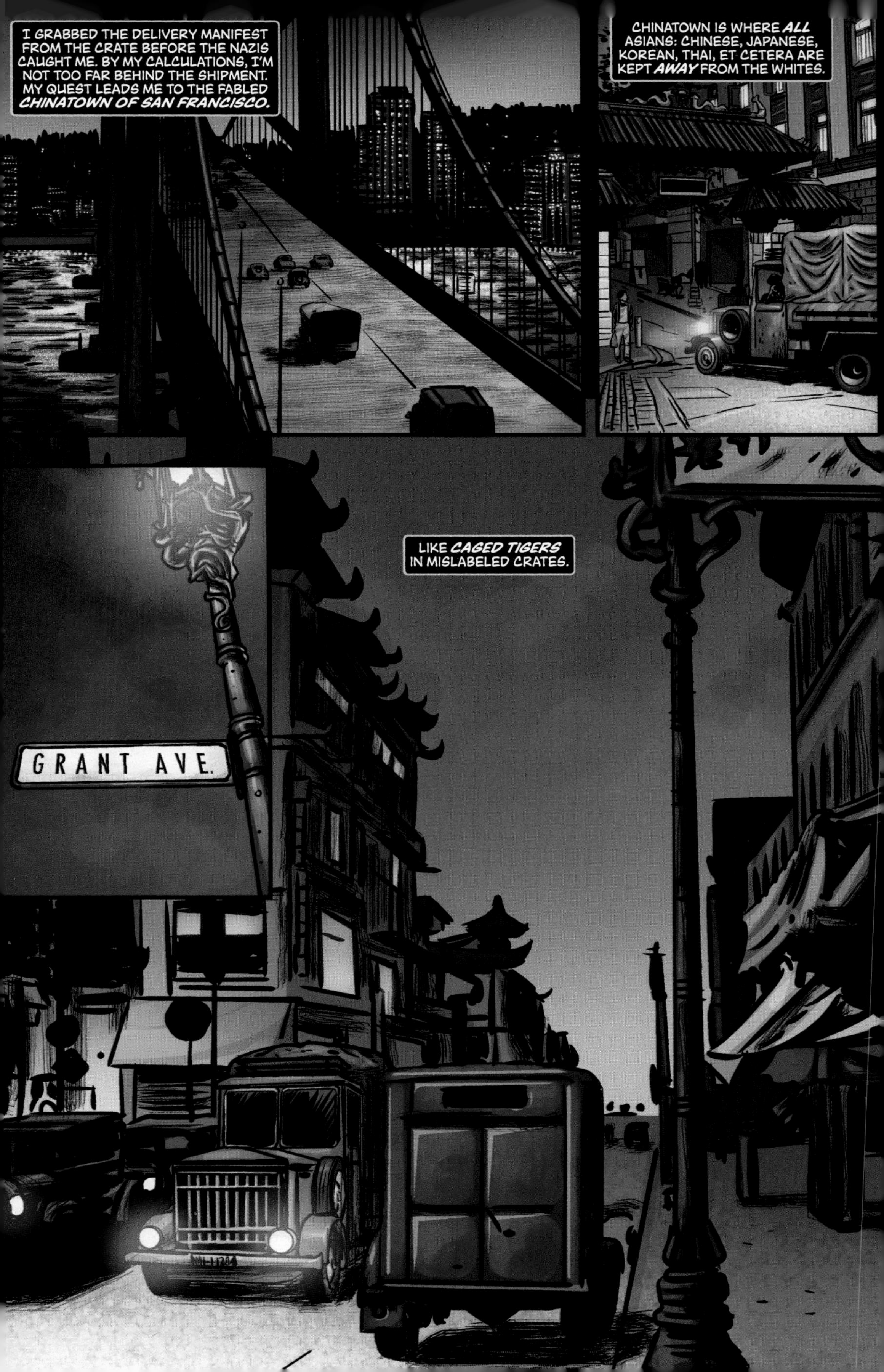
I GRABBED THE DELIVERY MANIFEST FROM THE CRATE BEFORE THE NAZIS CAUGHT ME. BY MY CALCULATIONS, I'M NOT TOO FAR BEHIND THE SHIPMENT. MY QUEST LEADS ME TO THE FABLED *CHINATOWN OF SAN FRANCISCO.*
CHINATOWN IS WHERE *ALL* ASIANS: CHINESE, JAPANESE, KOREAN, THAI, ET CETERA ARE KEPT *AWAY* FROM THE WHITES.
LIKE *CAGED TIGERS* IN MISLABELED CRATES.
GRANT AVE.

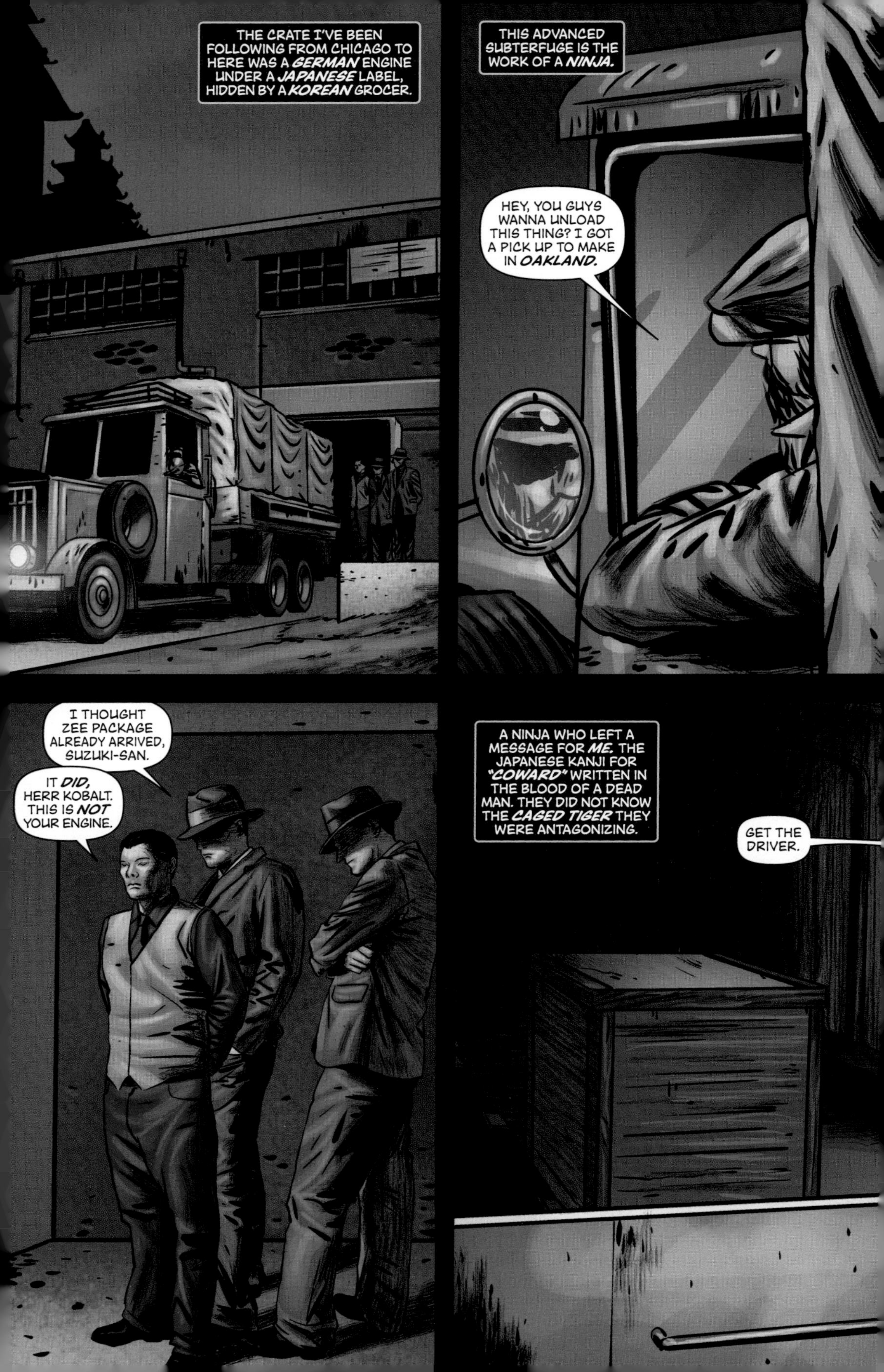
THE CRATE I'VE BEEN FOLLOWING FROM CHICAGO TO HERE WAS A GERMAN ENGINE UNDER A JAPANESE LABEL, HIDDEN BY A KOREAN GROCER.
THIS ADVANCED SUBTERFUGE IS THE WORK OF A NINJA.
HEY, YOU GUYS WANNA UNLOAD THIS THING? I GOT A PICK UP TO MAKE IN OAKLAND.
I THOUGHT ZEE PACKAGE ALREADY ARRIVED, SUZUKI-SAN.
IT DID, HERR KOBALT. THIS IS NOT YOUR ENGINE.
A NINJA WHO LEFT A MESSAGE FOR ME. THE JAPANESE KANJI FOR "COWARD" WRITTEN IN THE BLOOD OF A DEAD MAN. THEY DID NOT KNOW THE CAGED TIGER THEY WERE ANTAGONIZING.
GET THE DRIVER.

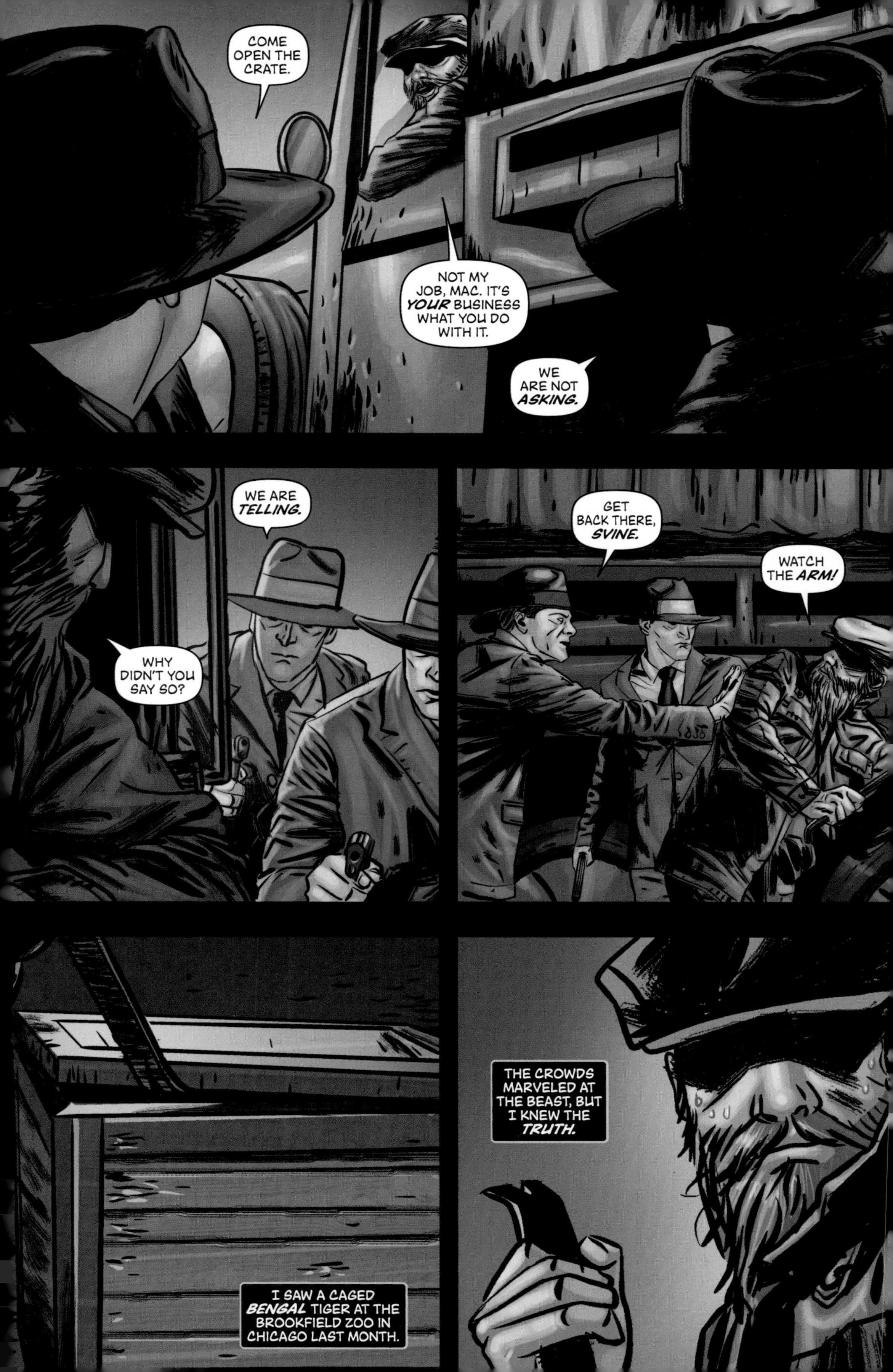
COME OPEN THE CRATE.
NOT MY JOB, MAC. IT'S *YOUR* BUSINESS WHAT YOU DO WITH IT.
WE ARE NOT *ASKING.*
WE ARE *TELLING.*
WHY DIDN'T YOU SAY SO?
GET BACK THERE, *SVINE.*
WATCH THE *ARM!*
I SAW A CAGED *BENGAL* TIGER AT THE BROOKFIELD ZOO IN CHICAGO LAST MONTH.
THE CROWDS MARVELED AT THE BEAST, BUT I KNEW THE *TRUTH.*

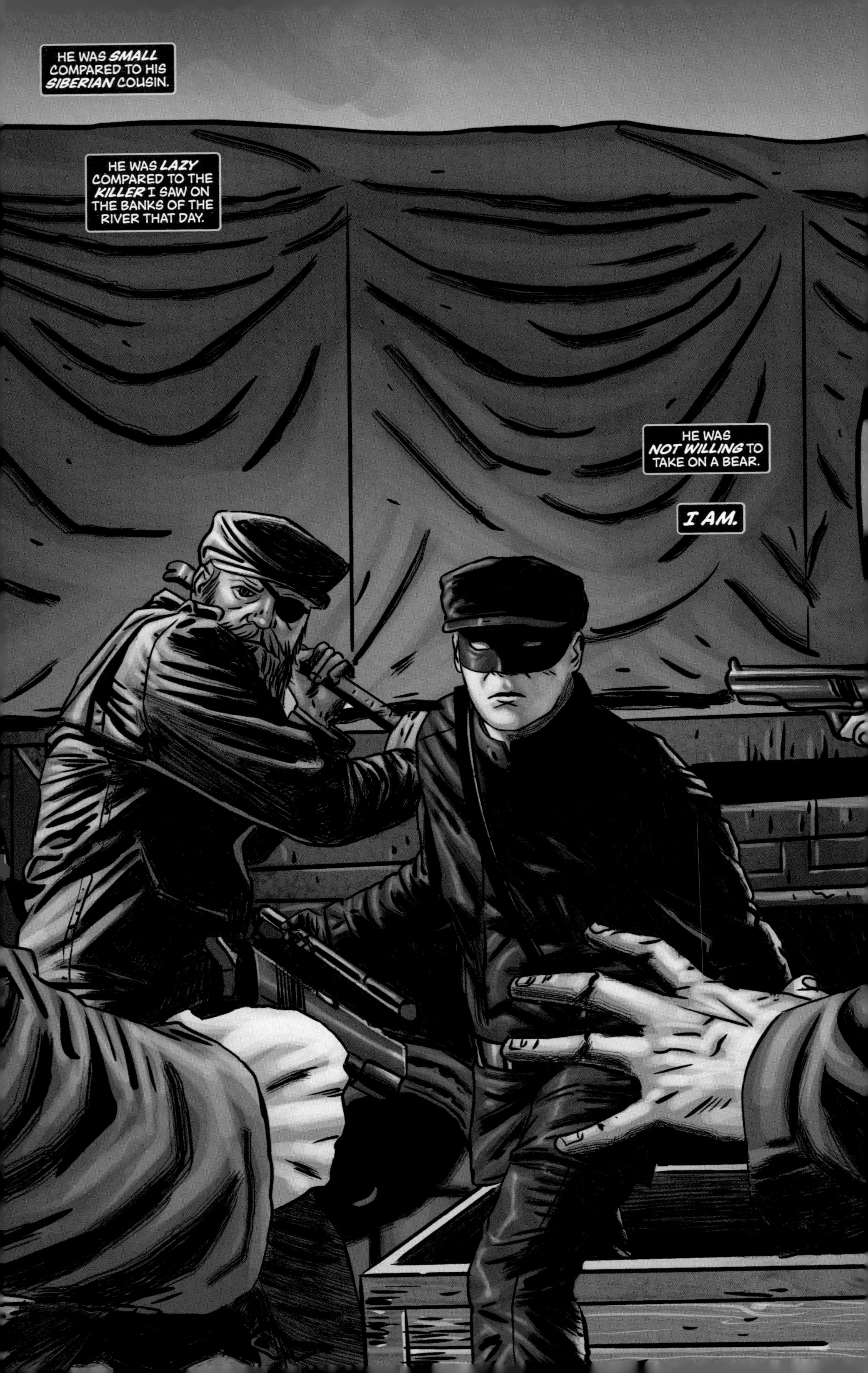
HE WAS SMALL COMPARED TO HIS SIBERIAN COUSIN.
HE WAS LAZY COMPARED TO THE KILLER I SAW ON THE BANKS OF THE RIVER THAT DAY.
HE WAS NOT WILLING TO TAKE ON A BEAR.
I AM.

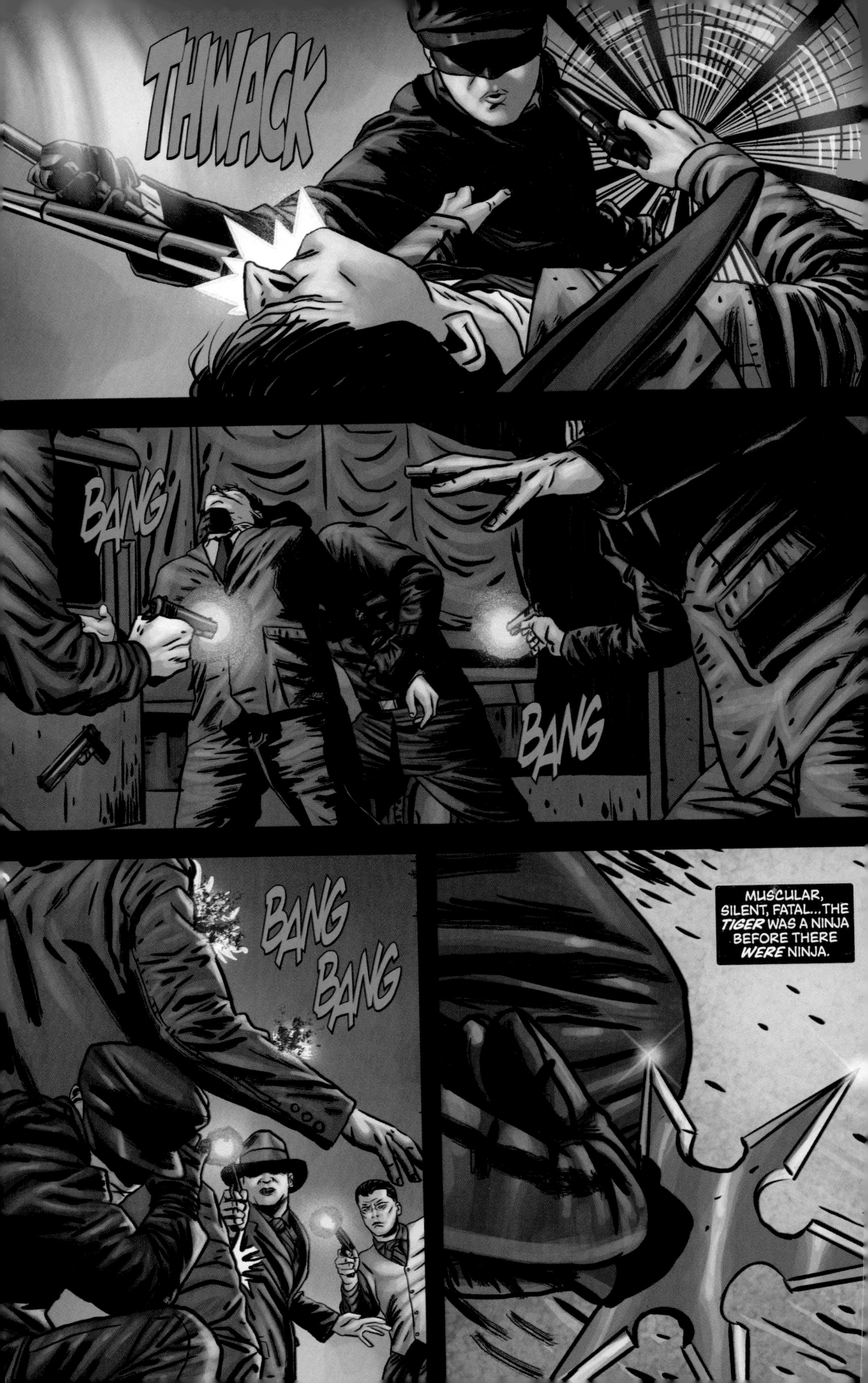
THWACK
BANG
BANG
BANG
BANG
MUSCULAR, SILENT, FATAL... THE TIGER WAS A NINJA BEFORE THERE WERE NINJA.

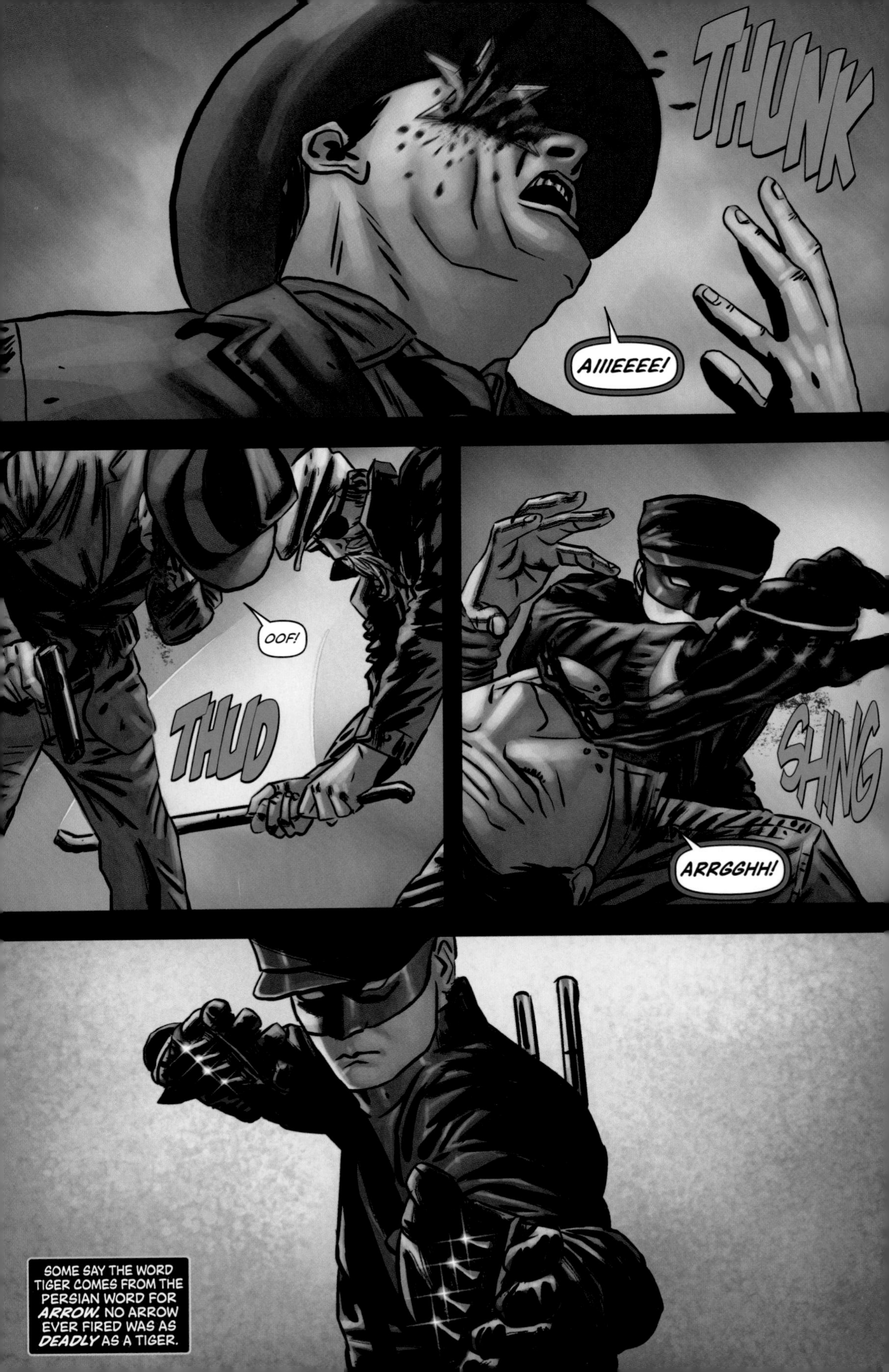
THUNK
AIIIEEEE!
OOF!
THUD
SHING
ARRGGHH!
SOME SAY THE WORD TIGER COMES FROM THE PERSIAN WORD FOR ARROW. NO ARROW EVER FIRED WAS AS DEADLY AS A TIGER.

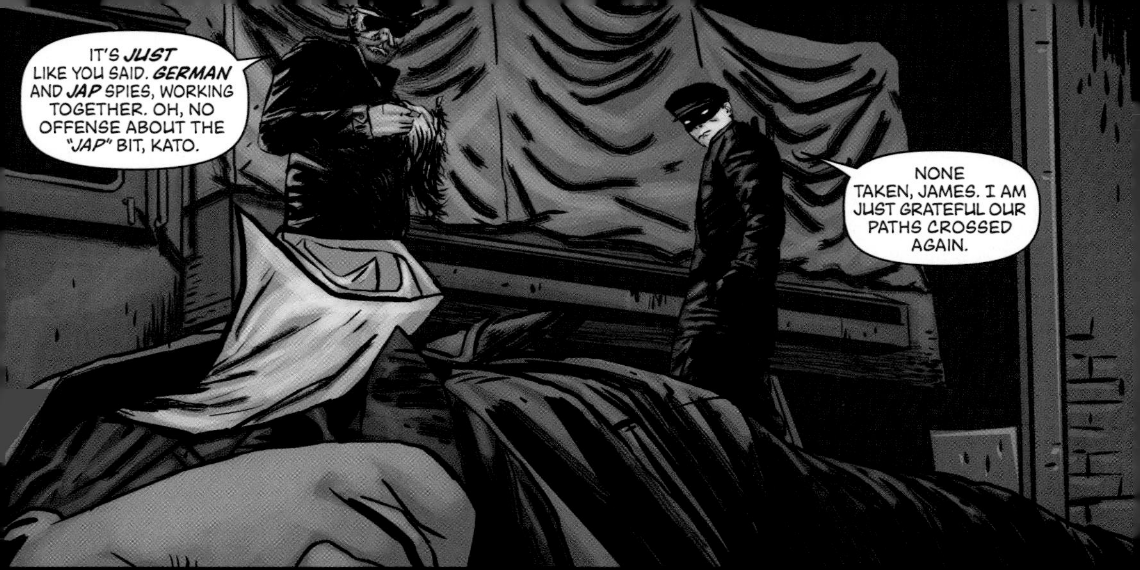
IT'S JUST LIKE YOU SAID. GERMAN AND JAP SPIES, WORKING TOGETHER. OH, NO OFFENSE ABOUT THE "JAP" BIT, KATO.
NONE TAKEN, JAMES. I AM JUST GRATEFUL OUR PATHS CROSSED AGAIN.
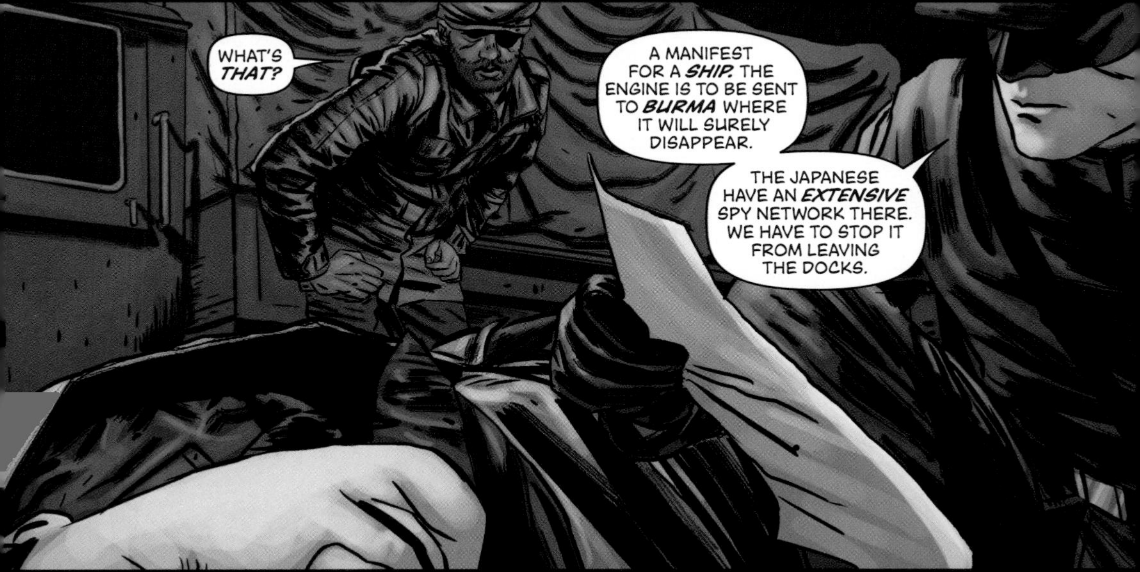
WHAT'S THAT?
A MANIFEST FOR A SHIP. THE ENGINE IS TO BE SENT TO BURMA WHERE IT WILL SURELY DISAPPEAR.
THE JAPANESE HAVE AN EXTENSIVE SPY NETWORK THERE. WE HAVE TO STOP IT FROM LEAVING THE DOCKS.
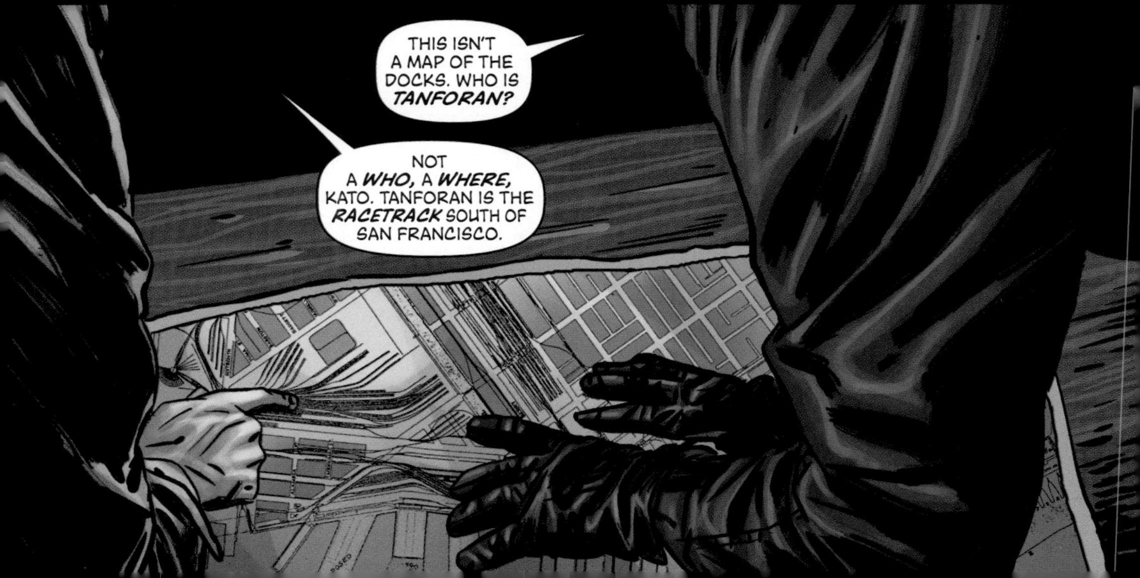
THIS ISN'T A MAP OF THE DOCKS. WHO IS TANFORAN?
NOT A WHO, A WHERE, KATO. TANFORAN IS THE RACETRACK SOUTH OF SAN FRANCISCO.

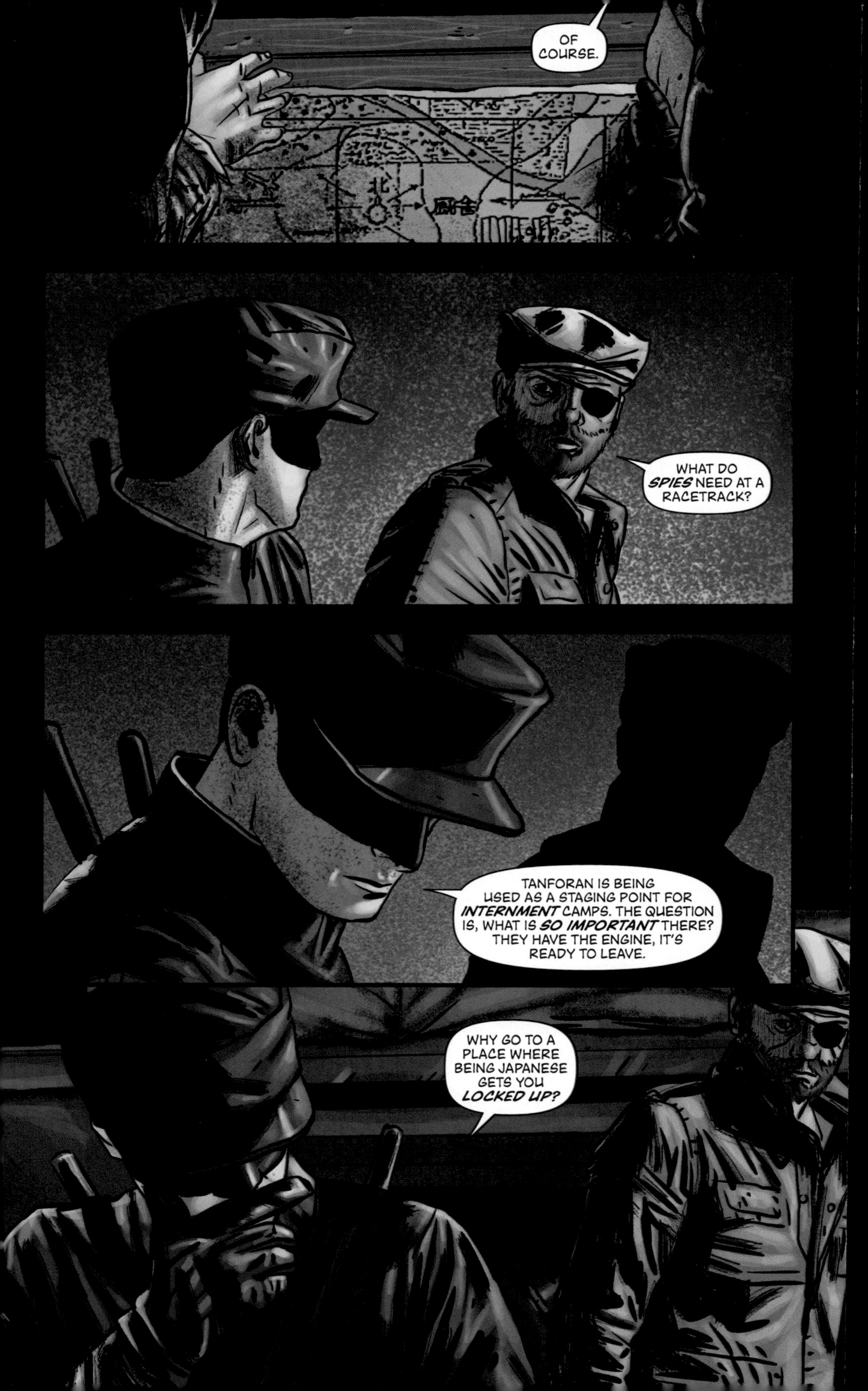
OF COURSE.
WHAT DO SPIES NEED AT A RACETRACK?
TANFORAN IS BEING USED AS A STAGING POINT FOR INTERNMENT CAMPS. THE QUESTION IS, WHAT IS SO IMPORTANT THERE? THEY HAVE THE ENGINE, IT'S READY TO LEAVE.
WHY GO TO A PLACE WHERE BEING JAPANESE GETS YOU LOCKED UP?

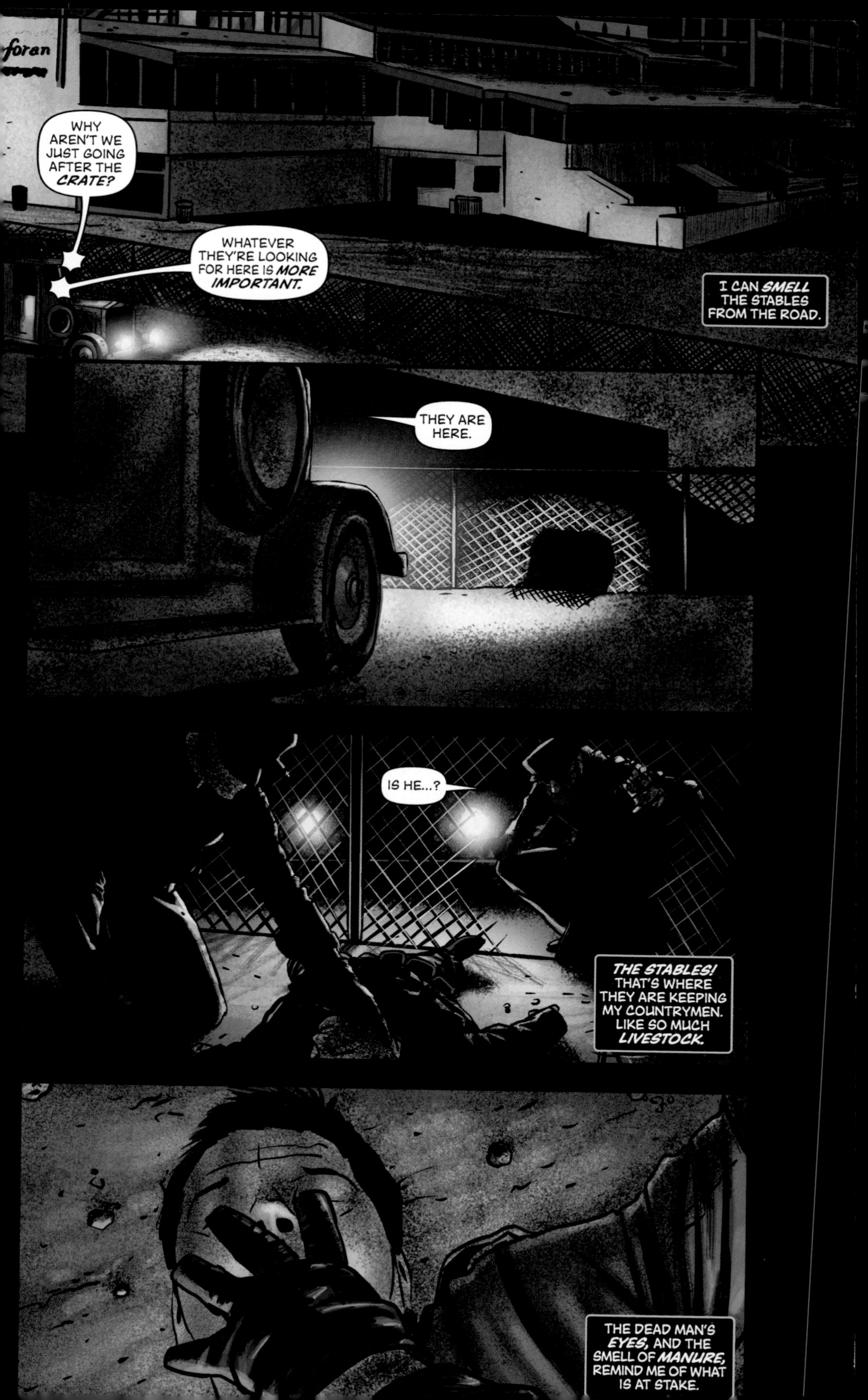
WHY AREN'T WE JUST GOING AFTER THE CRATE?
WHATEVER THEY'RE LOOKING FOR HERE IS MORE IMPORTANT.
I CAN SMELL THE STABLES FROM THE ROAD.
THEY ARE HERE.
IS HE...?
THE STABLES! THAT'S WHERE THEY ARE KEEPING MY COUNTRYMEN. LIKE SO MUCH LIVESTOCK.
THE DEAD MAN'S EYES, AND THE SMELL OF MANURE, REMIND ME OF WHAT IS AT STAKE.

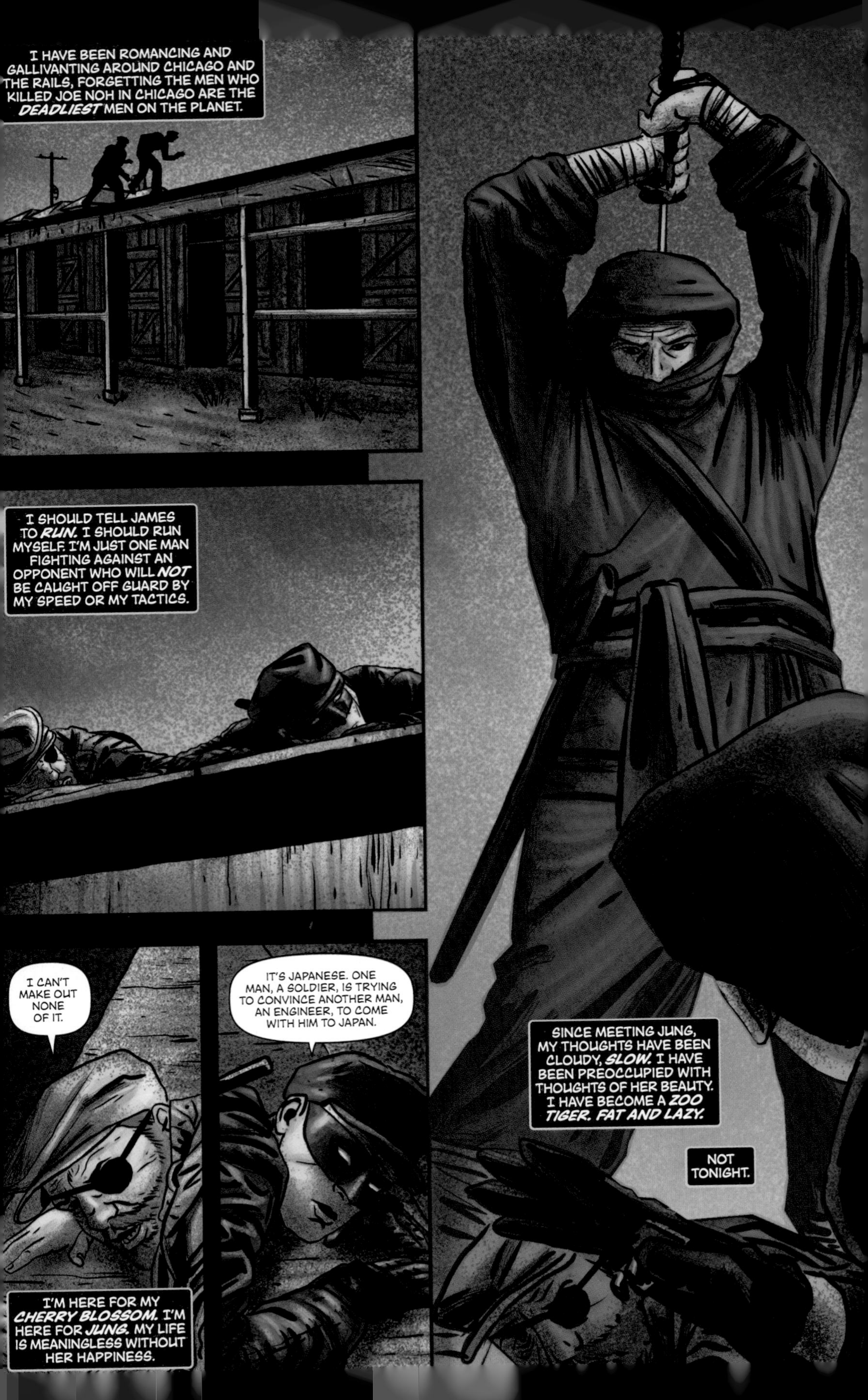
I HAVE BEEN ROMANCING AND GALLIVANTING AROUND CHICAGO AND THE RAILS, FORGETTING THE MEN WHO KILLED JOE NOH IN CHICAGO ARE THE DEADLIEST MEN ON THE PLANET.
I SHOULD TELL JAMES TO RUN. I SHOULD RUN MYSELF. I'M JUST ONE MAN FIGHTING AGAINST AN OPPONENT WHO WILL NOT BE CAUGHT OFF GUARD BY MY SPEED OR MY TACTICS.
I CAN'T MAKE OUT NONE OF IT.
IT'S JAPANESE. ONE MAN, A SOLDIER, IS TRYING TO CONVINCE ANOTHER MAN, AN ENGINEER, TO COME WITH HIM TO JAPAN.
I'M HERE FOR MY CHERRY BLOSSOM. I'M HERE FOR JUNG. MY LIFE IS MEANINGLESS WITHOUT HER HAPPINESS.
SINCE MEETING JUNG, MY THOUGHTS HAVE BEEN CLOUDY, SLOW. I HAVE BEEN PREOCCUPIED WITH THOUGHTS OF HER BEAUTY. I HAVE BECOME A ZOO TIGER. FAT AND LAZY.
NOT TONIGHT.

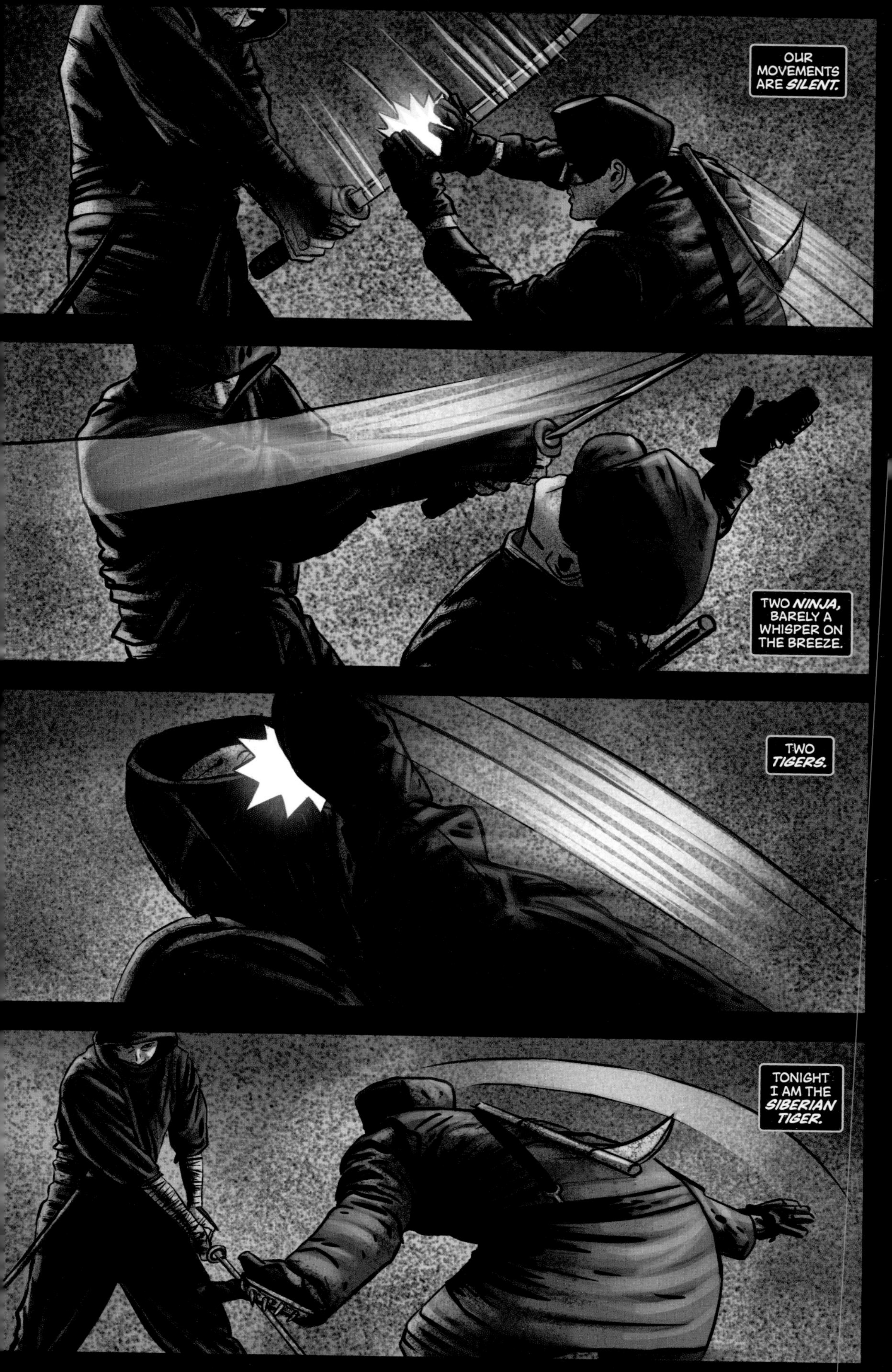
OUR MOVEMENTS ARE SILENT.
TWO NINJA, BARELY A WHISPER ON THE BREEZE.
TWO TIGERS.
TONIGHT I AM THE SIBERIAN TIGER.

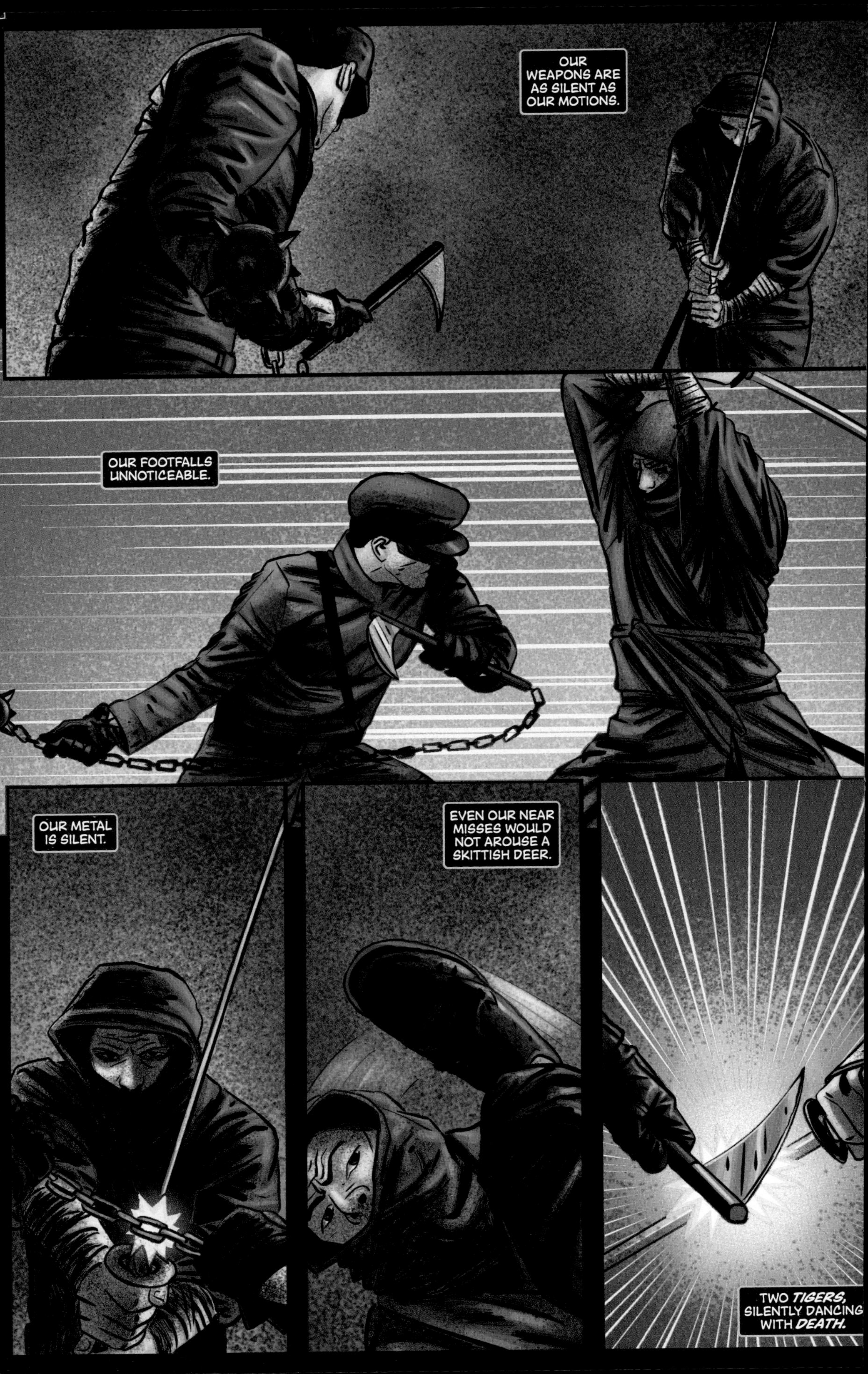
OUR WEAPONS ARE AS SILENT AS OUR MOTIONS.
OUR FOOTFALLS UNNOTICEABLE.
OUR METAL IS SILENT.
EVEN OUR NEAR MISSES WOULD NOT AROUSE A SKITTISH DEER.
TWO *TIGERS,* SILENTLY DANCING WITH *DEATH.*

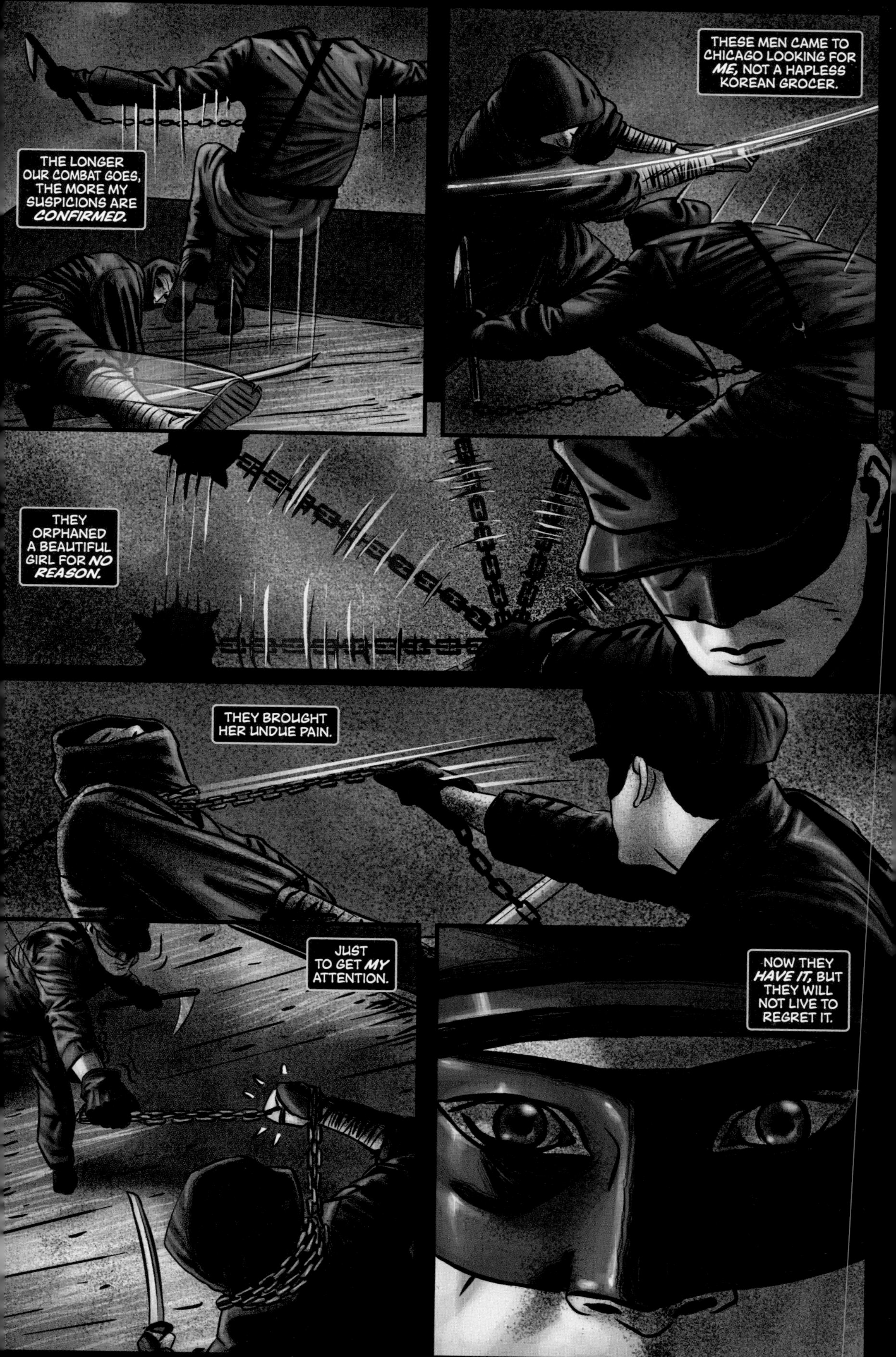
THE LONGER OUR COMBAT GOES, THE MORE MY SUSPICIONS ARE CONFIRMED.
THESE MEN CAME TO CHICAGO LOOKING FOR ME, NOT A HAPLESS KOREAN GROCER.
THEY ORPHANED A BEAUTIFUL GIRL FOR NO REASON.
THEY BROUGHT HER UNDUE PAIN.
JUST TO GET MY ATTENTION.
NOW THEY HAVE IT, BUT THEY WILL NOT LIVE TO REGRET IT.

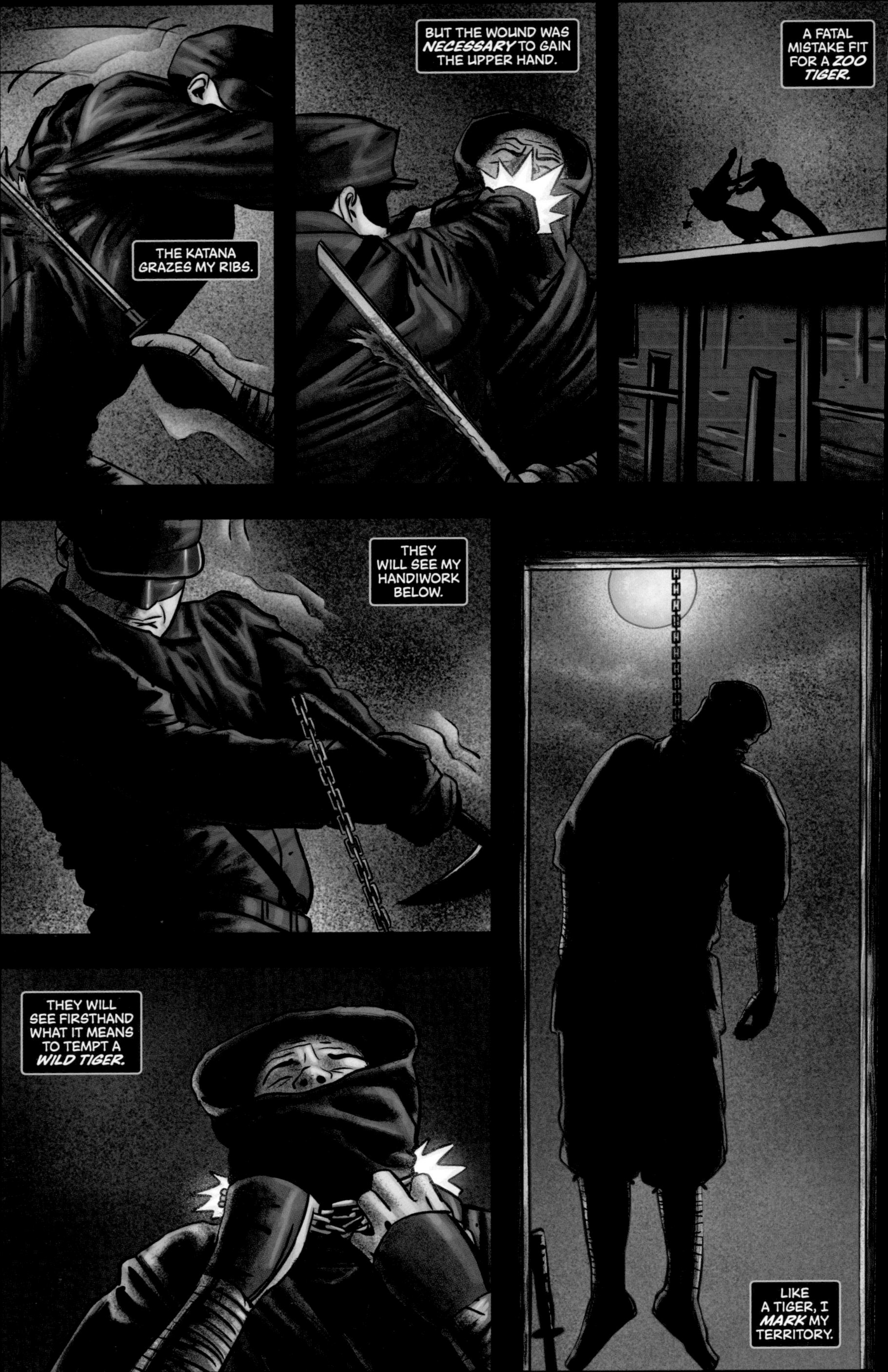
THE KATANA GRAZES MY RIBS.
BUT THE WOUND WAS NECESSARY TO GAIN THE UPPER HAND.
A FATAL MISTAKE FIT FOR A ZOO TIGER.
THEY WILL SEE MY HANDIWORK BELOW.
THEY WILL SEE FIRSTHAND WHAT IT MEANS TO TEMPT A WILD TIGER.
LIKE A TIGER, I MARK MY TERRITORY.

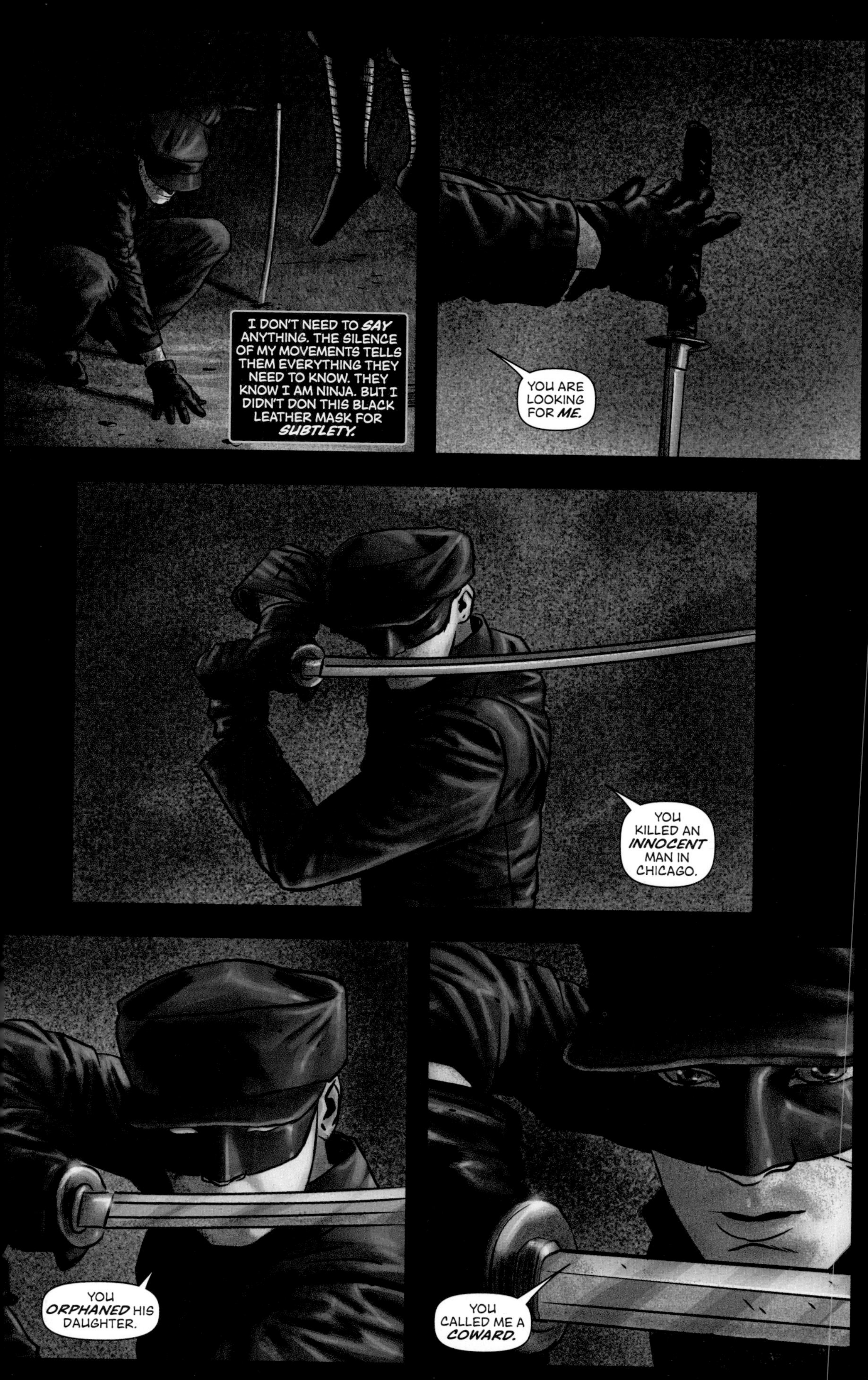
I DON'T NEED TO SAY ANYTHING. THE SILENCE OF MY MOVEMENTS TELLS THEM EVERYTHING THEY NEED TO KNOW. THEY KNOW I AM NINJA. BUT I DIDN'T DON THIS BLACK LEATHER MASK FOR SUBTLETY.
YOU ARE LOOKING FOR ME.
YOU KILLED AN INNOCENT MAN IN CHICAGO.
YOU ORPHANED HIS DAUGHTER.
YOU CALLED ME A COWARD.

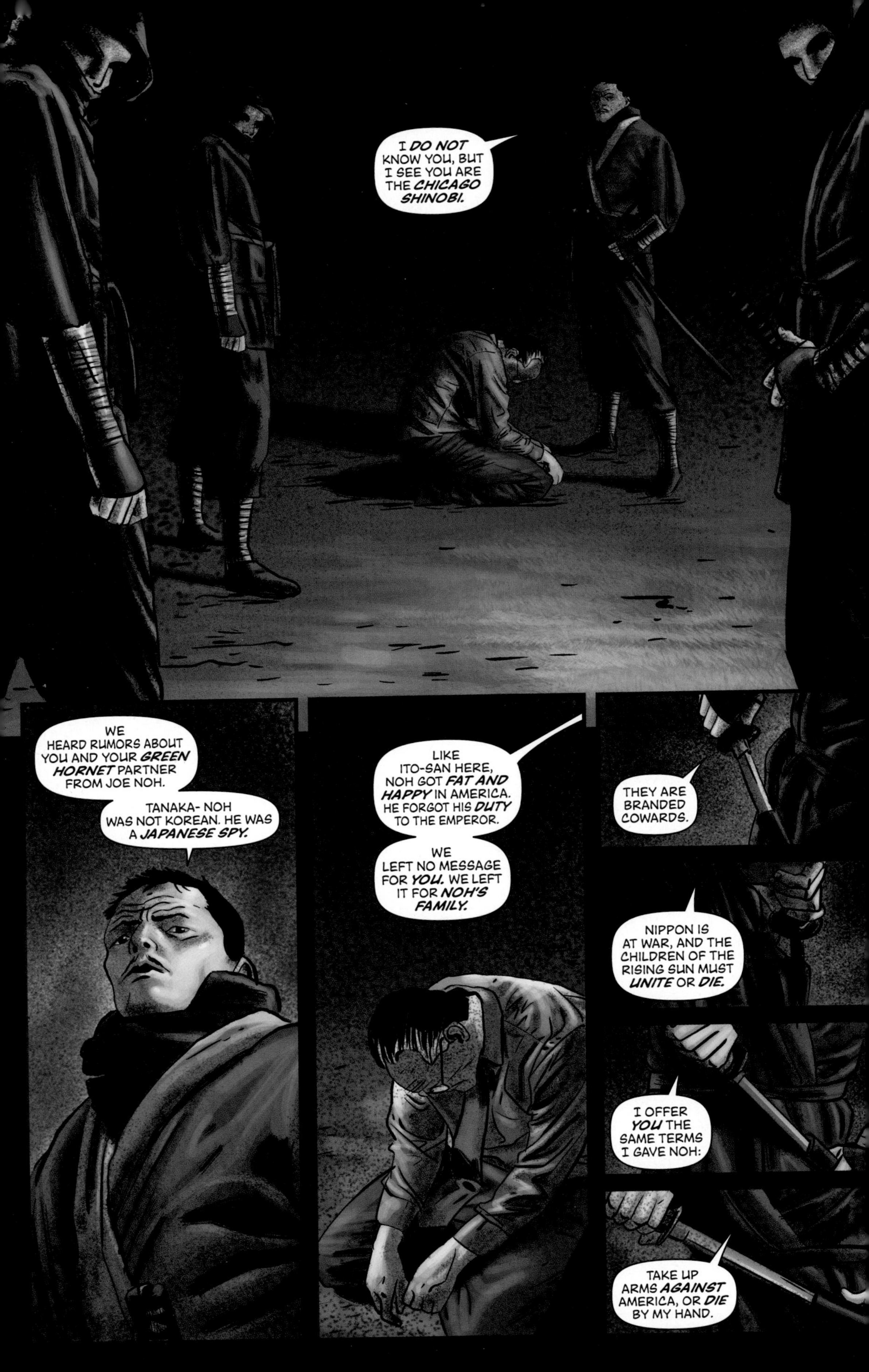
I DO NOT KNOW YOU, BUT I SEE YOU ARE THE CHICAGO SHINOBI.
WE HEARD RUMORS ABOUT YOU AND YOUR GREEN HORNET PARTNER FROM JOE NOH.
TANAKA- NOH WAS NOT KOREAN. HE WAS A JAPANESE SPY.
LIKE ITO-SAN HERE, NOH GOT FAT AND HAPPY IN AMERICA. HE FORGOT HIS DUTY TO THE EMPEROR.
WE LEFT NO MESSAGE FOR YOU. WE LEFT IT FOR NOH'S FAMILY.
THEY ARE BRANDED COWARDS.
NIPPON IS AT WAR, AND THE CHILDREN OF THE RISING SUN MUST UNITE OR DIE.
I OFFER YOU THE SAME TERMS I GAVE NOH:
TAKE UP ARMS AGAINST AMERICA, OR DIE BY MY HAND.

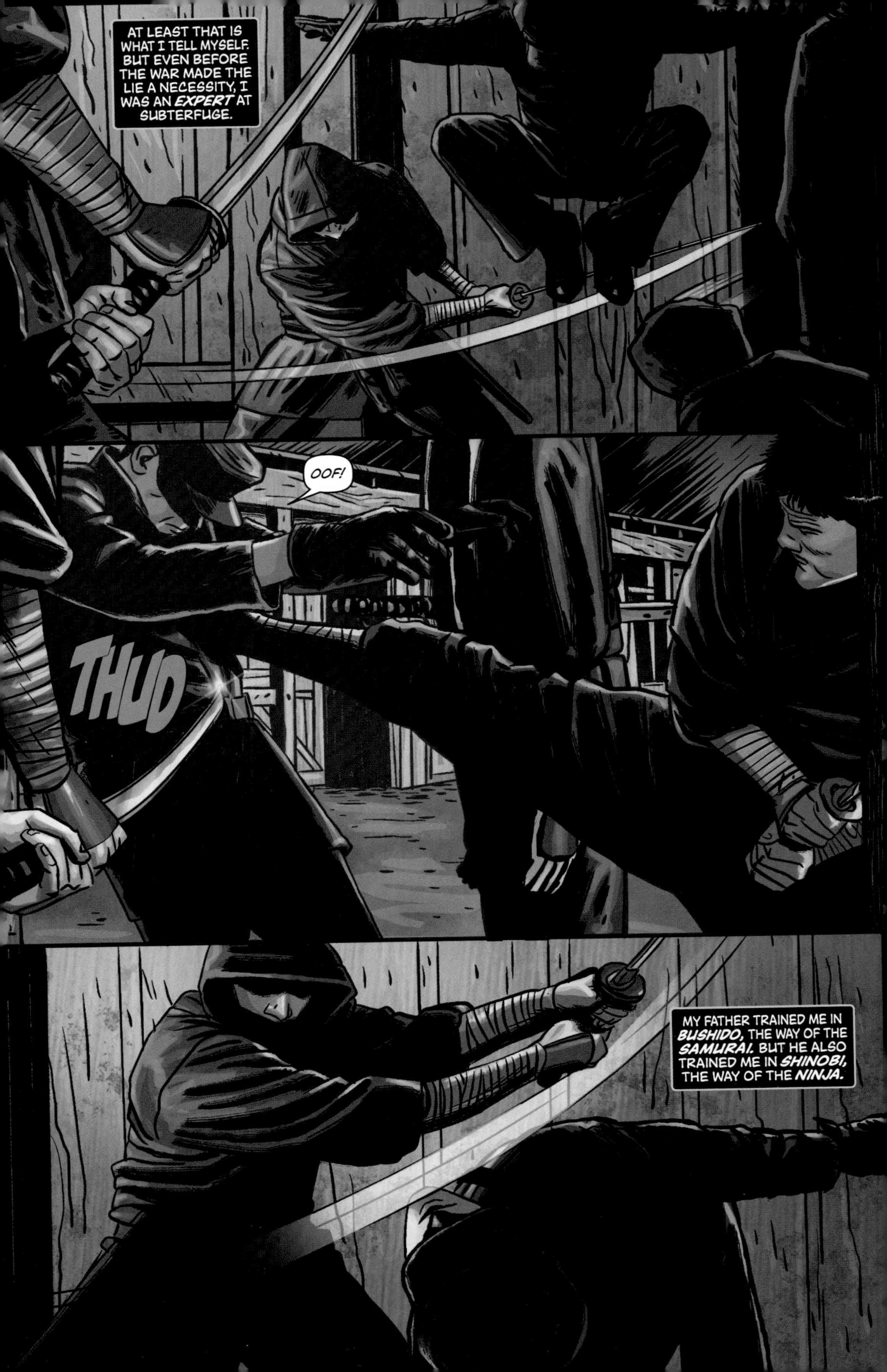
AT LEAST THAT IS WHAT I TELL MYSELF. BUT EVEN BEFORE THE WAR MADE THE LIE A NECESSITY, I WAS AN *EXPERT* AT SUBTERFUGE.
OOF!
THUD
MY FATHER TRAINED ME IN *BUSHIDO*, THE WAY OF THE *SAMURAI*. BUT HE ALSO TRAINED ME IN *SHINOBI*, THE WAY OF THE *NINJA*.

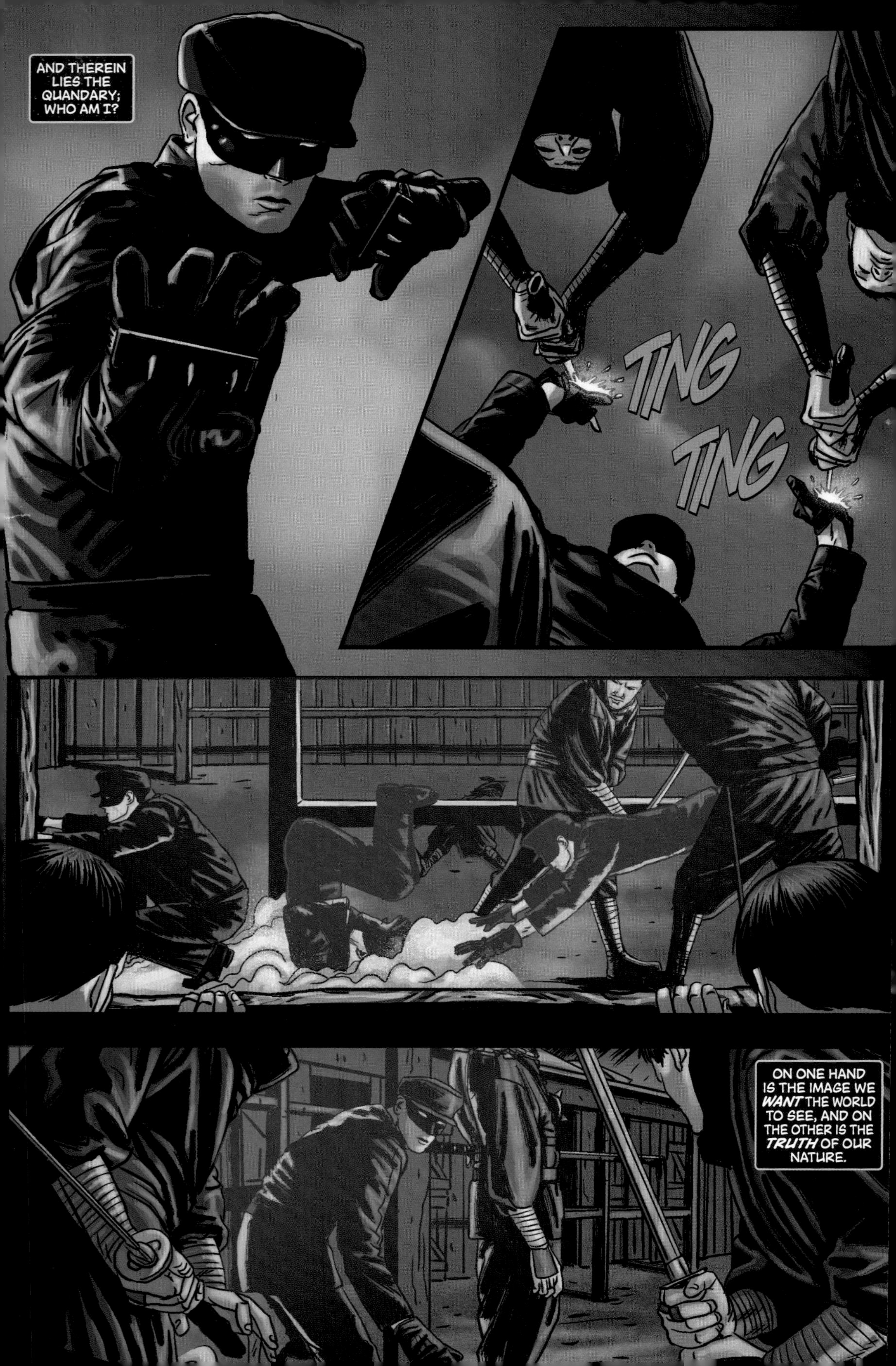
AND THEREIN LIES THE QUANDARY; WHO AM I?
TING
TING
ON ONE HAND IS THE IMAGE WE WANT THE WORLD TO SEE, AND ON THE OTHER IS THE TRUTH OF OUR NATURE.

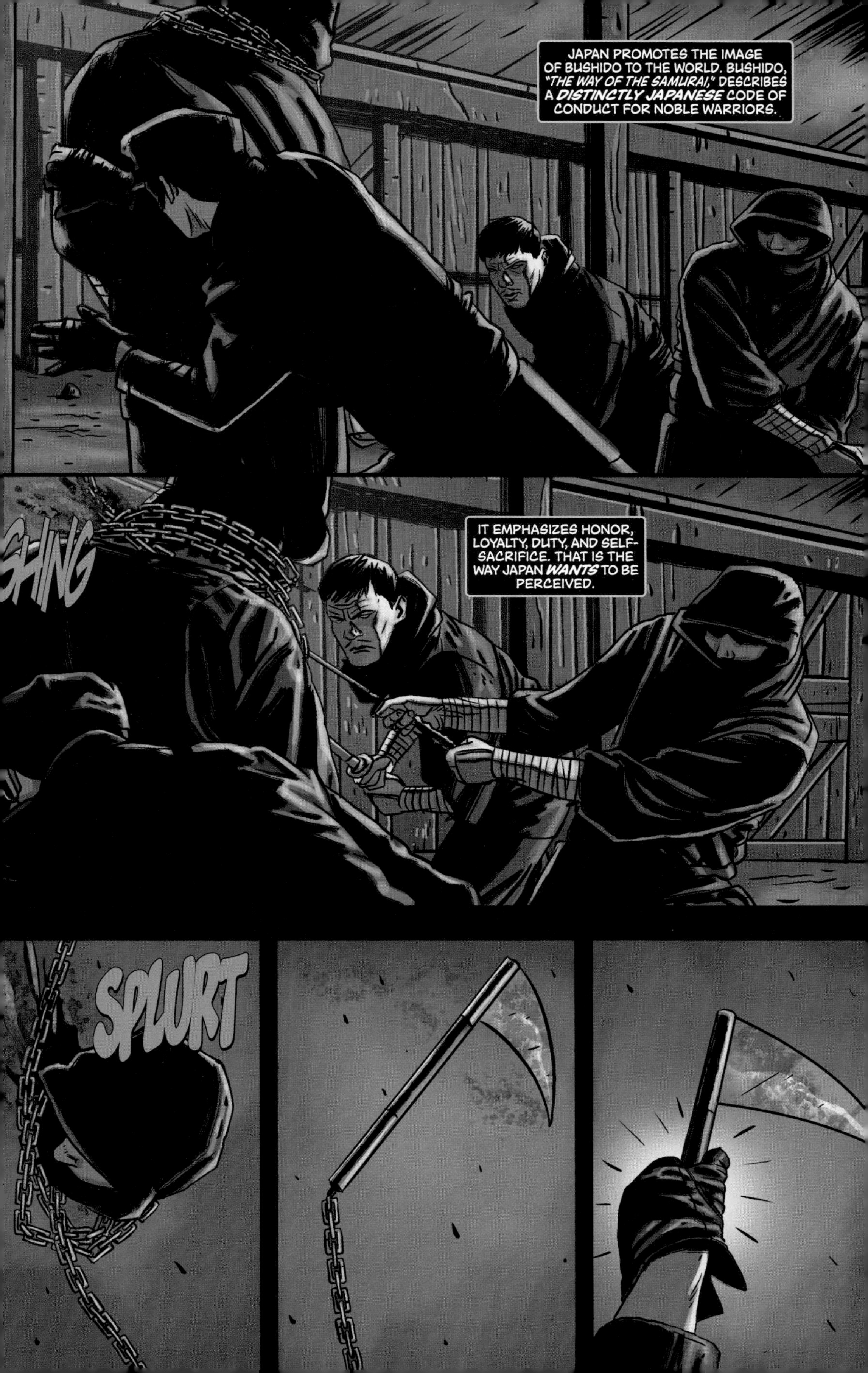
JAPAN PROMOTES THE IMAGE OF BUSHIDO TO THE WORLD. BUSHIDO, *"THE WAY OF THE SAMURAI,"* DESCRIBES A ***DISTINCTLY JAPANESE*** CODE OF CONDUCT FOR NOBLE WARRIORS.
SHING
IT EMPHASIZES HONOR, LOYALTY, DUTY, AND SELF-SACRIFICE. THAT IS THE WAY JAPAN ***WANTS*** TO BE PERCEIVED.
SPLURT

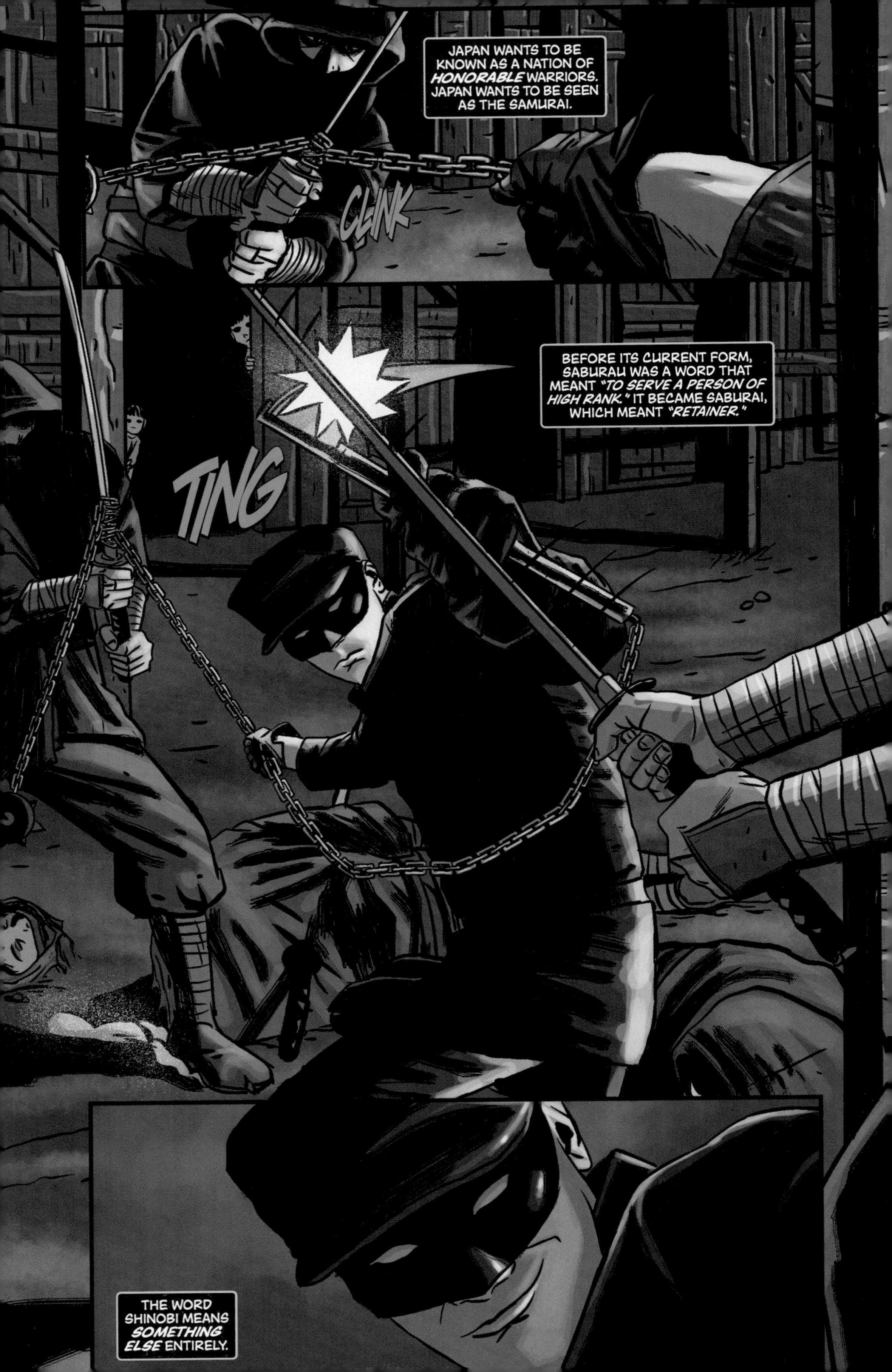
JAPAN WANTS TO BE KNOWN AS A NATION OF HONORABLE WARRIORS. JAPAN WANTS TO BE SEEN AS THE SAMURAI.
CLINK
BEFORE ITS CURRENT FORM, SABURAU WAS A WORD THAT MEANT "TO SERVE A PERSON OF HIGH RANK." IT BECAME SABURAI, WHICH MEANT "RETAINER."
TING
THE WORD SHINOBI MEANS SOMETHING ELSE ENTIRELY.

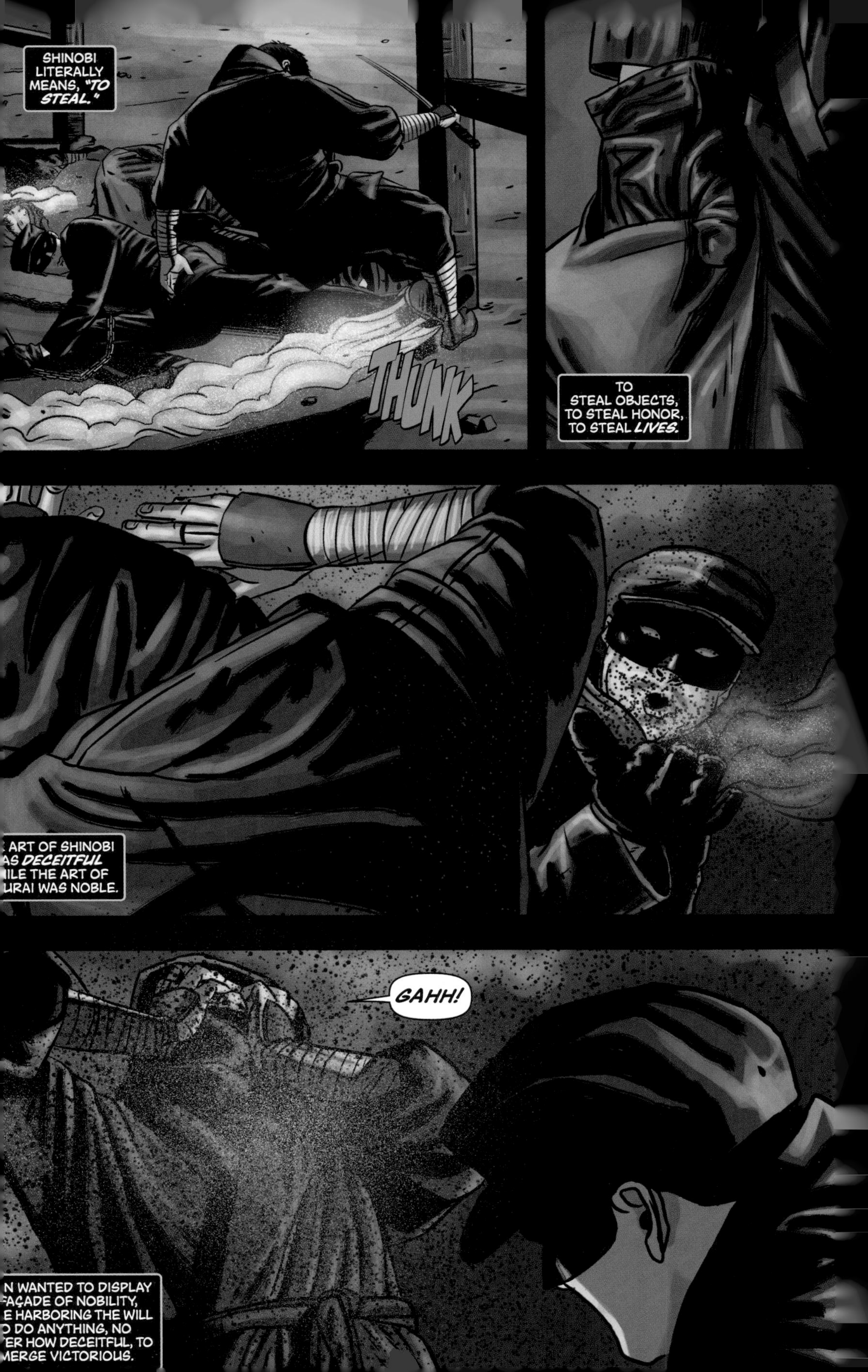
SHINOBI LITERALLY MEANS, "TO STEAL."
THUNK
TO STEAL OBJECTS, TO STEAL HONOR, TO STEAL LIVES.
ART OF SHINOBI AS DECEITFUL ILE THE ART OF URAI WAS NOBLE.
GAHH!
N WANTED TO DISPLAY FAÇADE OF NOBILITY, E HARBORING THE WILL O DO ANYTHING, NO ER HOW DECEITFUL, TO MERGE VICTORIOUS.

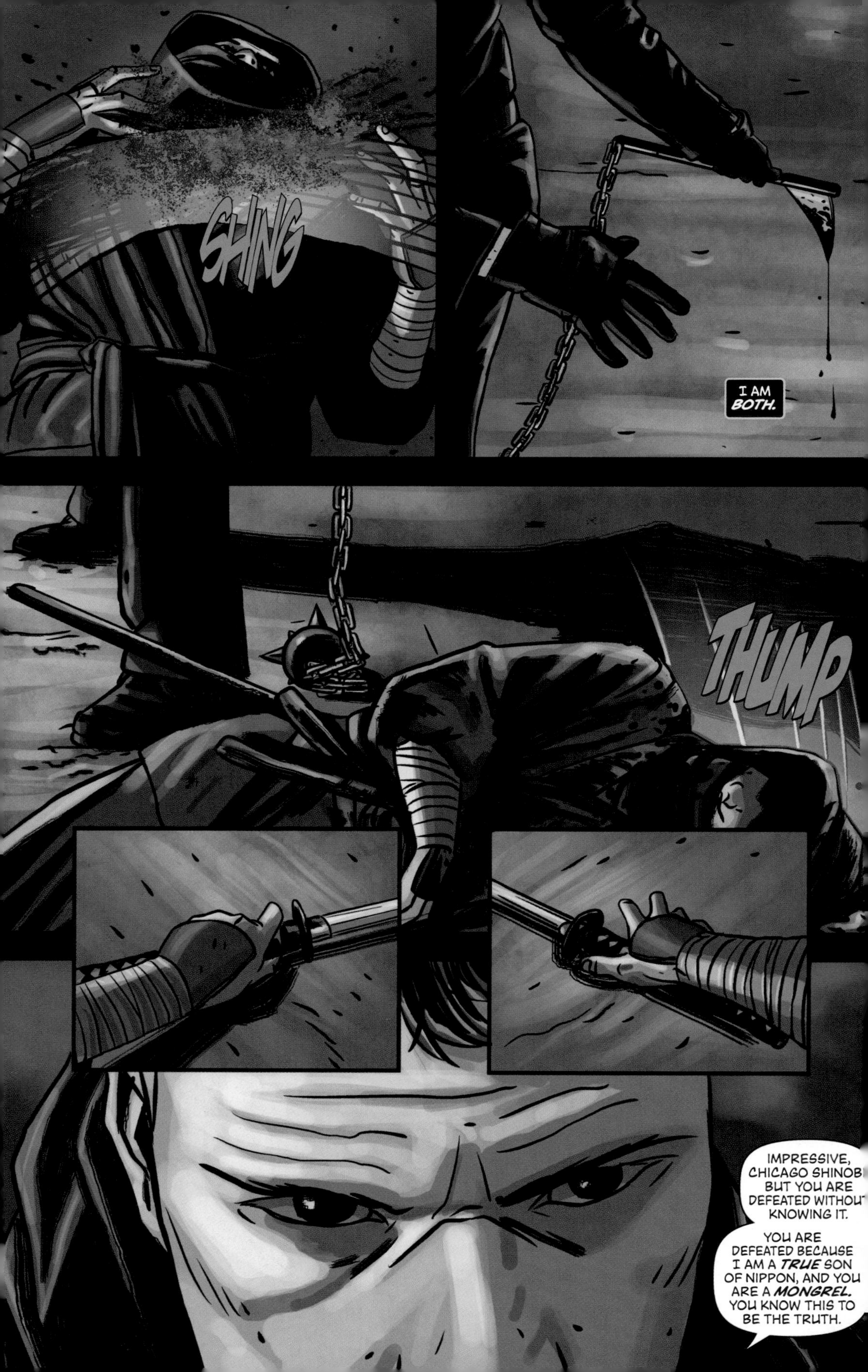
SHING
I AM BOTH.
THUMP
IMPRESSIVE, CHICAGO SHINOBI BUT YOU ARE DEFEATED WITHOUT KNOWING IT.
YOU ARE DEFEATED BECAUSE I AM A TRUE SON OF NIPPON, AND YOU ARE A MONGREL. YOU KNOW THIS TO BE THE TRUTH.

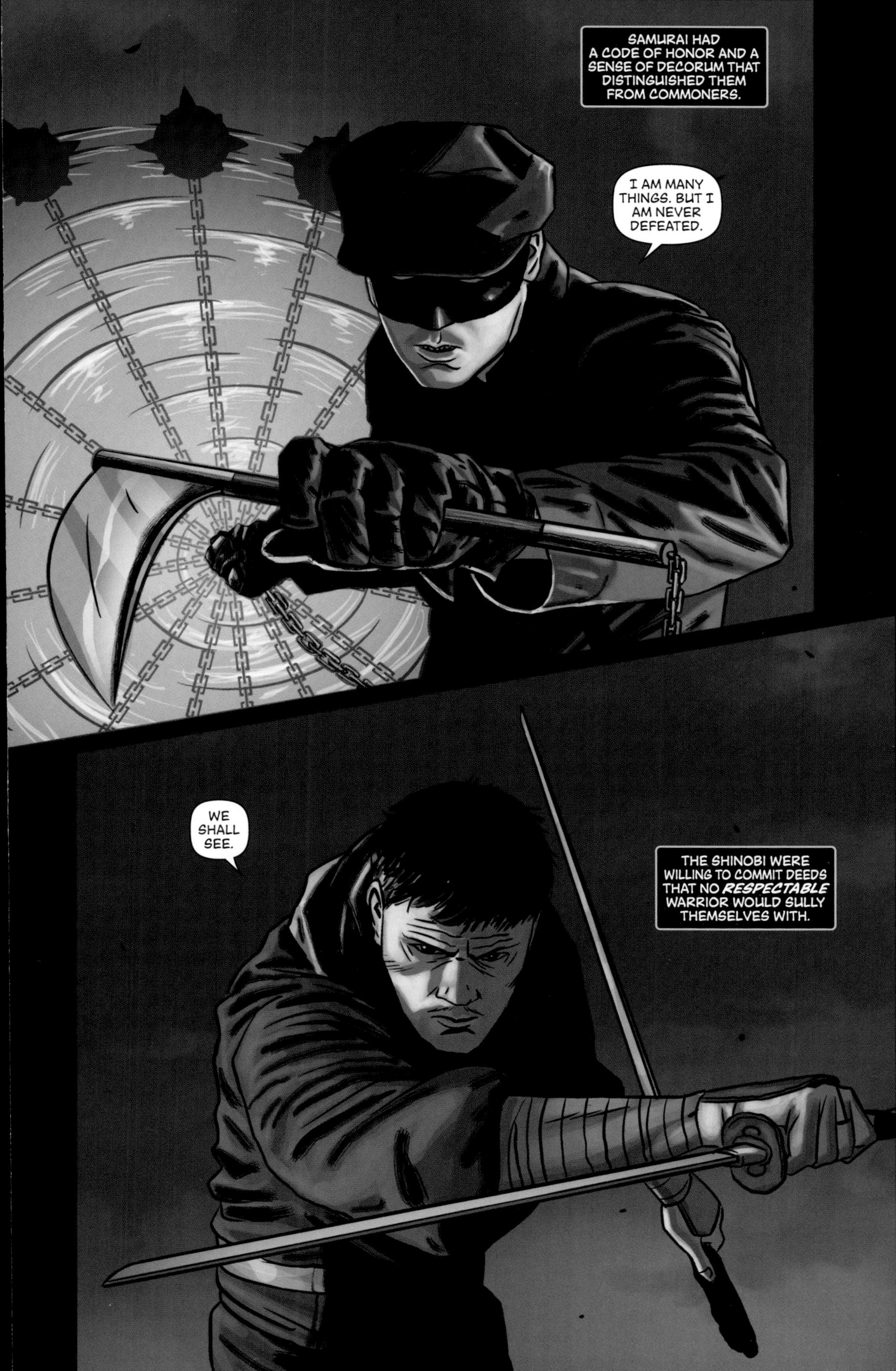
SAMURAI HAD A CODE OF HONOR AND A SENSE OF DECORUM THAT DISTINGUISHED THEM FROM COMMONERS.
I AM MANY THINGS. BUT I AM NEVER DEFEATED.
WE SHALL SEE.
THE SHINOBI WERE WILLING TO COMMIT DEEDS THAT NO RESPECTABLE WARRIOR WOULD SULLY THEMSELVES WITH.

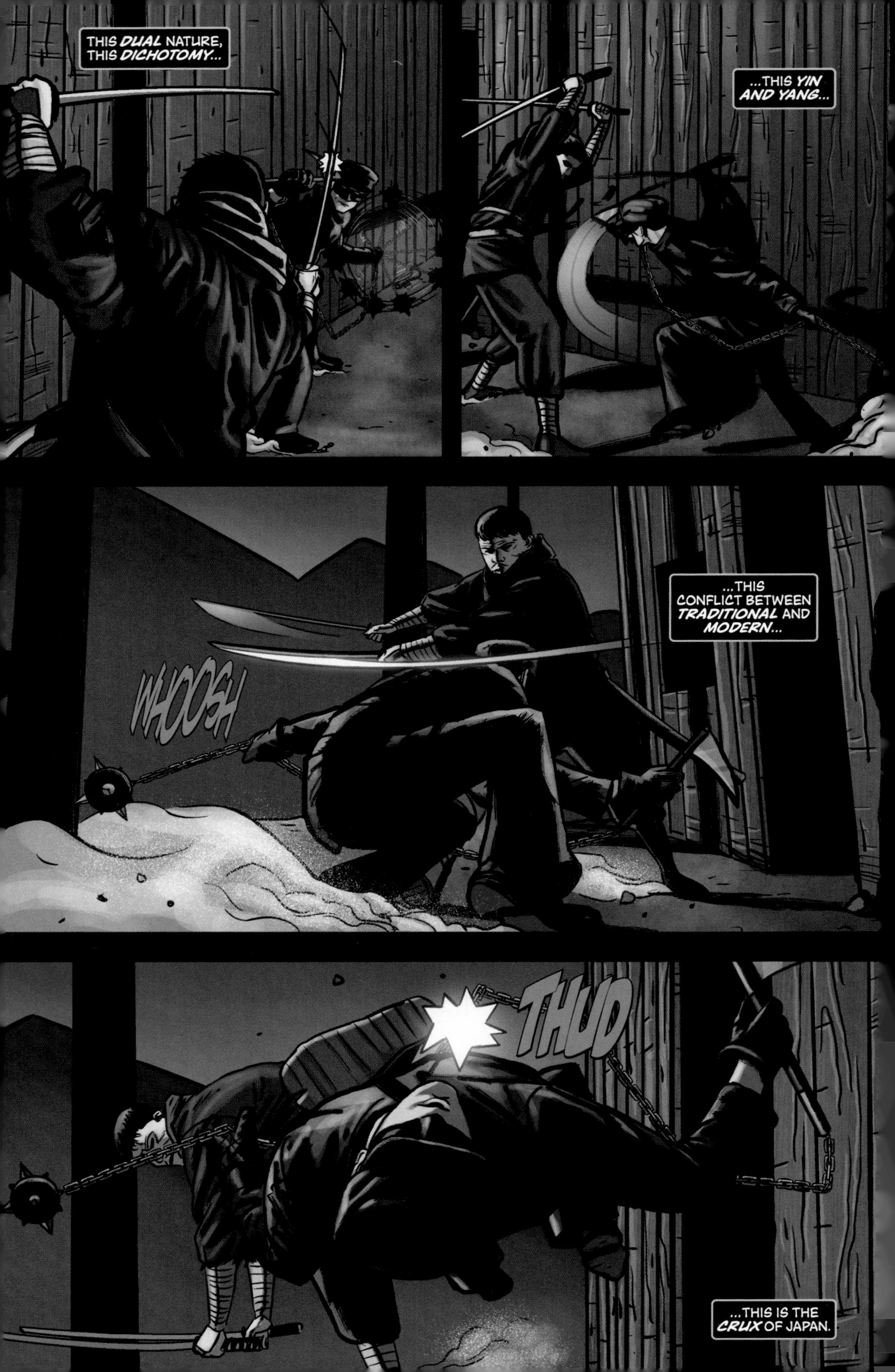
THIS DUAL NATURE, THIS DICHOTOMY...
...THIS YIN AND YANG...
...THIS CONFLICT BETWEEN TRADITIONAL AND MODERN...
WHOOSH
THUD
...THIS IS THE CRUX OF JAPAN.

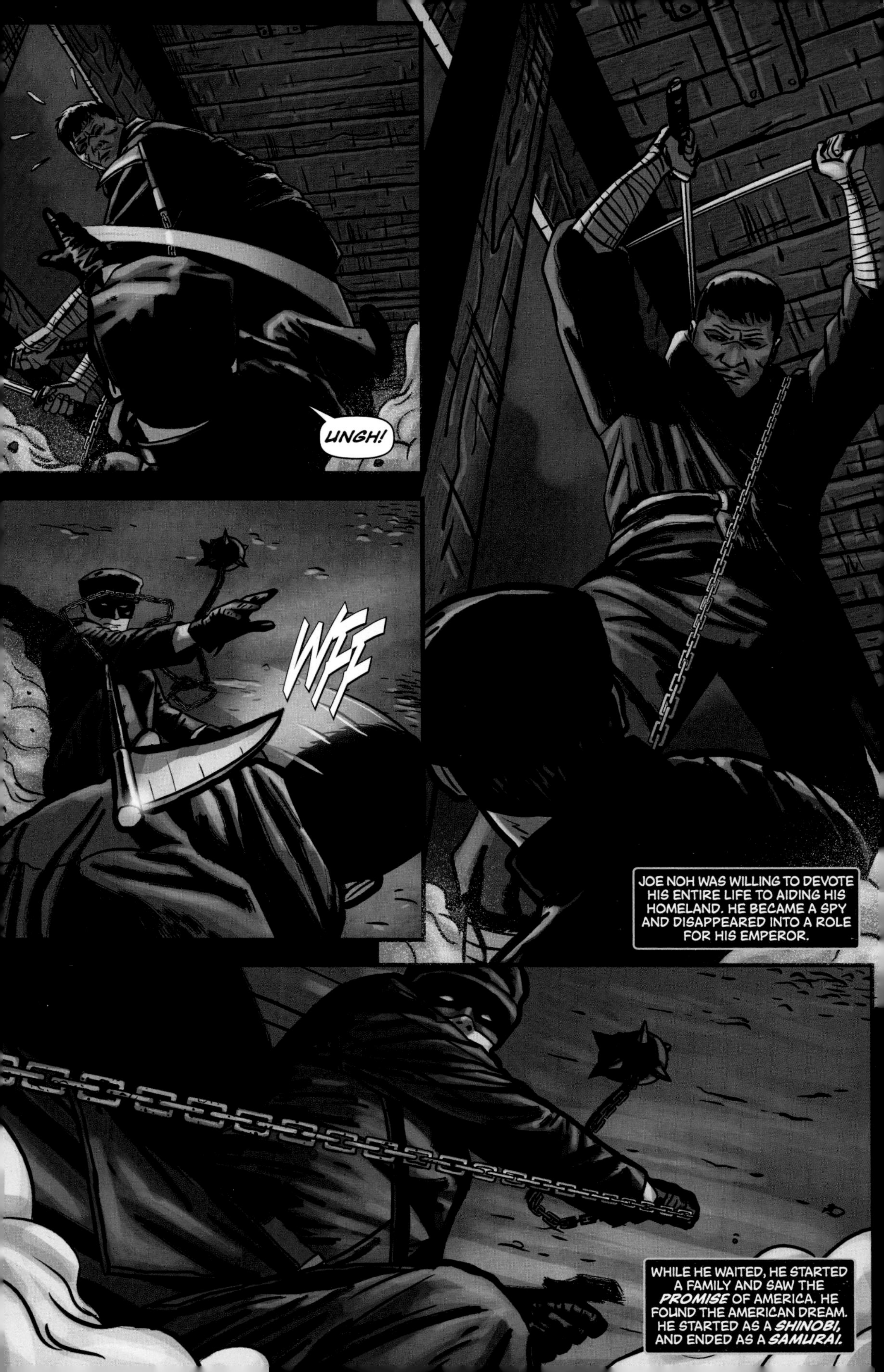
UNGH!
WFF
JOE NOH WAS WILLING TO DEVOTE HIS ENTIRE LIFE TO AIDING HIS HOMELAND. HE BECAME A SPY AND DISAPPEARED INTO A ROLE FOR HIS EMPEROR.
WHILE HE WAITED, HE STARTED A FAMILY AND SAW THE *PROMISE* OF AMERICA. HE FOUND THE AMERICAN DREAM. HE STARTED AS A *SHINOBI,* AND ENDED AS A *SAMURAI.*

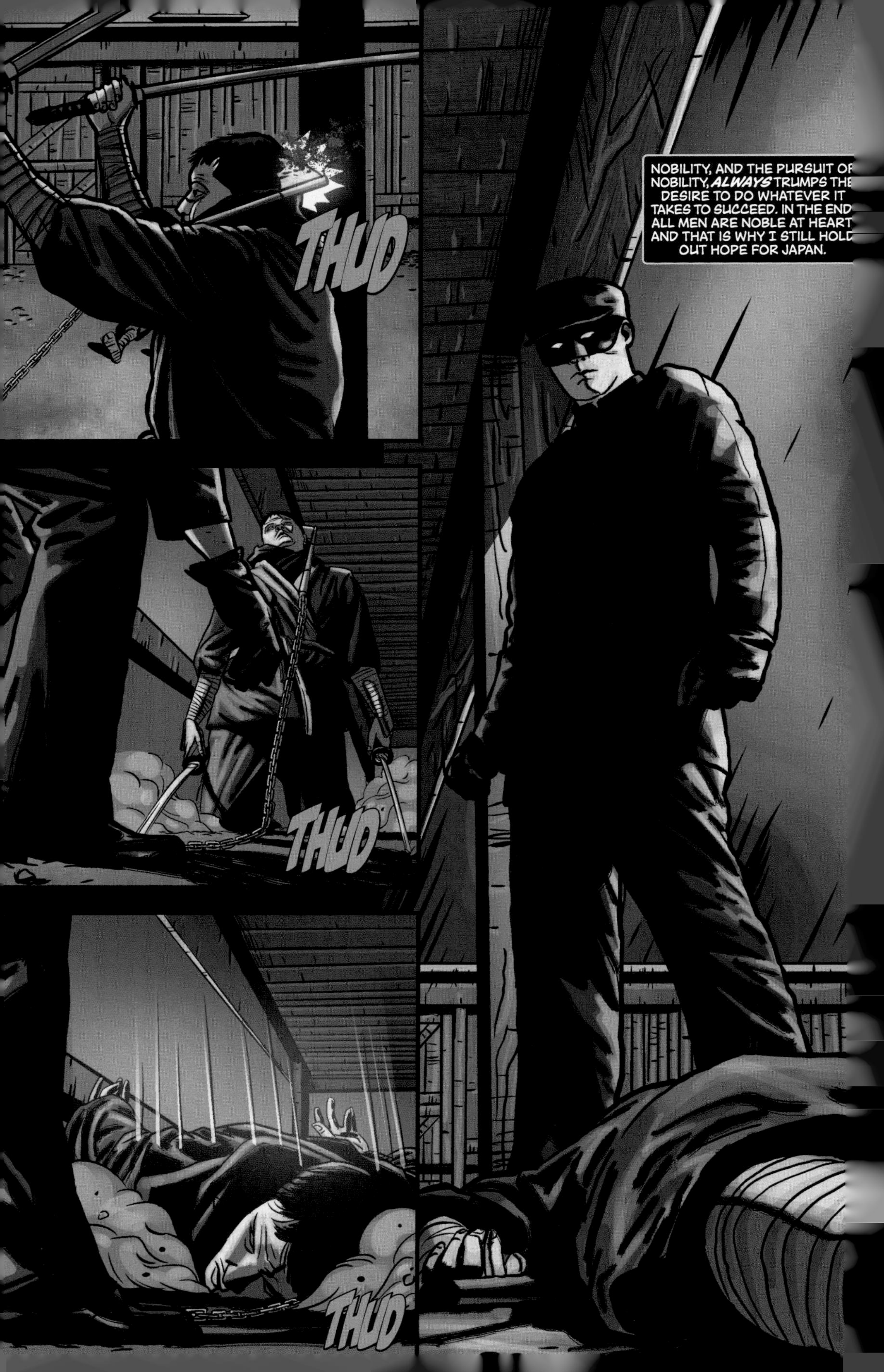
THUD
THUD
THUD
NOBILITY, AND THE PURSUIT OF NOBILITY, ALWAYS TRUMPS THE DESIRE TO DO WHATEVER IT TAKES TO SUCCEED. IN THE END ALL MEN ARE NOBLE AT HEART AND THAT IS WHY I STILL HOLD OUT HOPE FOR JAPAN.

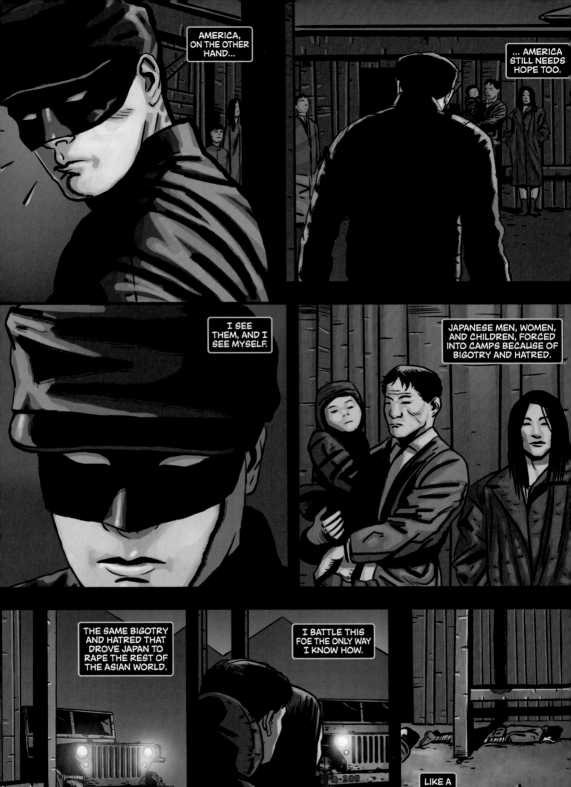

AMERICA, ON THE OTHER HAND...

... AMERICA STILL NEEDS HOPE TOO.

I SEE THEM, AND I SEE MYSELF.

JAPANESE MEN, WOMEN, AND CHILDREN, FORCED INTO CAMPS BECAUSE OF BIGOTRY AND HATRED.

THE SAME BIGOTRY AND HATRED THAT DROVE JAPAN TO RAPE THE REST OF THE ASIAN WORLD.

I BATTLE THIS FOE THE ONLY WAY I KNOW HOW.

LIKE A NINJA.

VRRRRRM

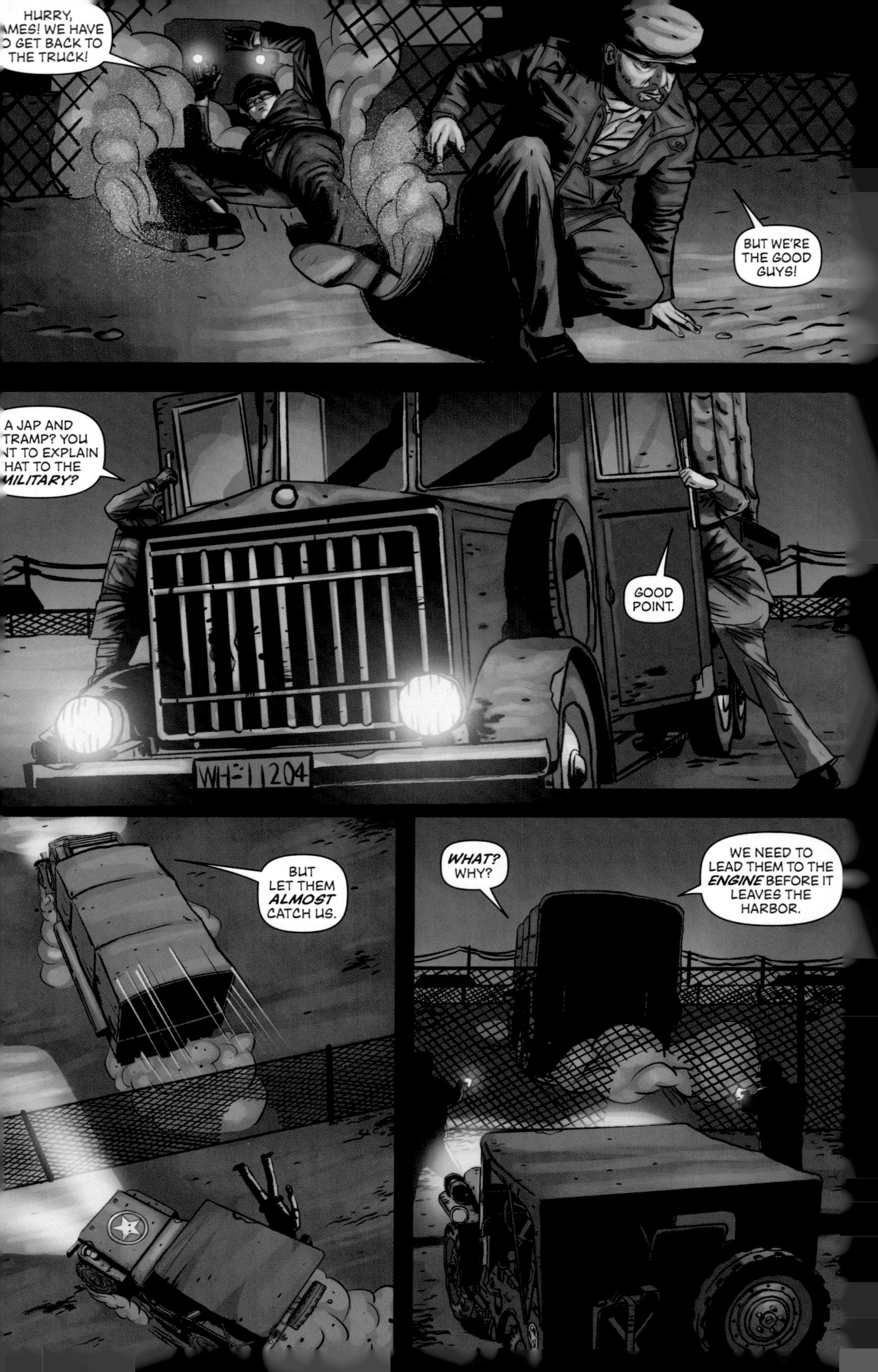
HURRY, AMES! WE HAVE O GET BACK TO THE TRUCK!
BUT WE'RE THE GOOD GUYS!
A JAP AND TRAMP? YOU NT TO EXPLAIN HAT TO THE MILITARY?
GOOD POINT.
WH-11204
BUT LET THEM ALMOST CATCH US.
WHAT? WHY?
WE NEED TO LEAD THEM TO THE ENGINE BEFORE IT LEAVES THE HARBOR.

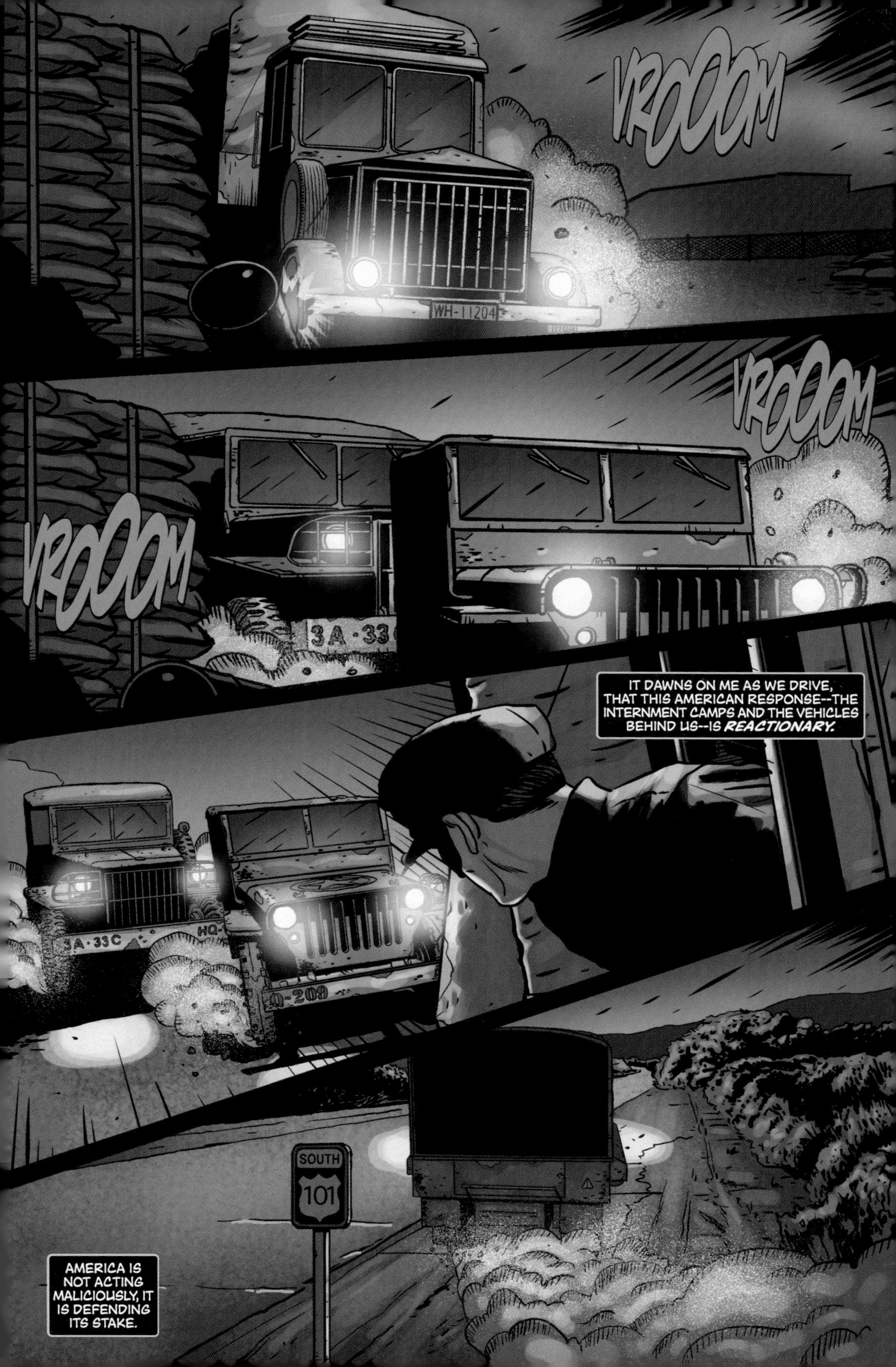
VROOOM
VROOOM
VROOOM
WH-11204
3A-33C
IT DAWNS ON ME AS WE DRIVE, THAT THIS AMERICAN RESPONSE--THE INTERNMENT CAMPS AND THE VEHICLES BEHIND US--IS REACTIONARY.
3A-33C
HQ-
Q-209
SOUTH
101
AMERICA IS NOT ACTING MALICIOUSLY, IT IS DEFENDING ITS STAKE.

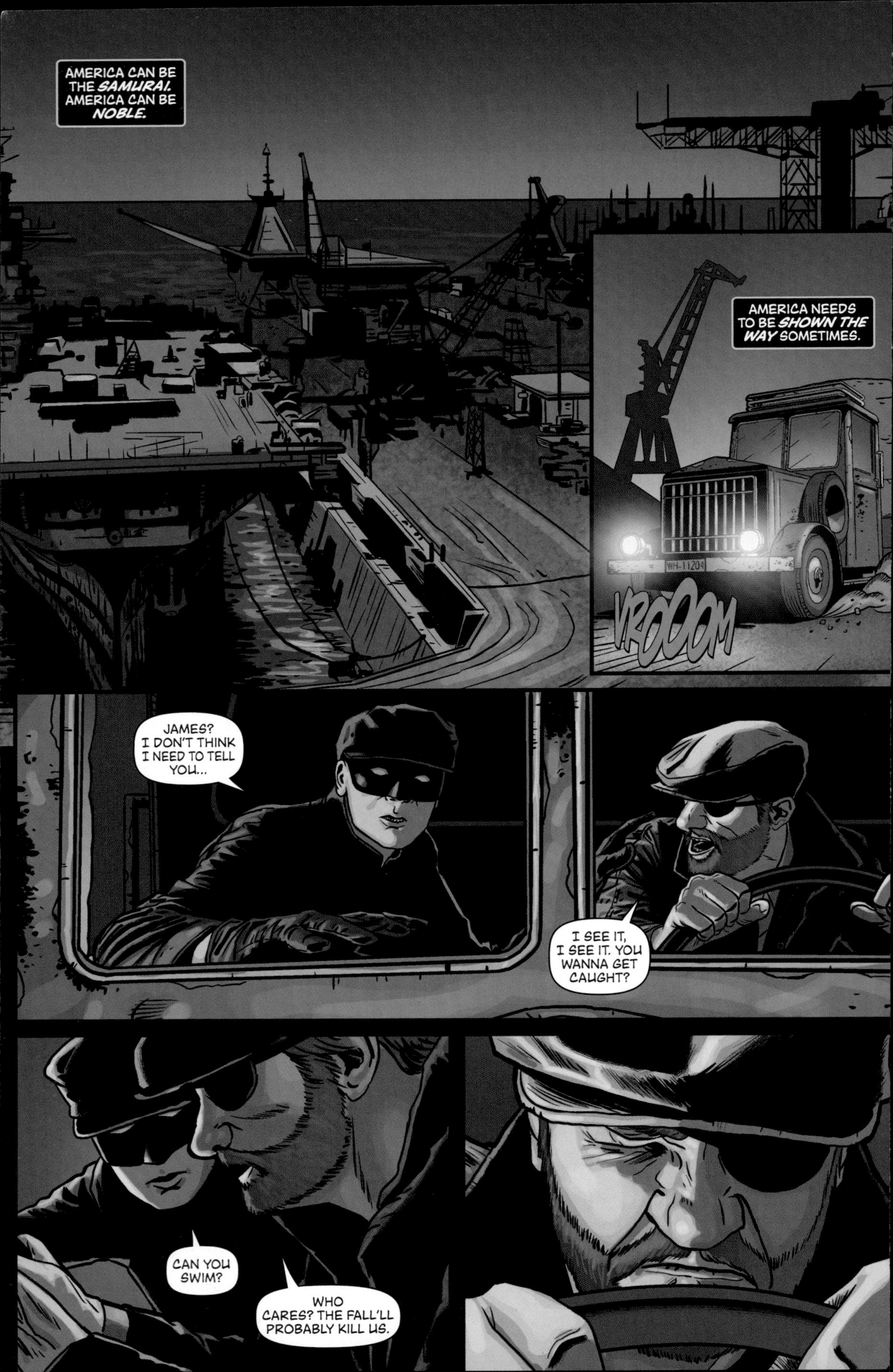
AMERICA CAN BE THE SAMURAI. AMERICA CAN BE NOBLE.
AMERICA NEEDS TO BE SHOWN THE WAY SOMETIMES.
WH-11204
VROOOM
JAMES? I DON'T THINK I NEED TO TELL YOU...
I SEE IT, I SEE IT. YOU WANNA GET CAUGHT?
CAN YOU SWIM?
WHO CARES? THE FALL'LL PROBABLY KILL US.

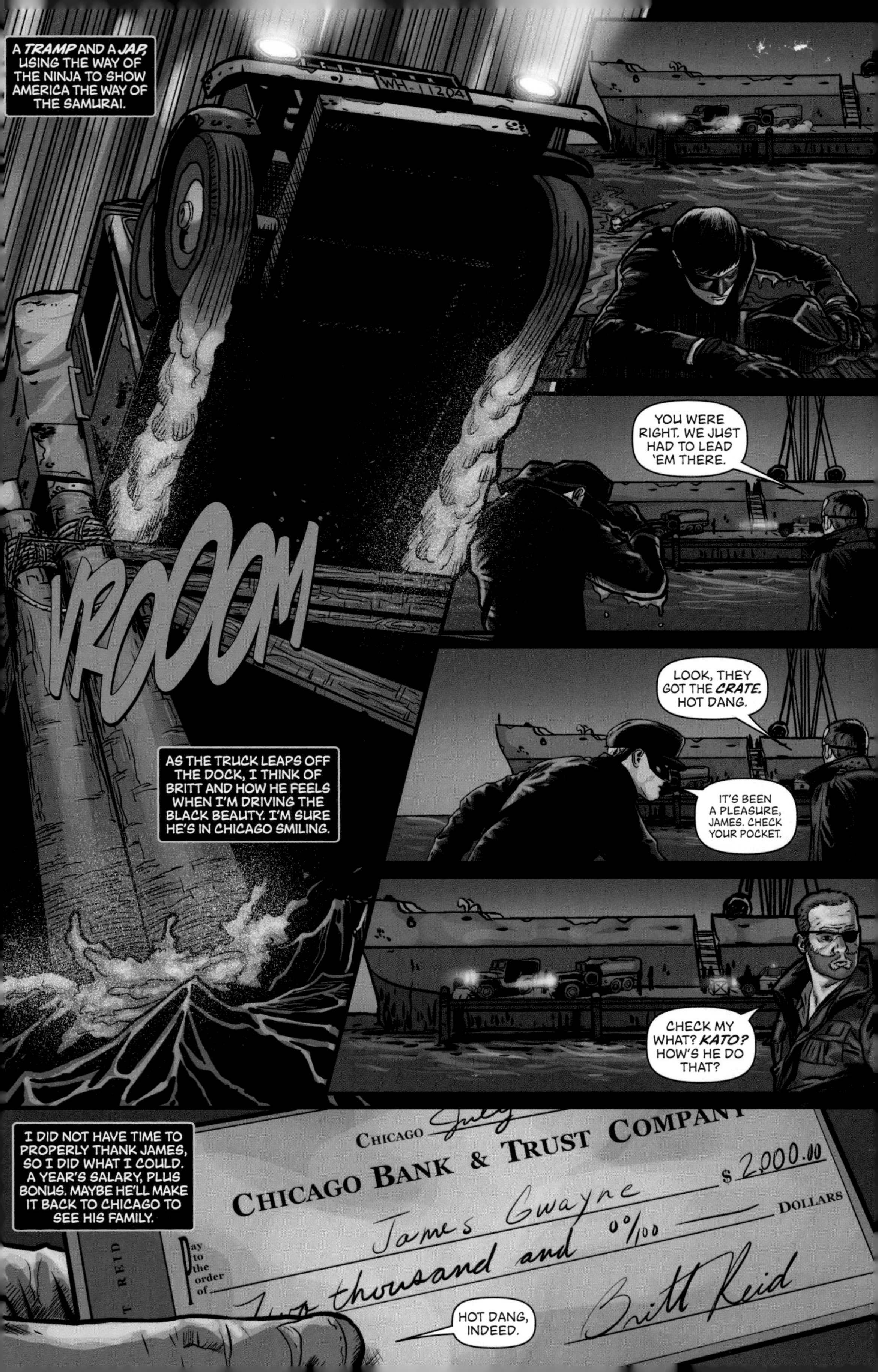
A *TRAMP* AND A *JAP*, USING THE WAY OF THE NINJA TO SHOW AMERICA THE WAY OF THE SAMURAI.
WH-11204
VROOOM
AS THE TRUCK LEAPS OFF THE DOCK, I THINK OF BRITT AND HOW HE FEELS WHEN I'M DRIVING THE BLACK BEAUTY. I'M SURE HE'S IN CHICAGO SMILING.
YOU WERE RIGHT. WE JUST HAD TO LEAD 'EM THERE.
LOOK, THEY GOT THE *CRATE.* HOT DANG.
IT'S BEEN A PLEASURE, JAMES. CHECK YOUR POCKET.
CHECK MY WHAT? *KATO?* HOW'S HE DO THAT?
I DID NOT HAVE TIME TO PROPERLY THANK JAMES, SO I DID WHAT I COULD. A YEAR'S SALARY, PLUS BONUS. MAYBE HE'LL MAKE IT BACK TO CHICAGO TO SEE HIS FAMILY.
CHICAGO
CHICAGO BANK & TRUST COMPANY
$ 2,000.00
Pay to the order of
James Gwayne
thousand and 00/100
DOLLARS
Britt Reid
HOT DANG, INDEED.

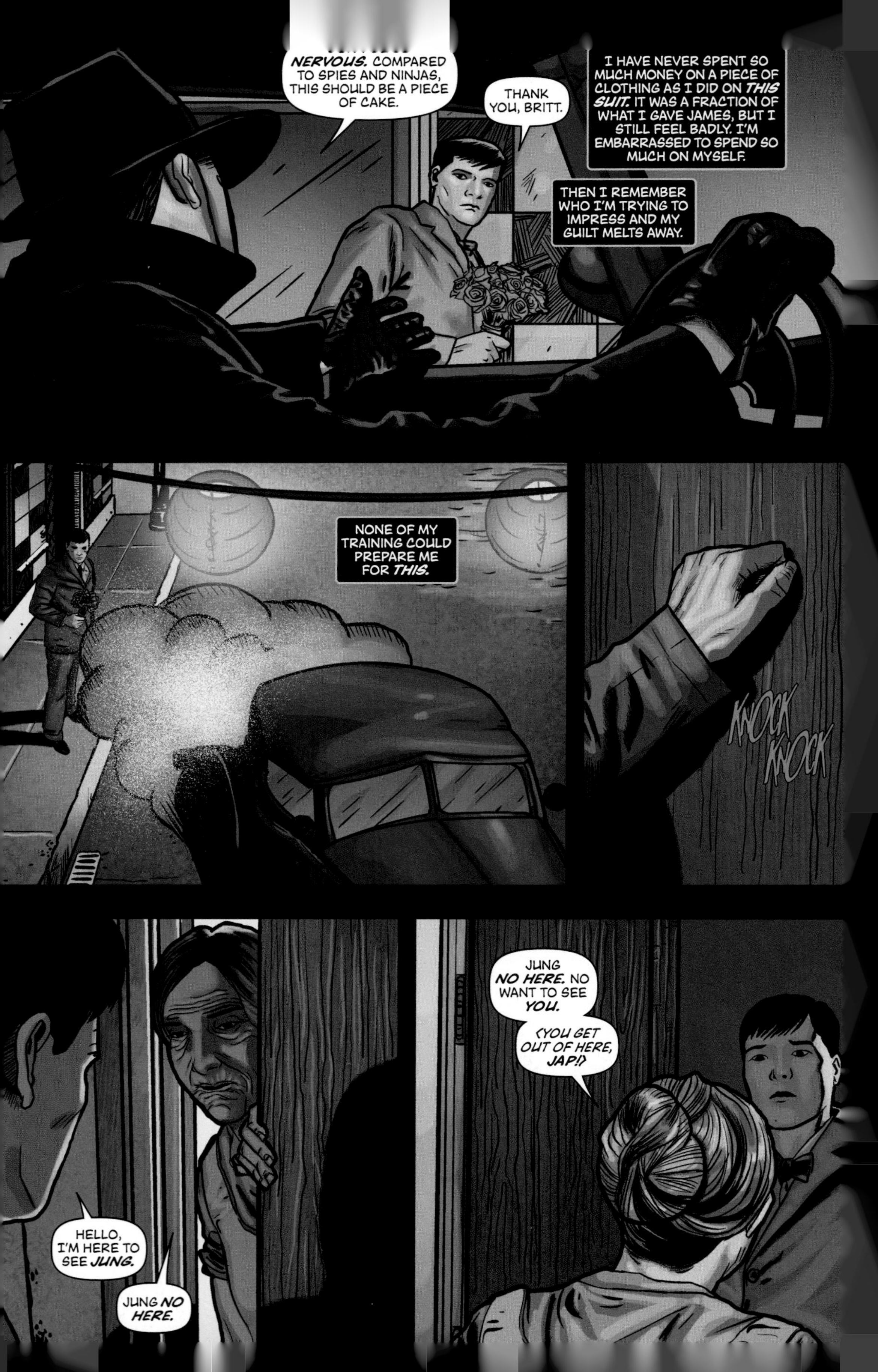
NERVOUS. COMPARED TO SPIES AND NINJAS, THIS SHOULD BE A PIECE OF CAKE.
THANK YOU, BRITT.
I HAVE NEVER SPENT SO MUCH MONEY ON A PIECE OF CLOTHING AS I DID ON THIS SUIT. IT WAS A FRACTION OF WHAT I GAVE JAMES, BUT I STILL FEEL BADLY. I'M EMBARRASSED TO SPEND SO MUCH ON MYSELF.
THEN I REMEMBER WHO I'M TRYING TO IMPRESS AND MY GUILT MELTS AWAY.
NONE OF MY TRAINING COULD PREPARE ME FOR THIS.
KNOCK KNOCK
HELLO, I'M HERE TO SEE JUNG.
JUNG NO HERE.
JUNG NO HERE. NO WANT TO SEE YOU.
<YOU GET OUT OF HERE, JAP!>

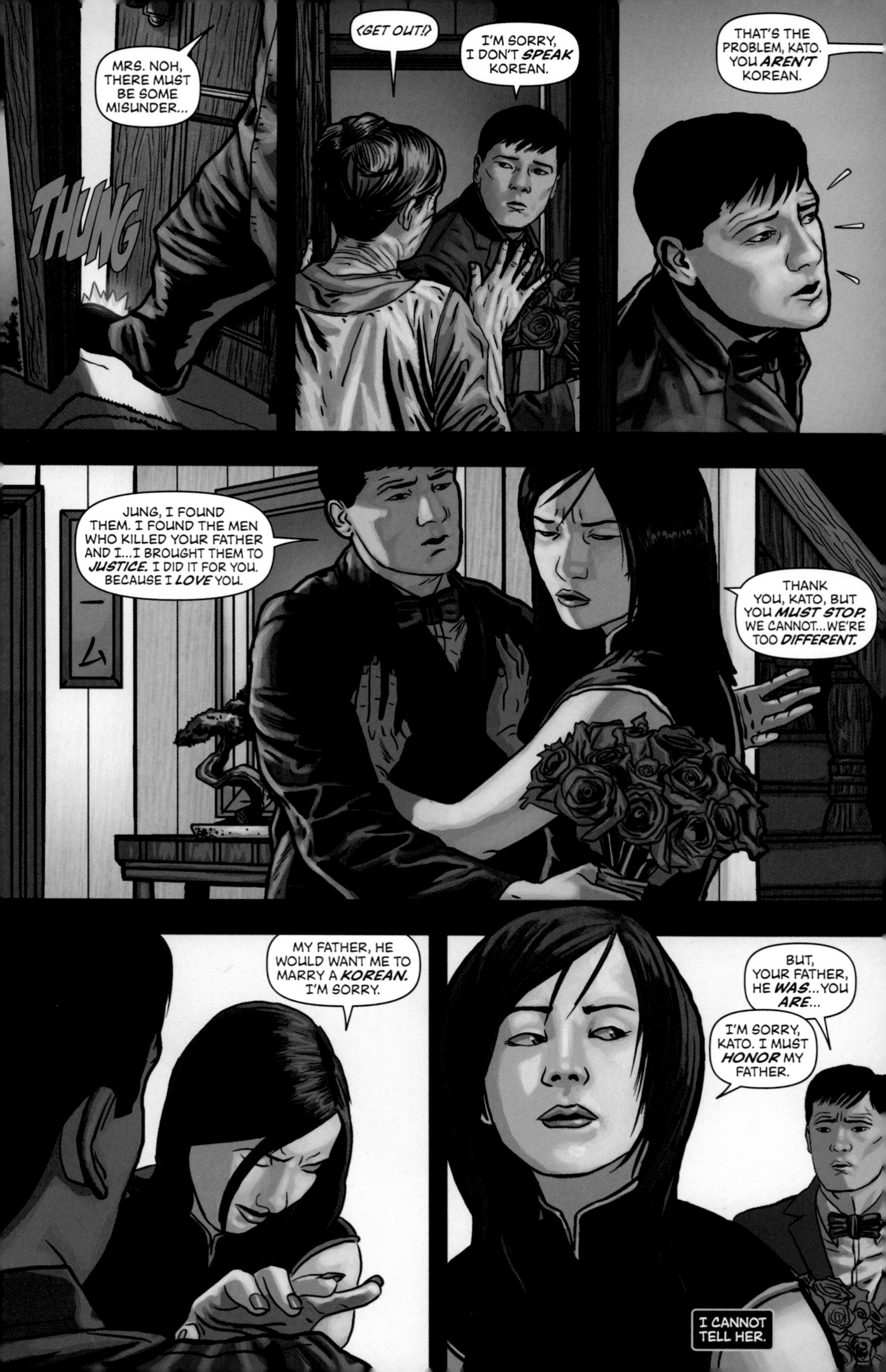
MRS. NOH, THERE MUST BE SOME MISUNDER...
THUNG
<GET OUT!>
I'M SORRY, I DON'T SPEAK KOREAN.
THAT'S THE PROBLEM, KATO. YOU AREN'T KOREAN.
JUNG, I FOUND THEM. I FOUND THE MEN WHO KILLED YOUR FATHER AND I...I BROUGHT THEM TO JUSTICE. I DID IT FOR YOU. BECAUSE I LOVE YOU.
THANK YOU, KATO, BUT YOU MUST STOP. WE CANNOT...WE'RE TOO DIFFERENT.
MY FATHER, HE WOULD WANT ME TO MARRY A KOREAN. I'M SORRY.
BUT, YOUR FATHER, HE WAS...YOU ARE...
I'M SORRY, KATO. I MUST HONOR MY FATHER.
I CANNOT TELL HER.

THE WAY OF THE NINJA IS FOUNDED ON DECEPTION AND OBFUSCATION. I USED MY TRAINING TO OVERCOME ALL OBSTACLES IN MY PATH. I BEAT CROOKED COPS AND GANGSTERS. I BEAT NAZI SABOTEURS AND JAPANESE NINJA SPIES. I BEAT POVERTY. I BEAT *RACISM.*

BUT I COULD NOT BEAT *DECEIT ITSELF.* THE SELF DECEPTION OF JOE NOH, INSTILLING KOREAN VALUES IN HIS FAMILY WHILE HE HIMSELF WAS A SPY OF THE RISING SUN. THE INHERENT NOBILITY OF THE AMERICAN DREAM, AND THE AMERICAN SPIRIT AGAINST THE JAPANESE IN A TIME OF WAR DEFEATED MY NINJA SKILLS.

I CANNOT TELL JUNG THAT HER FATHER'S LIFE WAS A *LIE.* I CANNOT BRING THAT SADNESS TO HER, EVEN IF IT IS THE TRUTH. SHE WOULD NEVER FORGIVE ME, AND SHE WOULD NEVER KNOW HAPPINESS WITH ME. I MUST ACT LIKE A SAMURAI AND *LOSE* THE WOMAN I LOVE.

I AM A NINJA, I AM JAPANESE, I AM AN AMERICAN, I AM A GAMBLER, I AM A TIGER, I AM A SCOURGE OF THE UNDERWORLD, I AM KATO. I AM *ALONE.*

BONUS MATERIALS

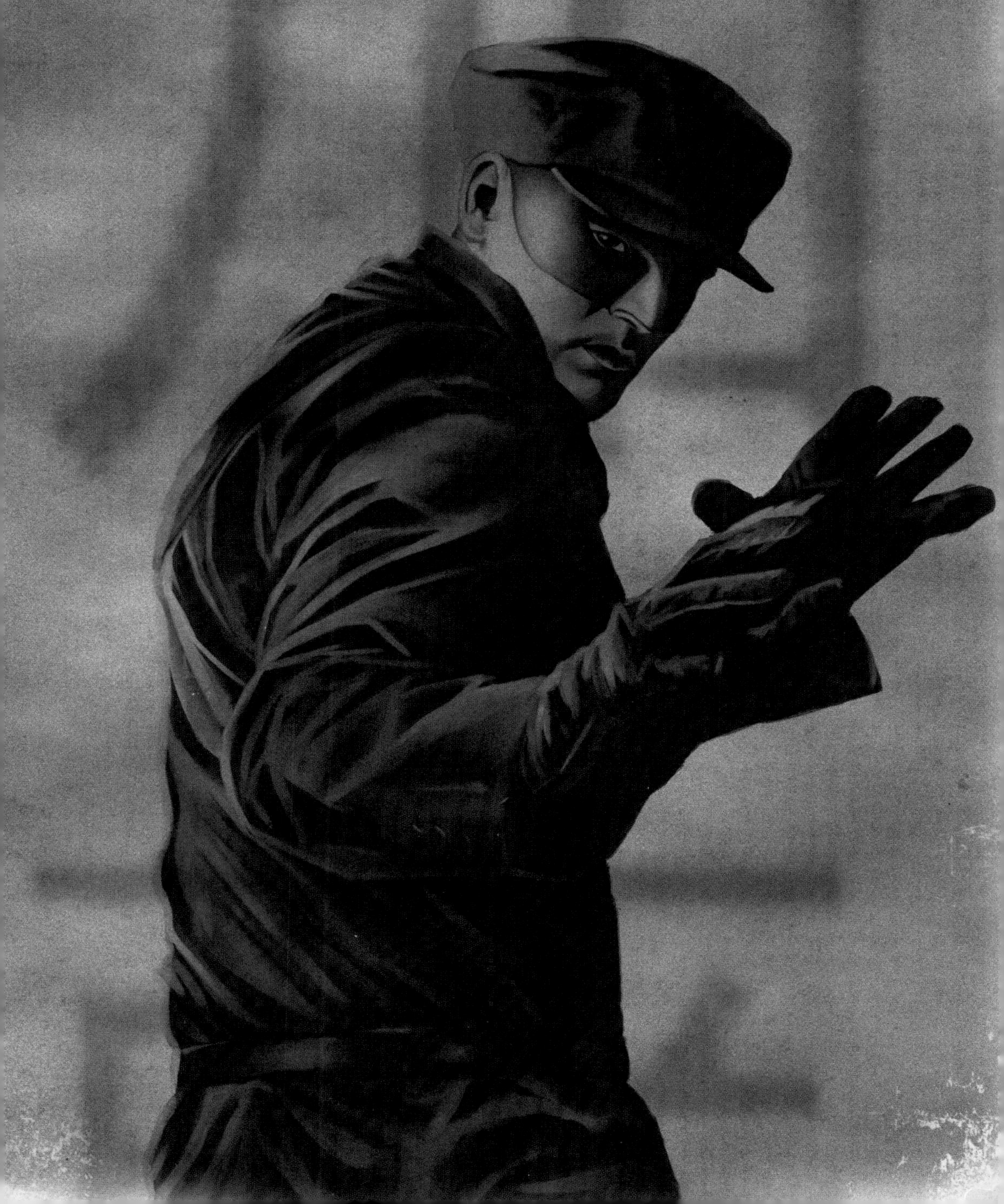

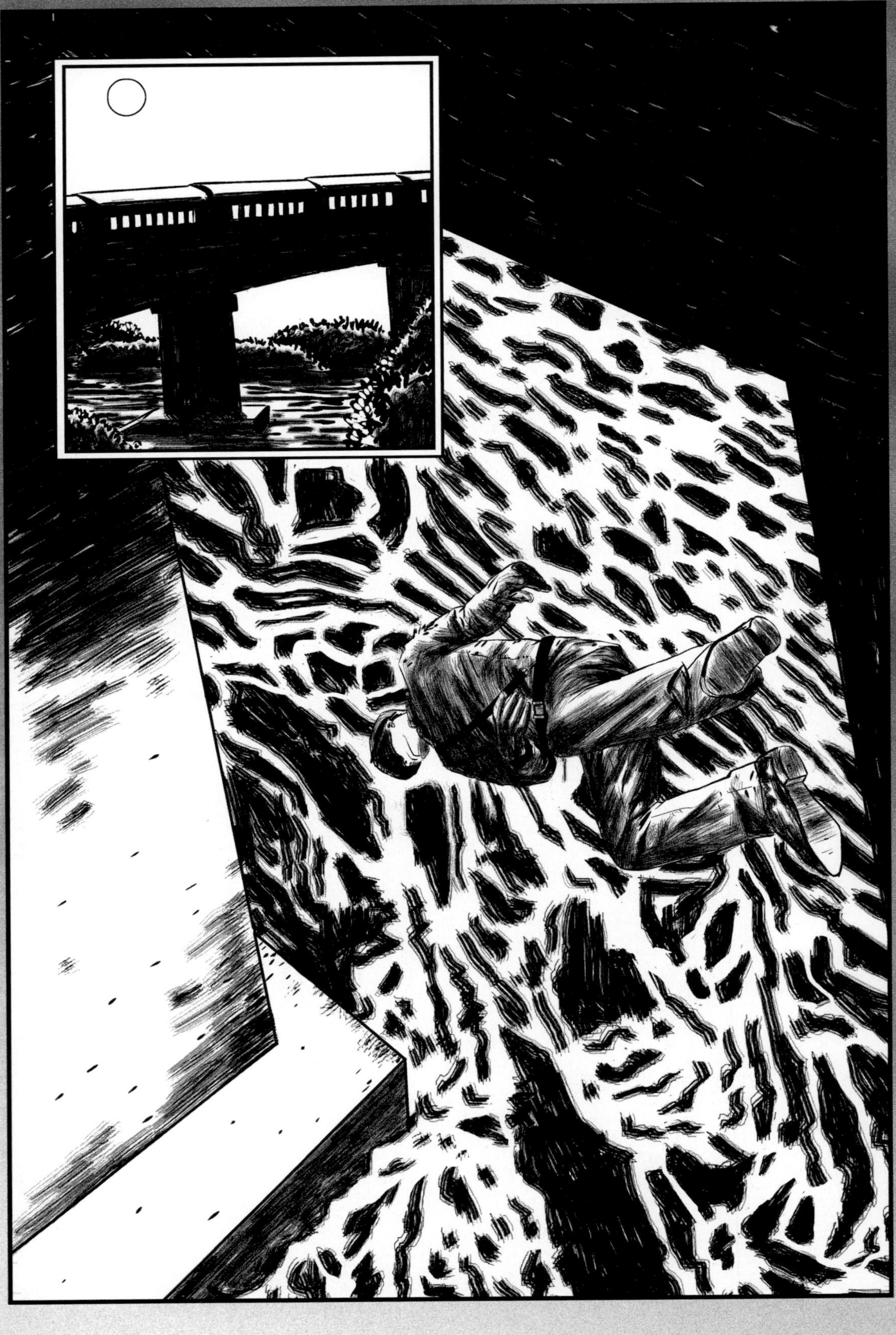

A BEHIND-THE-SCENES LOOK AT KATO ORIGINS #4 FEATURING COMMENTARY BY WRITER, JAI NITZ

Kato: Way of the Ninja Issue Four, Page One
Script by Jai Nitz

1.1 Inset panel of a train crossing over a high bridge at night. The silhouette of the train is lit by the moon.

Caption- Outside Sacramento, California.

1.2 Splash page of KATO falling to his death. He's falling off a moving train while it crosses a bridge, but into a river hundreds of feet below the tracks.

Kato (caption)- The first time I saw a tiger was the first time I got **shot.**

Kato (caption)- My current situation—shot by Nazis and thrown from a moving train—is a bit more **dramatic**, but the similarities are strong.

Jai Nitz on page one: One of my favorite pages Colton has drawn. Kato isn't jumping heroically, he isn't getting punched, he's falling. Falling is different than standing or sitting or running or sneezing. It's a weird thing to draw, and Colton nailed it.

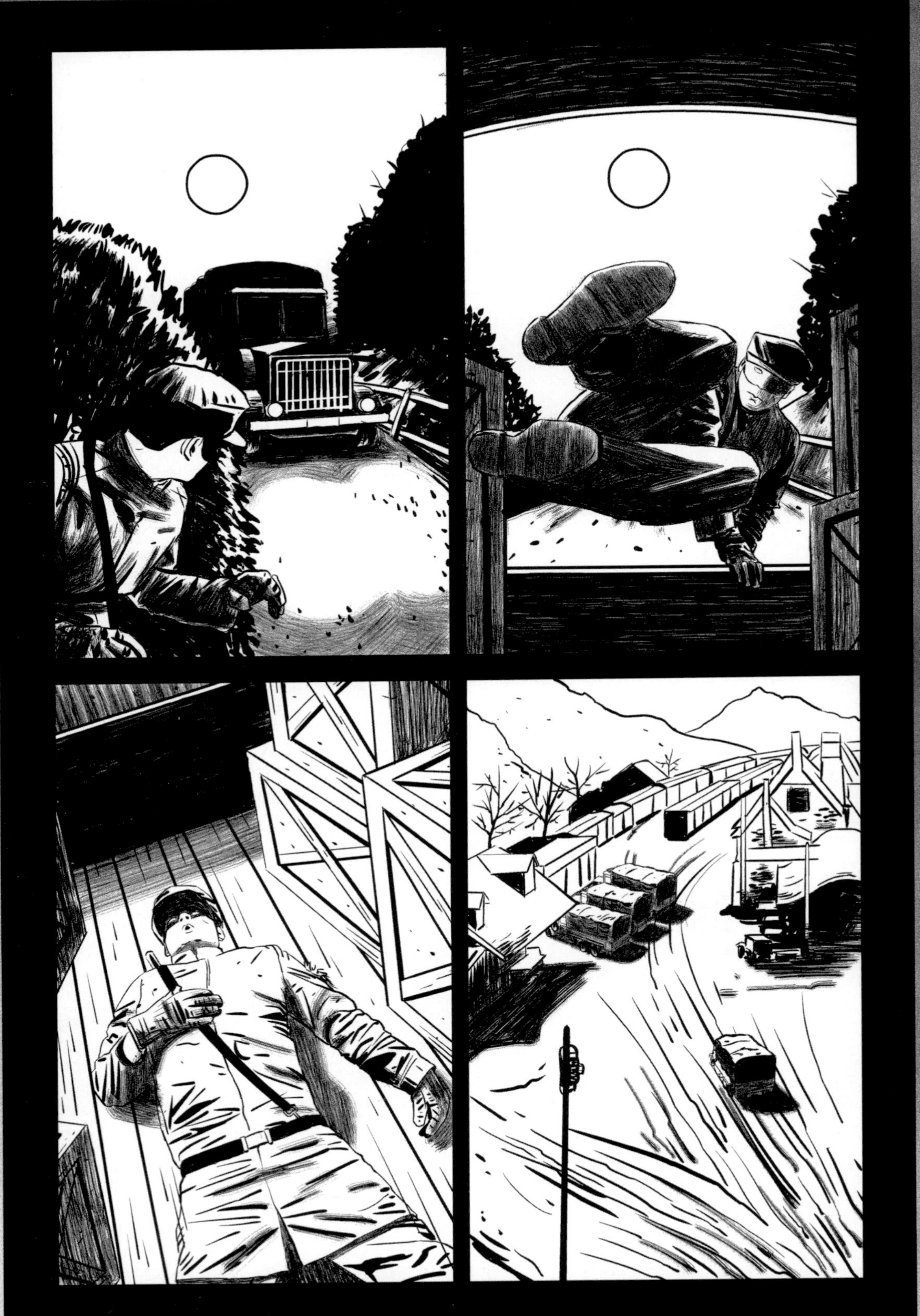

Kato: Way of the Ninja Issue Four, Page Three
Script by Jai Nitz

3.1 Still at night, Kato waits in the foliage as a shipping truck passes by.

Kato (caption)- There I saw a **bear** fishing on the shore.

Kato (caption)- I stopped and admired the symbol of Russia; it was bigger than any creature I'd ever seen.

3.2 Kato grabs on the back with his good arm.

Kato (caption)- Seconds later, a **male Siberian tiger** pounced on it.

3.3 Kato, weary and tired, rides on the back of a bumpy truck ride through the countryside.

Kato (caption)- I was trained in **Shinobi**, the way of the **ninja**, and I **still** didn't hear the half-ton beast coming.

3.4 Cut to a shot of the truck pulling into a train yard. Big overhead shot of the many trucks and trains at a delivery/loading area.

Kato (caption)- My ninja training seemed **inadequate** then, and again **tonight**. I have been tracking Japanese spies—and now Nazis—across the country from Chicago to here. I am trying to unravel the mystery of a Korean's death for his beautiful daughter. I feel like a **ragdoll** in the hands of a capricious child.

Jai Nitz on pages three and eleven: I am painfully aware of anachronisms. Kato notes the difference between Bengal tigers and Siberian tigers. He also talks about Burma. Siberian tigers are called Amur tigers now, because they're mostly in the Amur River valley. Would Kato have ever called them Amur tigers? No. Same thing with Burma; now Burma is recognized as Myanmar in most of the world. Then? It was Burma. Getting little details like that make the research feel really rewarding.

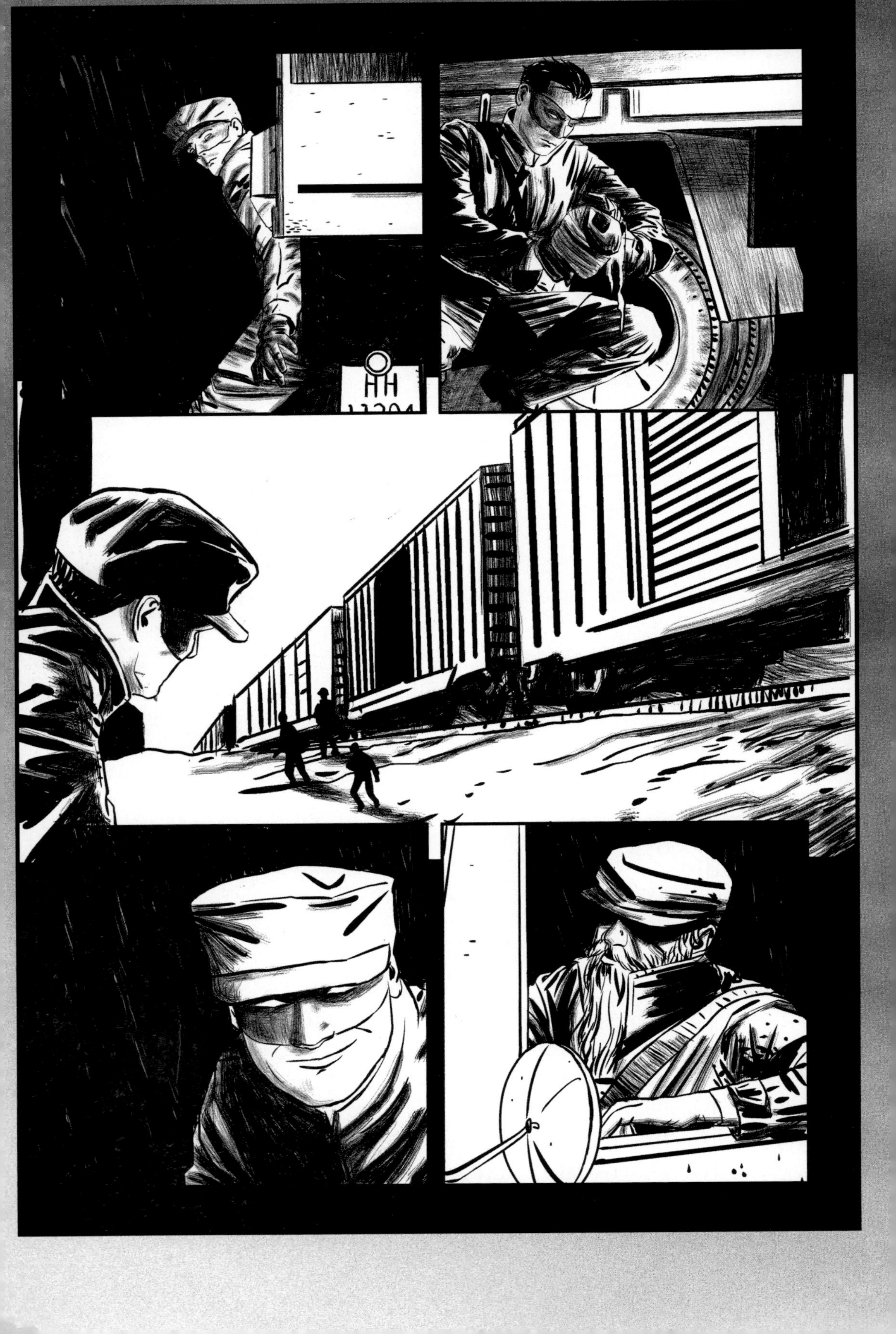
HH

Kato: Way of the Ninja Issue Four, Page Four

Script by Jai Nitz

4.1 Kato ducks into the shadows of the truck area.

Kato (caption)- The bear was like a child's toy in the maw of the **terrestrial** symbol of China.

4.2 Kato wrings the water out of his soaked disguise.

Kato (caption)- In China there are **two** royal symbols: the **Tiger** and the **Dragon**.

4.3 From Kato's hidden POV, we see tramps hopping off a train.

Kato (caption)- One is the king of **earth**, the other is the king of the **heavens**.

4.4 Close up of Kato smiling.

Kato (caption)- I recognize the **tramps** hopping off the train. In their own way, they are **kings** of earth.

4.5 Cut to a shot of Gwayne in disguise behind the wheel.

Kato (caption)- I've never seen a dragon, but I think even the master of the heavens would be **wise** to avoid the world's largest cat.

Jai Nitz on page four: I loved bringing back James Gwayne, the hobo from issue three, and putting him in Kato's disguise kit. He also had the line, "Hey, watch the arm," to add to the mystery. Is it Kato in disguise? What's in the box? I always liked television shows and comics that rewarded viewers for having a keen eye or viewers who stuck around for each installment. This was my little nod to that kind of storytelling.

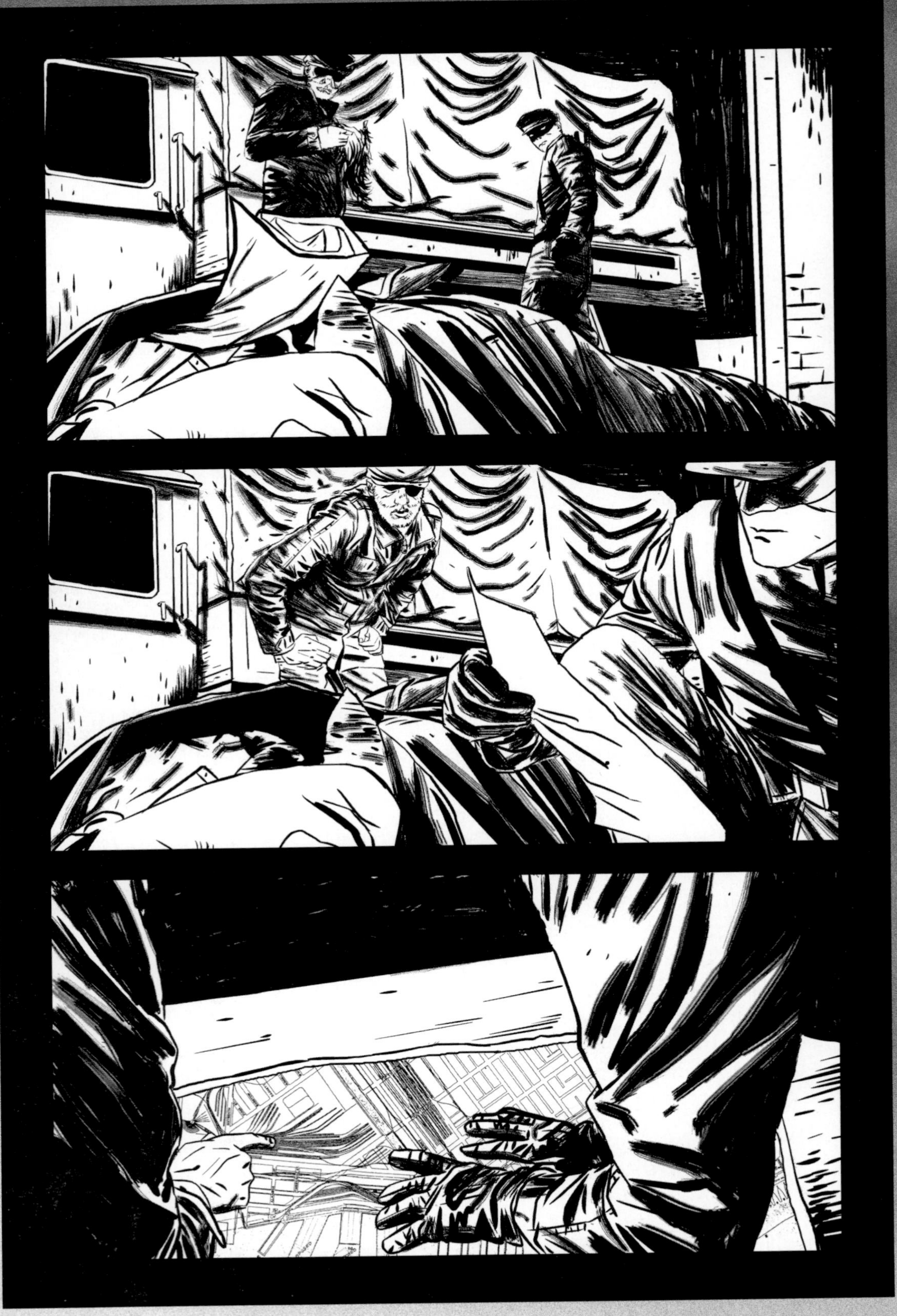

Kato: Way of the Ninja Issue Four, Page Eleven
Script by Jai Nitz

11.1 James removes his disguise. Kato sheathes his weapons.

James- It's **just** like you said. **German** and **Jap** spies, working together. Oh, no offense about the "Jap" bit, Kato.

Kato- None taken, James. I am just grateful our paths crossed again.

11.2 Kato investigates a piece of paper with Japanese kanji all over it. It lists the package going to a ship headed for Burma. It also has a series of numbers. James asks what it is; Kato tells him it's latitudinal and longitudinal coordinates.

James- What's **that**?

Kato- A manifest for a **ship**. The engine is to be sent to **Burma** where it will surely disappear. The Japanese have an **extensive** spy network there. We have to stop it from leaving the docks.

11.3 Kato and James plot the coordinates on a map. It's Tanforan, the racetrack ten miles south of San Francisco.

Kato- This isn't a map of the docks. Who is **Tanforan**?

James- Not a **who**, a **where**, Kato. Tanforan is the **racetrack** south of San Francisco.

Jai Nitz on pages eleven and twelve: Getting driving directions on the internet is second nature today. But finding a map of 1940s San Francisco and plotting a route from Chinatown to Tanforan was a chore. Those are the elements that make writing Kato Origins special. You can't fall back on modern thinking or technology. You have to get your hands dirty in research. I spend as much time at the library researching as I do at my desk writing.

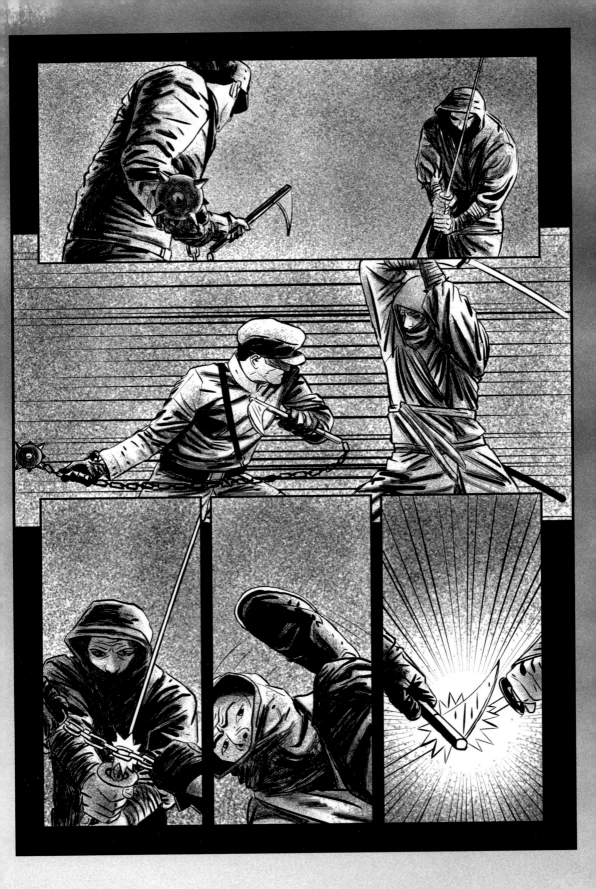

Kato: Way of the Ninja Issue Four, Page Sixteen
Script by Jai Nitz

16.1 Kato and the ninja square off. The ninja has a katana. Now Kato pulls out a kasurigama (the sickle and chain weapon from #2). Maybe show James, rolled over now, watching the fight.

Kato (caption)- Our weapons are as silent as our motions.

16.2 Kato and the ninja charge each other.

Kato (caption)- Our footfalls unnoticeable.

16.3 Kato blocks a katana attack with his chain.

Kato (caption)- Our metal is silent.

16.4 Kato misses with a kick as the ninja ducks under it.

Kato (caption)- Even our near misses would not arouse a skittish deer.

16.5 The ninja tries to attack with his katana again, but Kato blocks with his sickle this time.

Kato (caption)- Two **tigers**, silently dancing with **death**.

Jai Nitz on pages fifteen and sixteen: Kato's weapons are actual Shinobi weapons. He uses hand claws and a kusarigama. Both weapons would have been concealable, portable, and easily made. Since shinobi were drawn from lower castes (as opposed to Samurai who were of nobler stock), their weapons represented that. I wanted that to come through with Kato in this book.

MATT WAGNER – AARON CAMPBELL
The GREEN HORNET YEAR ONE

DYNAMITE.

THE GREEN HORNET: YEAR ONE VOL. 1 THE STING OF JUSTICE TRADE PAPERBACK

story by MATT WAGNER cover art by ALEX ROSS
interior art by AARON CAMPBELL & FRANCESCO FRANCAVILLA

Matt Wagner brings the The Green Hornet and Kato to their Golden-Age roots with this year one tale of the classic heroes!

Reprinting issues #1-6, along with a complete cover gallery.

FROM THE PAGES OF KEVIN SMITH'S GREEN HORNET

KATO

NOT MY
FATHER'S
DAUGHTER

DYNAMITE.

KEVIN SMITH'S KATO VOL. 1: NOT MY FATHER'S DAUGHTE

story by **ANDE PARKS** cover art by **ALÉ GARZA**
interior art by **DIEGO BERNARD** & **ALÉ GARZA**

From the pages of Kevin Smith's Green Hornet comes this thrilling lead-in story, starring
Mulan Kato, daughter of the Green Hornet's faithful companion, Kato! Learn the secrets of
Kato, his daughter, his wife's murder and the mysterious Black Hornet!

Collecting issues 1-5 of the prequal to Kevin Smith's Green Hornet • In stores November 201

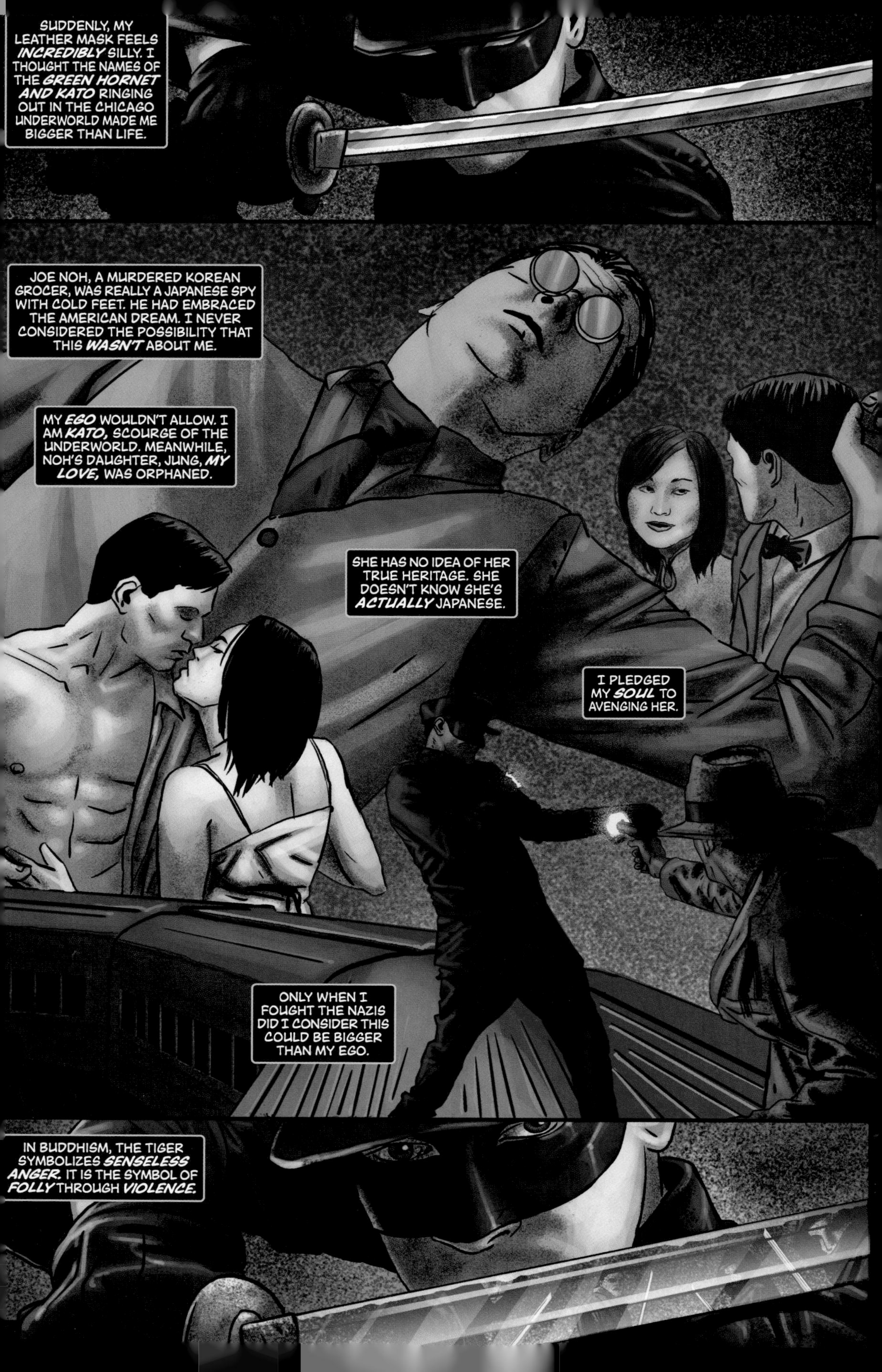
SUDDENLY, MY LEATHER MASK FEELS INCREDIBLY SILLY. I THOUGHT THE NAMES OF THE GREEN HORNET AND KATO RINGING OUT IN THE CHICAGO UNDERWORLD MADE ME BIGGER THAN LIFE.
JOE NOH, A MURDERED KOREAN GROCER, WAS REALLY A JAPANESE SPY WITH COLD FEET. HE HAD EMBRACED THE AMERICAN DREAM. I NEVER CONSIDERED THE POSSIBILITY THAT THIS WASN'T ABOUT ME.
MY EGO WOULDN'T ALLOW. I AM KATO, SCOURGE OF THE UNDERWORLD. MEANWHILE, NOH'S DAUGHTER, JUNG, MY LOVE, WAS ORPHANED.
SHE HAS NO IDEA OF HER TRUE HERITAGE. SHE DOESN'T KNOW SHE'S ACTUALLY JAPANESE.
I PLEDGED MY SOUL TO AVENGING HER.
ONLY WHEN I FOUGHT THE NAZIS DID I CONSIDER THIS COULD BE BIGGER THAN MY EGO.
IN BUDDHISM, THE TIGER SYMBOLIZES SENSELESS ANGER. IT IS THE SYMBOL OF FOLLY THROUGH VIOLENCE.

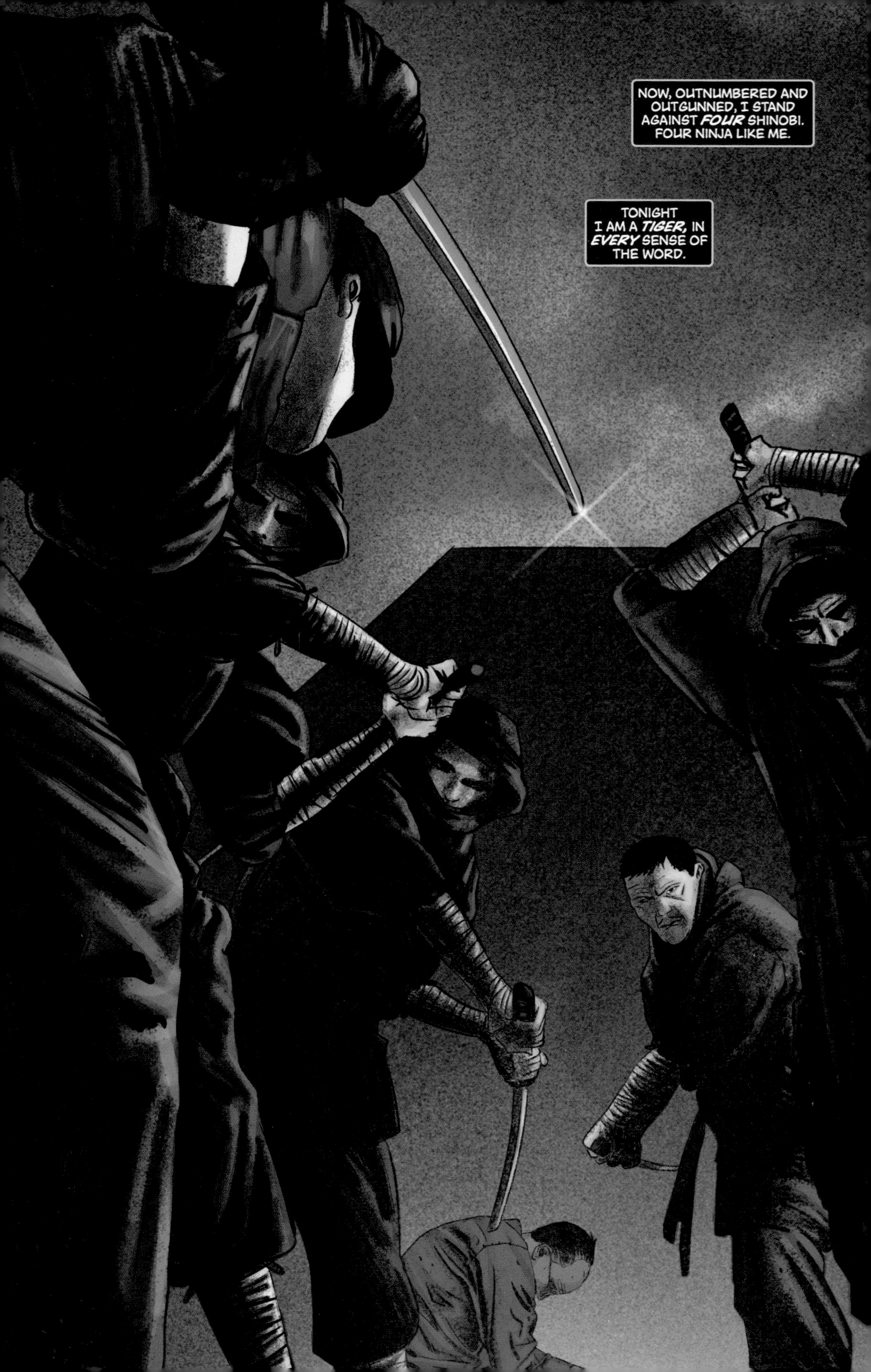
NOW, OUTNUMBERED AND OUTGUNNED, I STAND AGAINST *FOUR* SHINOBI. FOUR NINJA LIKE ME.
TONIGHT I AM A *TIGER,* IN *EVERY* SENSE OF THE WORD.

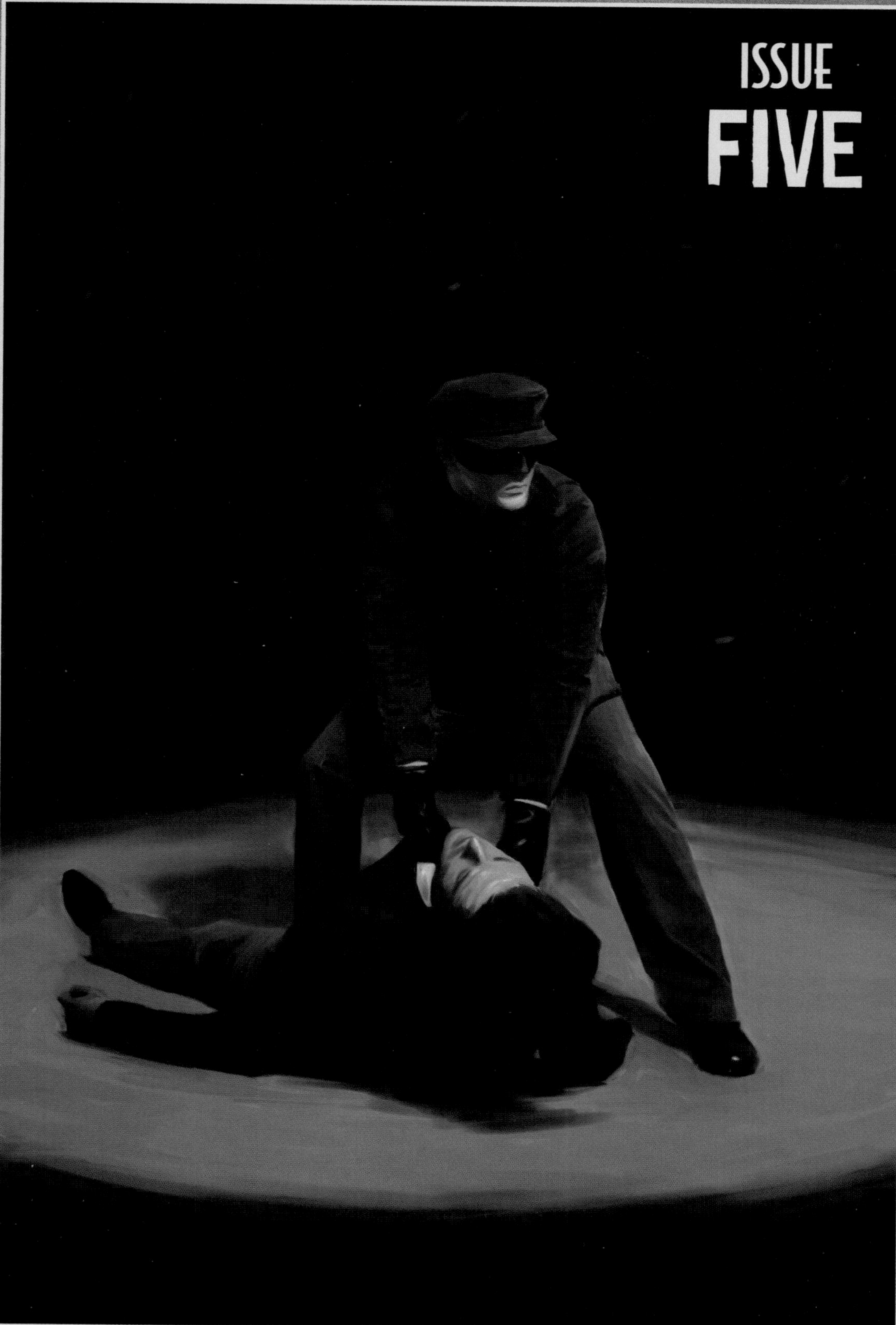
ISSUE
FIVE

Issue five cover by **COLTON WORLEY**

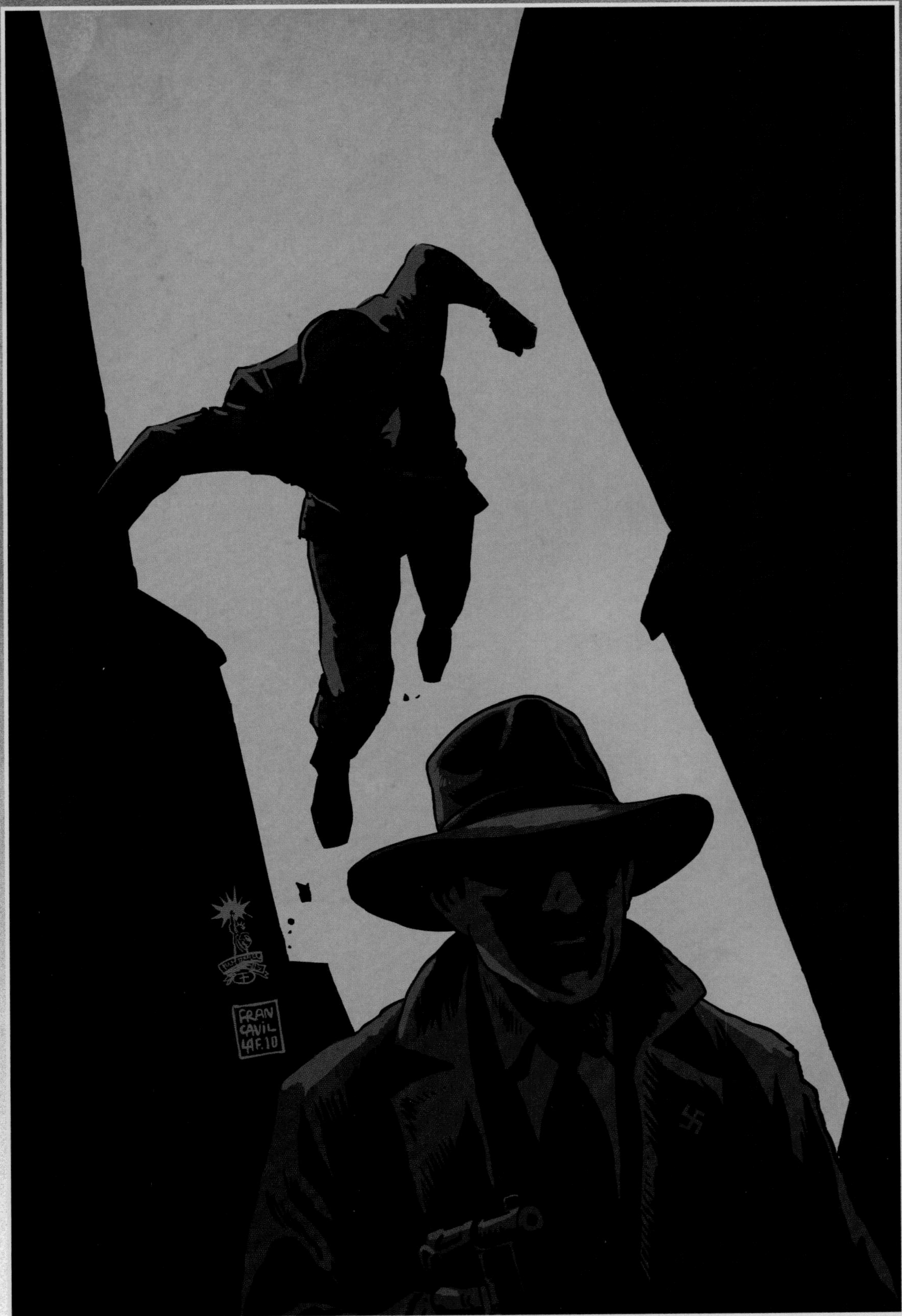
FRAN
CAVIL
4F.10

Issue five alternate cover by **FRANCESCO FRANCAVILLA**

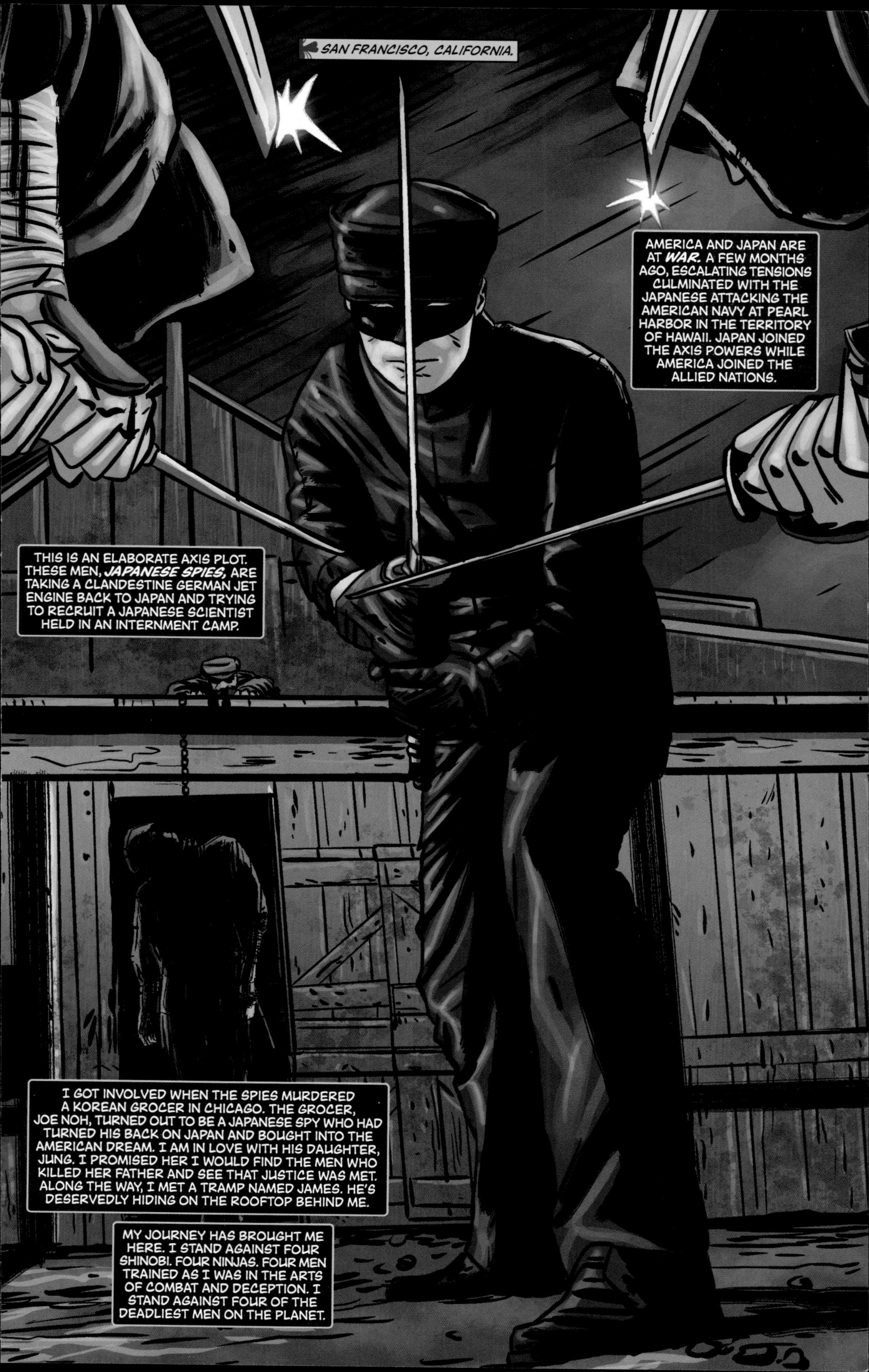
SAN FRANCISCO, CALIFORNIA.
AMERICA AND JAPAN ARE AT **WAR.** A FEW MONTHS AGO, ESCALATING TENSIONS CULMINATED WITH THE JAPANESE ATTACKING THE AMERICAN NAVY AT PEARL HARBOR IN THE TERRITORY OF HAWAII. JAPAN JOINED THE AXIS POWERS WHILE AMERICA JOINED THE ALLIED NATIONS.
THIS IS AN ELABORATE AXIS PLOT. THESE MEN, ***JAPANESE SPIES,*** ARE TAKING A CLANDESTINE GERMAN JET ENGINE BACK TO JAPAN AND TRYING TO RECRUIT A JAPANESE SCIENTIST HELD IN AN INTERNMENT CAMP.
I GOT INVOLVED WHEN THE SPIES MURDERED A KOREAN GROCER IN CHICAGO. THE GROCER, JOE NOH, TURNED OUT TO BE A JAPANESE SPY WHO HAD TURNED HIS BACK ON JAPAN AND BOUGHT INTO THE AMERICAN DREAM. I AM IN LOVE WITH HIS DAUGHTER, JUNG. I PROMISED HER I WOULD FIND THE MEN WHO KILLED HER FATHER AND SEE THAT JUSTICE WAS MET. ALONG THE WAY, I MET A TRAMP NAMED JAMES. HE'S DESERVEDLY HIDING ON THE ROOFTOP BEHIND ME.
MY JOURNEY HAS BROUGHT ME HERE. I STAND AGAINST FOUR SHINOBI. FOUR NINJAS. FOUR MEN TRAINED AS I WAS IN THE ARTS OF COMBAT AND DECEPTION. I STAND AGAINST FOUR OF THE DEADLIEST MEN ON THE PLANET.

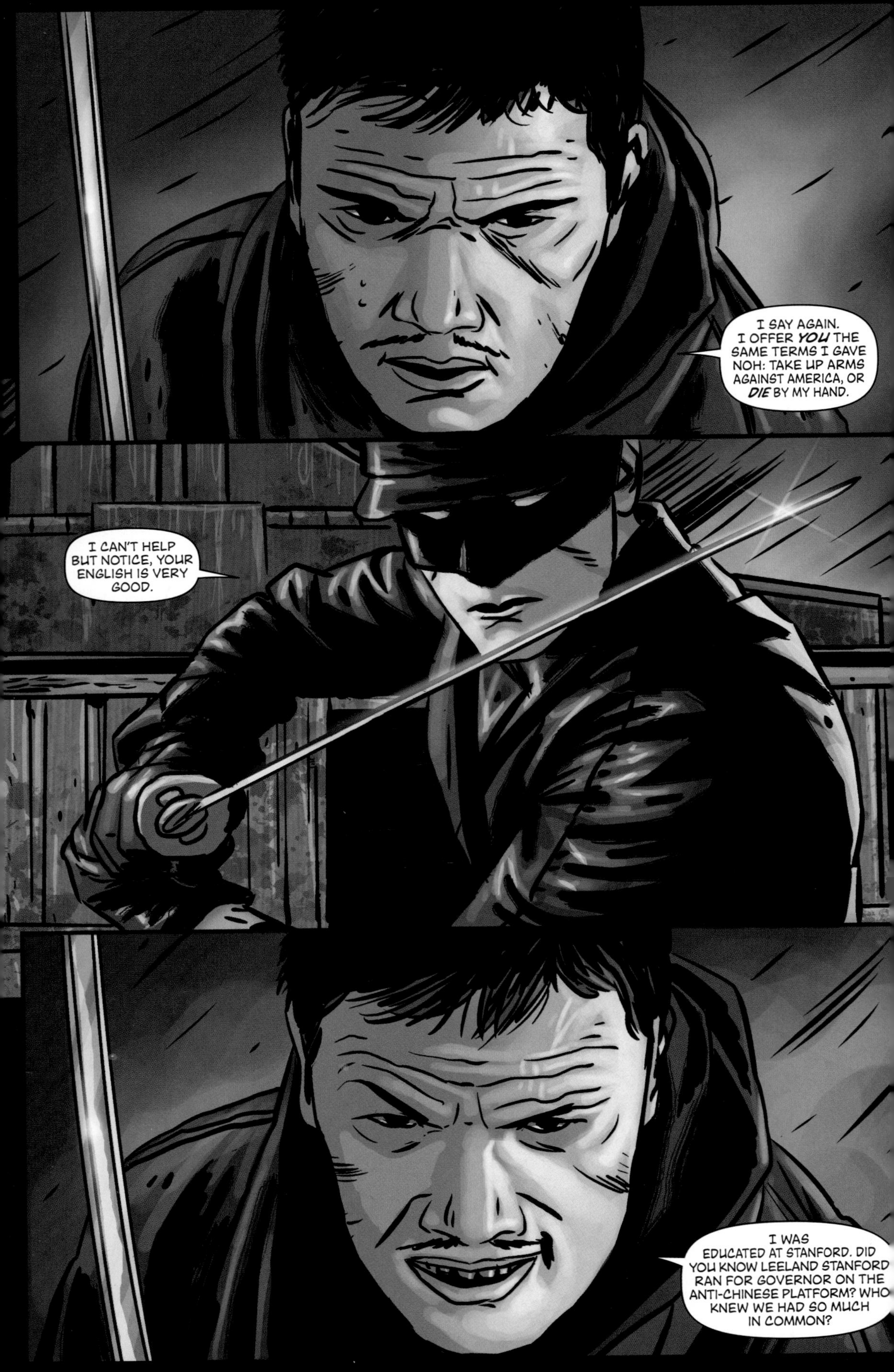
I SAY AGAIN. I OFFER *YOU* THE SAME TERMS I GAVE NOH: TAKE UP ARMS AGAINST AMERICA, OR *DIE* BY MY HAND.
I CAN'T HELP BUT NOTICE, YOUR ENGLISH IS VERY GOOD.
I WAS EDUCATED AT STANFORD. DID YOU KNOW LEELAND STANFORD RAN FOR GOVERNOR ON THE ANTI-CHINESE PLATFORM? WHO KNEW WE HAD SO MUCH IN COMMON?

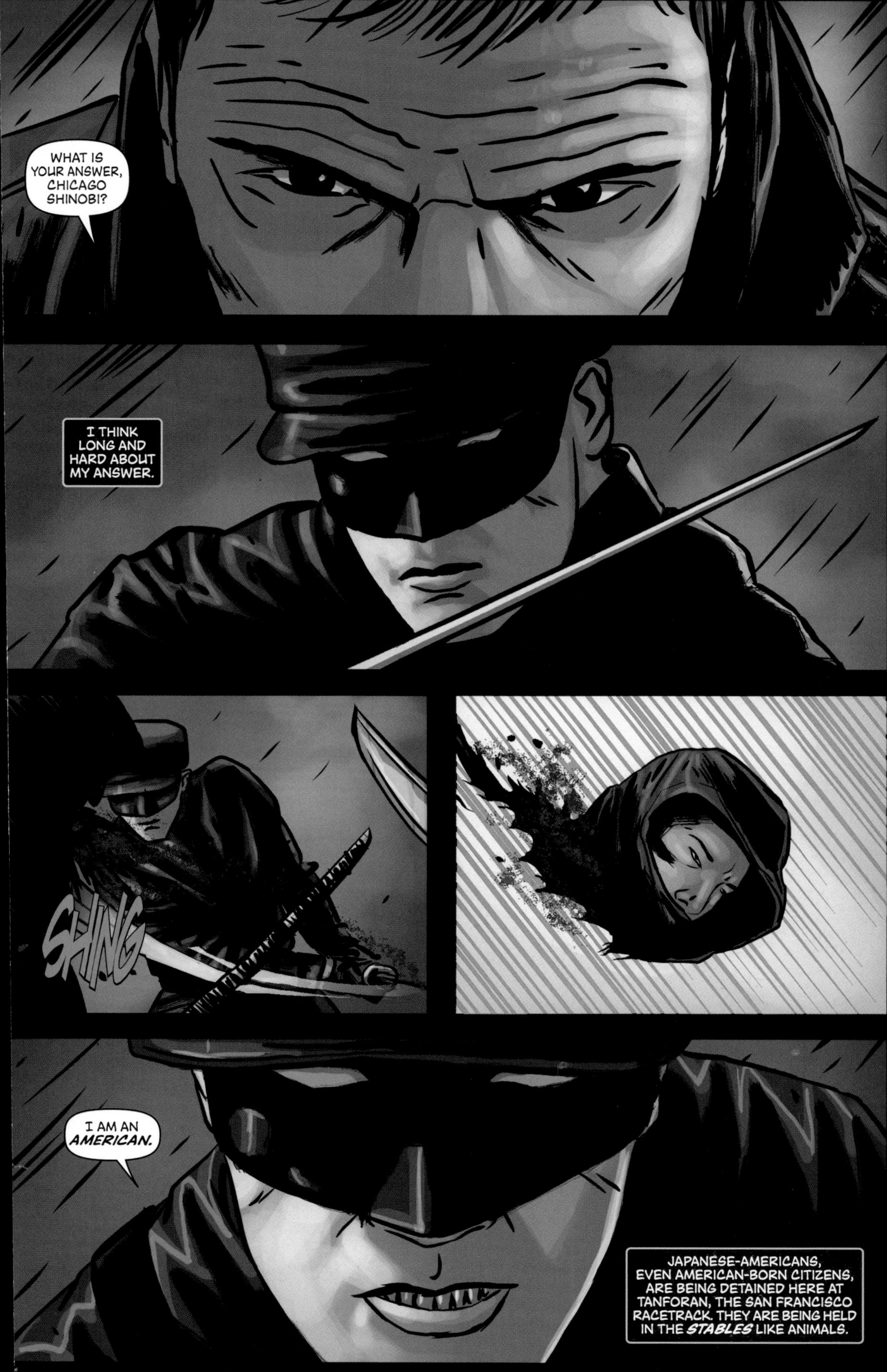
WHAT IS YOUR ANSWER, CHICAGO SHINOBI?
I THINK LONG AND HARD ABOUT MY ANSWER.
SHING
I AM AN *AMERICAN.*
JAPANESE-AMERICANS, EVEN AMERICAN-BORN CITIZENS, ARE BEING DETAINED HERE AT TANFORAN, THE SAN FRANCISCO RACETRACK. THEY ARE BEING HELD IN THE *STABLES* LIKE ANIMALS.

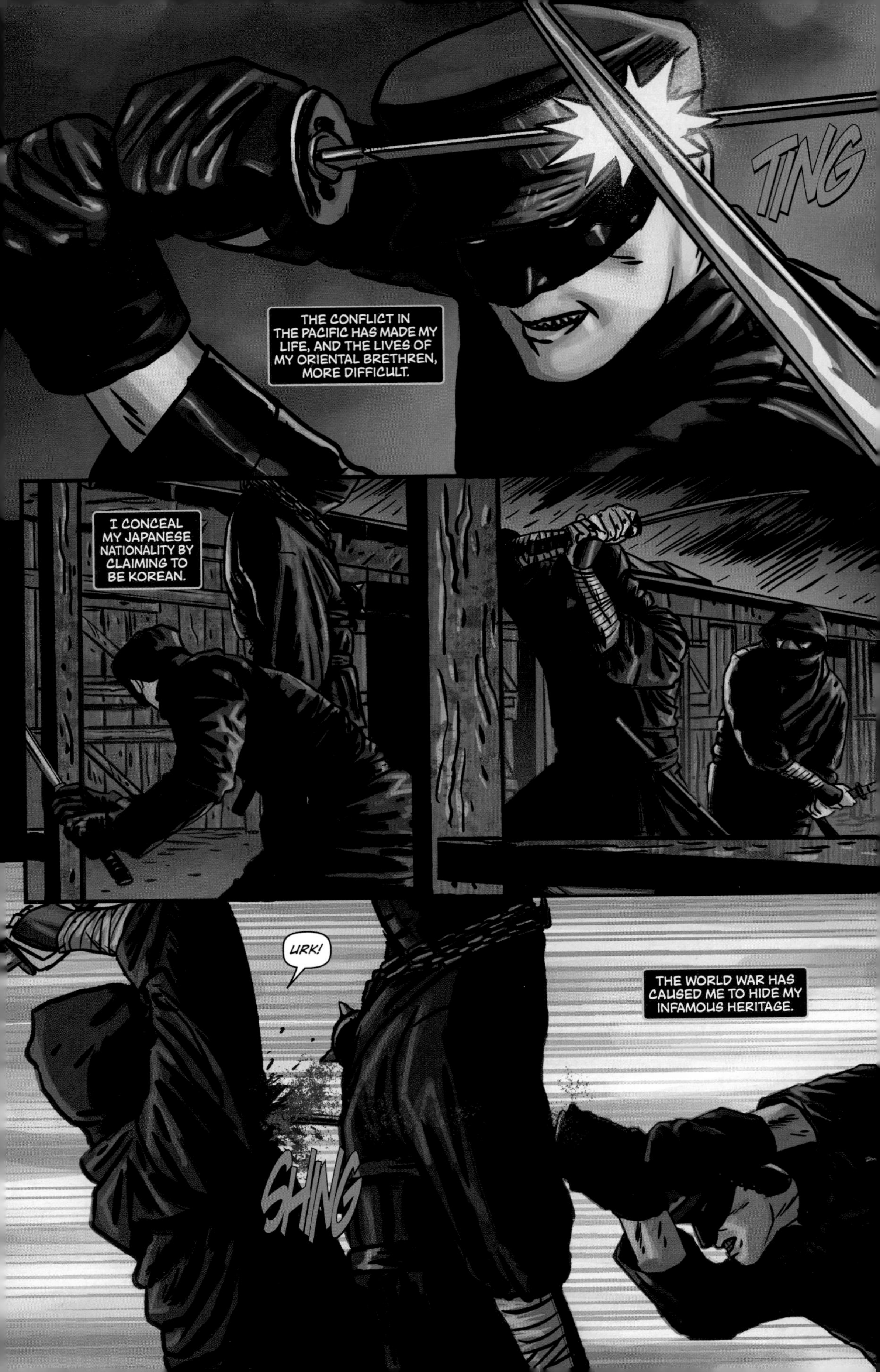
TING
THE CONFLICT IN THE PACIFIC HAS MADE MY LIFE, AND THE LIVES OF MY ORIENTAL BRETHREN, MORE DIFFICULT.
I CONCEAL MY JAPANESE NATIONALITY BY CLAIMING TO BE KOREAN.
URK!
THE WORLD WAR HAS CAUSED ME TO HIDE MY INFAMOUS HERITAGE.
SHING